Dog Tricks & Agility

FOR

DUMMIES®

2ND EDITION

Dog Tricks & Agility For Dummies®, 2nd Edition

Published by
Wiley Publishing, Inc.
111 River St.
Hoboken, NJ 07030-5774
www.wiley.com

Copyright © 2010 by Wiley Publishing, Inc., Indianapolis, Indiana

Published simultaneously in Canada

For general information on our other products and services, please contact our Customer Care Department within the U.S. at 877-762-2974, outside the U.S. at 317-572-3993, or fax 317-572-4002.

For technical support, please visit www.wiley.com/techsupport.

Wiley also publishes its books in a variety of electronic formats. Some content that appears in print may not be available in electronic books.

Library of Congress Control Number: 2010924561

ISBN: 978-0-470-53959-0

Manufactured in the United States of America

10 9 8 7 6 5 4 3 2

WILEY

About the Author

Sarah Hodgson is the author of nine books on dog training, including *Puppies For Dummies, Dog Tricks For Dummies, DogPerfect,* and *Miss Sarah's Guide to Etiquette for Dogs and Their People.* In addition, she has coauthored *Understanding Your Dog For Dummies* with world renowned dog behaviorist Stanley Coren. Her books have been translated into nine languages.

At an age when most kids were baby-sitting or mowing lawns, Sarah Hodgson was starting her career. At 10, she taught her own dog to jump through a tire swing and pull her on skis. At 12, she was showing her neighbors how to do it, and a dog trainer was born. In 1988, one year before graduating with a degree in biology, Sarah opened her professional practice in Bedford, New York, where she continues to help families demystify dog behavior. Through positive reinforcement, family conditioning, and her signature "loving touch," Sarah achieves profound results for people and their dogs.

With theories that link good behavior to having a solid foundation of fun in any relationship, Sarah believes that training must be simple and enjoyable for dogs and people. Blending traditional, time-tested techniques with bond-enhancing tricks and interactive activities, such as agility, flyball, and joring, Sarah shows people how to take charge of their dog in a humane, upbeat, and positive way. Sarah says: "Life is short — have fun!"

Sarah also works with shelters to temperament-test and recondition lost and abandoned dogs to improve their odds of finding permanent homes. Over the years, she has fostered many hard-to-place shelter dogs in her home, using her gentle, humane techniques to rebuild their trust and confidence.

Sarah has appeared as a guest expert on NBC, CNN, CNBC, ABC, FOX, CBS, Animal Planet, and the DIY Network. As a press escort for the Westminster Dog Show, Sarah worked alongside many news personalities, including Al Roker, David Fry, and Storm Phillips, creating segments for their networks. Sarah appeared on Animal Planet's *Dogs 101* series in December 2009.

A regular contributor to a variety of print publications, Sarah's columns have appeared in *Parenthood, Prevention,* and *Country Living* magazines as well as *The New York Times* and *The Record Review.*

A graduate of SUNY at Purchase with a Bachelor of Science degree in biology with an emphasis on human psychology and animal behavior, Sarah is also the inventor of the Teaching Lead. Its ingenious, patented design allows its use as a regular leash, a hands-free lead, or an indoor and outdoor training aid.

Sarah's famous clients have included TV personality Katie Couric; actors Richard Gere, Glenn Close, Susan Sarandon and Tim Robbins, Chazz Palminteri, Chevy Chase, and Lucie Arnez; business moguls George Soros, Tommy Hilfiger, Tommy Mottola, Peter and Sara Arnell, and Michael Fuchs; and sports greats Bobby Valentine and Alan Houston.

Sarah lives in Katonah, New York, with her husband, their two children, and their pets.

Dedication

For Lindsay, Bobo, Whoopsie, and Daisy: Always up to their tricks . . . always able to make their mama smile.

Author's Acknowledgments

The book you are holding is the product of many good, hard-working, creative people. I am so grateful for each of them! A special thanks to my personal assistant, Moira Clune — your suggestions add life to my words, like a soft breeze on a sunny day. You are one of a kind. Thank you to the crew of editors and readers at Wiley Publishing, Inc., who harp — but in a good way. I am grateful to Tracy Boggier for conceiving this idea and pursuing it. And finally, many thanks to my husband, my top agility performer — who regularly juggled meals, kids, and dogs to keep things stable so I could complete this book. Thank you all!

Publisher's Acknowledgments

We're proud of this book; please send us your comments at http://dummies.custhelp.com. For other comments, please contact our Customer Care Department within the U.S. at 877-762-2974, outside the U.S. at 317-572-3993, or fax 317-572-4002.

Some of the people who helped bring this book to market include the following:

Acquisitions, Editorial, and Media Development

Senior Project Editor: Christina Guthrie

Project Editor: Jennifer Connolly

Acquisitions Editor: Tracy Boggier

Senior Copy Editor: Danielle Voirol

Copy Editor: Christine Pingleton

Assistant Editor: Erin Calligan Mooney

Senior Editorial Assistant: David Lutton

Technical Editor: Laura VanArendonk Baugh

Editorial Manager: Christine Meloy Beck

Editorial Assistants: Jennette ElNaggar, Rachelle Amick

Art Coordinator: Alicia B. South

Cover Photos: iStock

Cartoons: Rich Tennant (www.the5thwave.com)

Composition Services

Project Coordinator: Lynsey Stanford

Layout and Graphics: Joyce Haughey

Special Art: Interior illustrations by Barbara Frake

Proofreaders: Lindsay Littrell, Shannon Ramsey

Indexer: Glassman Indexing Services

Publishing and Editorial for Consumer Dummies

    Diane Graves Steele, Vice President and Publisher, Consumer Dummies

    Kristin Ferguson-Wagstaffe, Product Development Director, Consumer Dummies

    Ensley Eikenburg, Associate Publisher, Travel

    Kelly Regan, Editorial Director, Travel

Publishing for Technology Dummies

    Andy Cummings, Vice President and Publisher, Dummies Technology/General User

Composition Services

    Debbie Stailey, Director of Composition Services

Contents at a Glance

Table of Contents

Introduction

I'm a dog maniac who, for years, has been trying to take the edge off serious training and inject the whole process with a little fun. One of the reasons we share our lives with dogs is to enjoy their company, while they help us loosen our grip on this no-nonsense, career-driven world.

Don't get me wrong! I'm not negating the whole training process. After all, I am a dog trainer, and basic lessons are essential to let your dog know who's in charge. But once you've made that point, you can lighten up. Though obedience lessons teach your dog how to act in everyday situations, they're pretty streamlined and relatively predictable. A sit is a sit is a sit . . . not a whole lot of variety!

Playing games and learning tricks, however, invites and encourages liveliness, excitement, and creativity. Sharing your life with a dog shouldn't be a militaristic venture, designed around what you want your dog to do; owning a dog is about joining two different species, two different spirits, in a way that makes the world better for both. So let the fun begin!

About This Book

Tricks and games are open to dogs of all sizes, shapes, and ages. Of course, there are 300 and some-odd pages here dedicated to games and tricks, and not every page will be for you and your dog. You'd have to be a magician to transform a pack of Pekingese into a dogsled team. But that many pages leave plenty of room for a whole array of games and tricks for the everyday dog and owner, and some extra space for more complex maneuvers and team hobbies, such as agility and pet therapy. Every dog can learn to do something.

Discover what gets your dog's tail wagging. Dogs love food, toys, and praise — with varying levels of enthusiasm. You'll find out what works best for your dog within the pages of this book and use that knowledge to build a stronger relationship with your dog.

As with the other *For Dummies* books, you can surf the table of contents and create your own starting point, or you can read this book cover to cover. I've arranged the parts to invite interaction from the start, organizing tricks in each chapter in order of complexity: simple stuff first, then fancy tricks with movie-star potential — and dog sports like agility and flyball a little farther down the road.

There is no one right method for teaching dogs, but if you steer the course to positive reinforcement — treating your dog with respect and leading him with enthusiasm and compassion — you'll have a wonderful time learning together.

Conventions Used in This Book

I use several standard conventions throughout this book:

- New terms are *italicized,* followed by definitions in layman's terms. Italics may also be used occasionally for emphasis.

- Key words in bulleted and numbered lists are **bold,** indicating the most important info.

- Web site addresses are in monofont. Some addresses may have needed to break across two lines of text. In those instances, no extra characters (such as hyphens) were put in to indicate the break. So, when using one of these Web addresses, just type in exactly what you see in this book, pretending the line break doesn't exist.

- With reference to dogs, I've alternated the use of gender-related pronouns by chapter — no preferential treatment is intended!

- Commands that you'll use with your dog are placed in quotation marks, with the first word of each command capitalized. When two commands are given in succession, you'll see them separated by an en dash, for example, "Sit–Stay."

Foolish Assumptions

As I wrote this book, I made a few assumptions. See whether the following statements apply to you:

- You want to bond with your four-legged friend, keeping lessons fun and upbeat. You'd like to share cool tricks and games, do a performance together, coach your dog to navigate an agility course, try some competitions, or just have fun in the backyard.

- You're looking for a way to give your dog — and perhaps yourself — a fun and healthy workout.

- You're relatively new to trick training or dog agility. Please don't think I'm patronizing you if I explain a term you've known for years — I just don't want to leave anyone out in the cold.

- Your dog knows basic obedience commands, such as "Sit," "Stay," "Down," and "Come." To make sure you have this foundational training down, I include a refresher in Chapter 4.

What You're Not to Read

While you're more than welcome to read every word of text in this book, I understand that you're busy, and you might want to read only the essential material. If you want to skip a few things, you can safely skip the following:

✔ Sidebars (shaded gray boxes) contain information that's fun and interesting, but not critical to your understanding of the basics.

✔ The Technical Stuff icon marks text that offers more in-depth information about a concept or how something works. Paragraphs marked with this icon can be skimmed over quickly or skipped altogether if you're not interested in the technical details.

How This Book Is Organized

This book is divided into parts, with each one having its own colorful theme. Here's a quick rundown.

Part I: Getting Started: The Foundations of Training

Ready to jump right in? Whether your dog is savvy enough with the basic commands to start your trick training or you need to review the basics, this section helps you formulate where to begin. Sections spotlight clicker and target training, and the motivational influence of rewards and praise. This part also looks at how your dog's temperament and breed characteristics may enhance (or discourage) her cooperation and enthusiasm.

Part II: Teaching Tricks with Positive Reinforcement

Let the tricks begin! It's time to take all those natural dog movements and behaviors, like tail-wagging, pawing, and carrying stuff around, and redirect them into amusing, useful tricks. Each chapter explains different approaches to training so that you can see what works best for your dog.

Part III: Tackling More Advanced Tricks

From legendary parlor tricks to the more complex stuff like barking on cue, jumping through hoops, and picking up the trash or the laundry, this section excites your dog and challenges your trick training abilities.

Part IV: Exploring the World of Agility

Are you ready to learn more about dog agility? Agility is the up-and-coming, feverishly popular sporting event where dogs are directed through a virtual obstacle course and (when competitive) judged on their timed performances. It's fun, it's fast-paced, and it's very addicting.

If you find that agility has stolen your and your dog's heart, the rest of this part is for you! Obstacle by obstacle you'll be introduced to the most current approach to positive reinforcement training. Once you've mastered each obstacle individually, you'll learn about sequencing a series of them, as well as get all the know-how on troubleshooting common frustrations. Once you've got the course down pat, you'll be lured, quite literally, into competition. Before you take the plunge, learn all there is to know about the different organizations and what's involved on the big day!

Part V: Getting Hip to Hobbies, Events, and Earning Credentials

Part V covers the many other adventures and sporting events you and your dog can enjoy together. Certain canine activities have been around for ages — herding, sledding, hunting, and drafting (pulling) are as much a part of dog evolution as fur and a tail. I help you make connections to other people who share your interests and would welcome your newbie fascination and participation.

Part VI: The Part of Tens

In this part, you find cool agility maneuvers you can try at home, either inside or out. They're a great way to test your dog's affinity for this sport. You also discover more about your dog's make-up and how to keep sports injuries at bay. Finally, you can check out a top-ten list for ensuring your dog stays fit and healthy throughout your life together!

Icons Used in This Book

The icons in this book point out certain special bits of information. This is what they mean:

The Tip icon marks useful tidbits and helpful advice.

Friendly reminders about things you shouldn't forget, like warming up your dog before vigorous trick training, are marked with the Remember icon.

When you see the Warning icon, take care and read carefully. It alerts you to avoid common errors and dangerous habits.

The Technical Stuff icon marks text that provides greater detail or background on a particular concept. While you may find this information interesting, it isn't essential to your understanding.

Where to Go from Here

Because every dog and owner's situation is unique, not everyone will approach this book in the exact same way. Some cover-to-cover folks will read each page; others may be agility-focused and want to start at Chapter 11. Perhaps you're dying to learn how to teach your dog to high five, roll over, or catch a disc. Feel free to check out the Table of Contents to find what best meets your needs or appeals to you most.

If you need a quick brush up on training basics, flip to Chapters 4 and 5 for a quick review. Not sure what your dog might be best in? Chapter 3 teaches you about breed and body basics to help you select the best tricks for your dog. After you've mastered some of the simpler tricks, you can check out Chapters 8–10 for other dramatic, multi-step moves that are fun to learn and will wow any crowd. Eager for athletics? The chapters in Parts IV and V highlight many sporting activities open to dogs and dog lovers.

As you're reading my book, know that I wrote it eager for you to feel what I feel — that having a loving, interactive relationship with your dog is one of the most special gifts in life. To know another species so well that you can sense their feelings, without words, and trust their reactions are always genuine, is a priceless connection indeed. It doesn't matter who you are or where you've been or what you've done. Your dog loves you today. Limitless is their devotion. Please feel open to share your experiences and stories with me. You can visit me online at whendogstalk.com. I'd be thrilled to hear from you.

Part I
Getting Started: The Foundations of Training

"Down Skippy, down!! Mike has tried so hard to socialize this dog so we can have people over without being embarrassed, but evidently he needs a few more lessons."

In this part . . .

No matter which chapter you find yourself in, the insights in Part I help you communicate and train your dog with utmost compassion. Chapter 2 examines the all-important question: Are you training your dog, or is he training you? You learn basic commands here as you're encouraged to take charge, not as a dictator but as a patient and all-knowing teacher, eager to teach your student new and exciting lessons. In the following chapters, you learn how to recognize your dog's personality, temperament, and breed-specific talents and limitations. Other topics include an introduction to clicker training, targeting, and teaching off-leash control with basic commands like "Come," "Stand," and "Down," used throughout the book.

Chapter 1

Exploring the Fun that Awaits You

In This Chapter

▶ Discovering the rewards of working with your dog

▶ Looking at the basic concepts of trick training

▶ Getting an overview of dog agility

1 wrote this book for the fun of it — fun for me and, I hope, fun for you. Having fun with your dog usually tops the list of reasons we share our lives with dogs in the first place. They bring us back to a time when pleasure was our only priority.

Nobody has to teach a dog tricks or go the extra mile to explore new adventures. No one needs to get involved in agility or other activities with their dog. After all, training is time-consuming, sometimes costly, and requires incredible patience and understanding. But if you've chosen to go this extra mile, I know that your relationship with your dog is a special one. Your dog is a special gift to you, and you have chosen to give back to him.

As you progress in your training, you'll find out more about your dog: how he thinks and what he likes. You'll gain insight into the way your dog learns and better understand how to shape that learning process, from the length of the lessons to the various teaching approaches. You'll discover how to reward and encourage your dog in fun, engaging, and constructive ways.

In this chapter, I highlight the many benefits of teaching your dog tricks, familiarize you with the basic concepts of trick training, and introduce you to the sport of dog agility. Ready to go? Your dog can hardly wait!

Beyond Obedience: The Value of Tricks

Why teach your dog to do tricks? After all, he's not joining the circus anytime soon. The answer is simple: Most dogs will jump at the opportunity to perform for fun, praise, treats . . . almost anything! Dogs are active by nature and love to *do stuff* — just jiggle your car keys or utter the word W-A-L-K if you don't believe me. Tricks give your dog the chance to release his inner, audience-starved vaudevillian, expend pent-up energy, and use his innate dog skills — jumping, barking, sock-stealing — in positive ways.

A well-trained dog also serves as an ambassador for us all. Whether you're just clowning around in your living room or putting on an act at a local fair, the work and time you devote to your dog shines through wherever you take him. Sure, your dog may never star in a commercial or show off his routines at the local Elks Club, but that doesn't rob you of one undeniable fact: If you love your dog, he's a star. And the size of your star is not measured by how many people share your pride; it's measured by you. When I listen to my friends and clients talk about their dogs, I feel the warmth in their hearts, and when I see the dog face-to-face, I already know that dog's worth.

You'll be surprised at the new friends your dog wins over with simple tricks and basic good behavior, which I discuss in Chapter 5. Watching your dog strut his stuff makes everyone feel a little bit happier. Dog-phobic kids lose some of their fear, busy people find a little time to watch, and total strangers share a smile. Those of us who love dogs congratulate you on your efforts toward making the world a more dog-friendly place.

Starting with Trick Training

Classic obedience lessons utilize a lot of leash work. Dogs must be trained to obey and follow, which generally involves a lot of ordering about and corrections for misbehavior. It's serious stuff. Not so with trick training and other adventures like agility and flyball. These activities depend on an invisible leash — a strong tie that brings you together in a flow of excitement and trust, like a coach guiding an eager athlete.

Are you concerned about how your dog will handle the freedom? Chapter 4 walks you through the basics and guides you toward the freedom of off-lead control. In this section, I give you an overview of trick training and some things you can do to get started today.

Figuring out who's teaching who

The first thing you need to explore is your relationship as it exists now. Does your dog look to you for direction, eager to follow you and learn new things? Or does your dog's schedule look something like this:

- **Paw for attention:** Promptly at 7 a.m.
- **Bark at the window:** 1–3:30 p.m.
- **Scratch at the door:** 8 a.m., 3:30 p.m., 9 p.m.
- **Steal socks and get the family to chase me:** 4 p.m.

If your dog's day is one long human training session, all hope is not lost! This is a sign of a smart and clever dog; he'll be easy to train. At the moment, though, he's training you. Chapter 2 helps you restructure your relationship so that you're the teacher, not the student. Chapter 4 gets you up to speed on basic obedience commands your dog should know.

Trying lessons without words

Dogs learn in ways that are both simple and complex. Dogs are so eager to earn rewards and attention that it's amazingly easy to teach them simple things. Get five super-savored treats or a toy your dog loves to play with, and then try the following lessons.

Heeding the four-paw rule: All paws on the floor

Stand upright in front of your dog and wave the treat above his head. If he jumps for it, lift the treat up and look to the sky. If he scratches at you frantically, wear a trench coat and completely ignore your dog. When he pauses, reward him immediately with the treat or toy. Repeat this five times in a row, three times a day. My hunch? In three or four days, your dog will hold still when you offer him treats and toys. Give it a try!

Sitting for a toy or before dinner

Try this wordless lesson, building on the preceding four-paw rule. If your dog doesn't know the command "Sit," flip to Chapter 4 and practice it first.

Wave your dog's toy or hold his dinner bowl above his head and wait. Don't look at or talk to your dog if he jumps or barks at you. Ignore him so he understands that these behaviors will not work with you. No sirree! Be patient with your dog and keep your eyes peeled for success. The moment he sits, reward him immediately. If he stands calmly, position him or maneuver the toy or bowl above his head so that he moves into a sitting position himself. After five repetitions, surprise — he won't bark or jump —he'll sit automatically! Good dog. Good person. You make a great team.

Deciding which tricks to teach

When thinking through the tricks in this book, consider your dog and what he's likely to enjoy learning. Work on routines that complement his natural abilities first. For example, if you have a canine athlete who's in constant motion on your hands, he'll likely take to jumping (Chapter 8), dog agility (Part IV), and other movement-based tricks like crawling and playing "Hide and Seek" (Chapters 10 and 5, respectively). That said, if he's the silent type, avoid putting "teach him to bark" (Chapter 9) at the top of your list. Chapter

3 relates breed type, personality, and age factors to selecting tricks and adventures that your dog will enjoy and can accomplish.

As you work through your tricks, start with the simplest routines first to build your dog's success rate and eagerness to learn new things. For example, teach "Paw" before you work on "High five" and "Wave" (Chapter 6).

Using the sequencing approach

When teaching fun and useful tricks, keep your training sessions short and sweet — no more than five minutes each to start. Because your dog can't master an entire routine in five minutes, you need to isolate each step and build on your dog's successes using the sequencing approach. The *sequencing approach* is fairly simple: Each new routine has steps to follow, and you need to perfect each step before moving on to the next. Mastering small steps helps your dog feel empowered as you progress to more-difficult tasks.

I say a lot more about sequencing and steps throughout the book, but to illustrate quickly, suppose you want to teach your dog how to jump through a hoop. Chaining together the following steps makes this trick a four-step program (you can find more details on hoop-jumping in Chapter 8):

1. **Create a low jump, and then take the jump with your dog as you command "Over."**

   Use a broom to create a low jump across a threshold, like a doorway. Prop up the broom with two objects of equal height, like soup cans or, for a small dog, Dixie cups. Let your dog sniff the setup.

   Then take him five doggie paces back. Command "Over" as you run toward the setup and take the jump together. Good dog! Repeat this jumping sequence three to five times per session until your dog is eager to run in front of you and take the jump himself. When you've perfected this, you're ready for Step 2.

2. **Let your dog explore the hoop, and then have him walk through the hoop at ground level, introducing the command "Through."**

   Show your dog the hoop, placing it flat on the ground so that your dog can step around and sniff it.

   Holding the hoop at ground level, lure your dog through it with a toy or treat. As he walks through, give the command "Through."

3. **Ask a helper to hold the hoop to the broom and have your dog jump through it, combining the commands you introduce in Steps 1 and 2 by instructing "Over–Through."**

   Recruit someone to hold the hoop directly in front of the broom. The bottom of the hoop should be at the same level as the broom.

Take your dog back down the runway, instruct "Over–Through," run up to the obstacle, and encourage your dog to jump through.

4. **Phase out the broom, progress to practicing in other doorways, and then move away from doorways altogether.**

Continue to work in the same threshold until once again your dog is eagerly running ahead of you to leap over the broom. Now, remove the broom and encourage "Over–Through." Good dog! Slowly raise the hoop to the height of your dog's elbow. Once your dog perfects the jump in this threshold, you can branch out to other thresholds in the house. Got that? Now you're ready for the big time! Encourage your dog to jump through the hoop wherever it is placed.

Repeat your three- to five-minute training sessions one to four times a day, whatever your day allows. Some days I'm busy and I get only one lesson in. Other days, I have time for two or three. No worries — my dogs are up for anything. Your dog will learn, too, as long as you're positive and use the sequencing approach.

Sequencing also comes into play as you decide to teach more and more advanced tricks. For instance, your dog may need to understand ideas such as targeting (see Chapter 2) to do tricks like waving or rolling over at various locations in a room or on a stage. Before you blend two concepts like these, make sure your dog is happy with doing the trick and moving away from you.

A technique called *back-chaining* involves teaching the last step first. It sounds — well, backwards — and confusing, but it's especially useful with certain tricks like fetching (Chapter 7) and in agility (Part IV) because it makes your dog aware of the end goal.

Rewarding good behavior

As you're working with your dog, think of yourself as equal parts coach, teacher, parent, and friend. Because many of the routines and adventures in this book will be new to your dog, you'll need to sell him on why he needs to leap over broomsticks, bark to ten, and help you pick up the laundry. If you approach these tasks with the right attitude (mainly fun, fun, fun . . . plus rewards!), he'll be eager to participate. Consider how you'd like to be treated when learning something new — and remember what my grandmother always said, "You attract a lot more bees with honey than with salt."

To be an effective teacher, you have to identify what thrills your dog. You can use food, toys, and attention to encourage your dog's cooperation. For my treat-loving dogs, I schedule training around feeding times. I do a lesson before breakfast, and because they're hungry, the dogs are even spunkier. I end the lesson on a positive note and reward them with a yummy meal.

The timing of rewards influences your dog's understanding and works hand-in-paw with incentive training. If you want to teach your Chihuahua how to jump up and "dance" but you reward him after he has landed on the ground, you'll actually be reinforcing not-jumping. Remember your dog isn't the only one who needs to learn new techniques: Helping your dog master tricks quickly and without confusion requires you to learn a few tricks, too.

I cover all these ideas in Chapter 2, and I throw in a few other techniques, such as clicker and target training, to really get the motivational ball rolling.

Getting Active with Agility and Other Sports and Hobbies

If parlor tricks aren't enough to keep your dog down and you're enthusiastic about exploring other activities, you have many to pick from in Parts IV and V. Most of the events are open to all dogs, regardless of their pedigree, and many invite social interaction and competitions. One of the most popular and publicized sporting events for dogs is agility, a relatively new activity on the scene. Agility was first practiced in England in the 1980s and has attracted enthusiasts around the world like nothing else.

While many dogs love the challenge of agility and the time spent with their owners, there are other sporty activities that can be easier to master and require less of a commitment. Read through these sections to find one that may be perfectly tailored to the energy levels and passions of both you and your dog. These include flyball, flying disc, and pulling sports like sledding, skijoring, and derivations of skijoring like scootering and skim-joring. Of course, if rigorous involvement is not your game, there are other ways to socialize and further your dog's training, from obedience trials to pet therapy and good citizenship certification.

What is agility?

Dog agility is a fun sporting event that challenges teams — one dog and one person — to navigate through a series of obstacles in a race to get the highest score for their performance. Think dog park meets Olympic equestrian event meets *Dancing with the Stars*. You and your dog perform choreographed moves — over jumps, through tunnels, and over balance boards — as you race together to finish an obstacle course. Wow, huh?

Deciding whether agility is right for you and your dog

Is your dog up for the adventure? While agility is open to all breeds of dogs as well as mixed breeds, it does require a certain get-up-and-go. Often the dogs who excel at this sport are the very ones whose enthusiasm and excitement often land them in the proverbial doghouse at home. Does your dog jump on everything and everyone? Believe it or not, you may be harboring an agility champion. Is your dog barely winded after a 6-mile run? Tirelessness is a cherished trait in agility!

There are some restrictions — age and safety limitations that you must consider before you begin. Personality also factors in — both yours and your dog's. Agility requires patience, persistence, and an über-positive attitude. But there's no room for dictators on the agility field — dogs (like people) do not respond well to human frustration or impatience. To take part in this adventurous activity, you need to check your inner despot at the door, put on a smiling face, and encourage your dog through every step of the learning process. To discover more about the sport and whether it may be a good fit for your dog, flip to Chapter 11.

Training for agility

If you choose to go forward, you'll witness a fascinating transformation. At first, you and your dog will feel bewildered by the enormity of the effort. You'll need to learn all the obstacles and then choreograph a routine that involves up to 16 obstacles in succession. But if you show up day after day, week after week, and work together — often next to people who share the same goals and passion for their dogs as you — you'll develop a trust and kinship with your dog that only forms from the camaraderie of a shared goal. You'll learn to manage and communicate with one another until your motions are synchronized and fluid . . . two bodies moving together. Friends for life.

Getting ready for agility requires a lot of training, so you need to become familiar with some basic commands and equipment. Many people sign up for agility classes with their dogs, hire instructors, and/or join agility clubs. Chapter 12 reviews up-to-date training methods and *PRAT* (Positive Reinforcement Agility Training), a well-studied and effective way of introducing your dog to this new sport. PRAT uses the latest tools and props and takes your dog's species-specific learning capacities to heart, minimizing anxiety and buoying enthusiasm.

Part IV of this book introduces you to the sport. In Chapters 13 and 14, you learn the basics about the various obstacles. While each dog is an individual, universal training techniques exist to help ensure every dog's safety and guarantee a positive experience while learning the ropes. If your dog hesitates or you're concerned about how he may respond to a certain obstacle, read through the troubleshooting section of Chapter 15 — while you may feel your dog's issues are unique, you're likely to find yourself in good company.

Competing and having fun

Mastering each of the agility obstacles takes time and effort, but once your dog is eager and confident and you've learned to sequence a pre-designed field, you may find yourself daydreaming about competing and earning titles.

Weekend events that classify teams by size and experience are held across the country. If you decide to jump into competitive agility, you'll compete against others in your experience bracket. Chapter 16 introduces you to agility competitions.

If the thought of judges and time clocks overwhelms you, no worries! Many people do agility just for the fun of it and never choose to compete. Whatever you decide, agility is a fun time for everyone involved. You get to share special one-on-one time with your dog, exploring new experiences and hanging out with others who are excited by the very same thing!

Trying dog sports, trials, and backyard games

Agility, though popular, fun, and *everywhere,* isn't the only competitive or social dog event on the scene. Frisbee and flyball are two challenging games that pair a dog's predatory instincts with a focused activity. At a competitive level, you and your dog will be judged against comparative performances and/or against the clock or set standard.

There are other activities that you can enjoy together with or without other people. From organized obedience training to more breed-specific efforts, you can work to hone your dog's talents and compete against others for titles. Many dog organizations, such as the American Kennel Club (AKC) and United Kennel Club (UKC), offer competitive trials, clearly outlining their specifications and granting awards to dogs who show excellence in their performance. Earned titles at every level represent the determined effort you and your dog underwent to perform tasks that, while no longer necessary for our survival, represent skills that did in fact aid in our evolution. Breed-specific events include lure coursing for Sighthounds, scent trails for Scenthounds, hunting and field trials for Retrievers, earthdog trials for Terriers, and herding trials for herding breeds. Competitions judge how a dog's breed-specific inclinations have been fine-tuned through training and how well they can perform their "duties" under stress.

Finally, there are activities and certifications that are open to all dogs and often sponsored by various groups and clubs. These events include *pet therapy,* where dogs earn certification to work in therapeutic environments (such as nursing homes, libraries, or hospitals), and *canine freestyle,* where a dog and handler perform a choreographed dance to music. Hard to envision? Search YouTube — you'll be impressed!

Who knew? So much for you and your dog to explore together!

Chapter 2

Prepping for Training — Mentally and Physically

In This Chapter

▷ Recognizing the power of your approval

▷ Speaking the same language

▷ Equipping yourself with all the right tools

▷ Preparing your dog to respond to special training gadgets

*B*efore you begin training, you need to do a little prep work. Part of it's physical; for example, you have to get all your training gear in order. And some of your preparation is mental — getting an idea of how your dog thinks, for example, and figuring out how all your training gadgetry works.

Although your dog isn't born knowing the English language, you can teach her just like you'd teach a baby — speaking in a clear voice and repeating a word until your dog makes the connection. Some of life's little consistencies can light your way, too. For example, dogs like to know things. They focus on anyone who acts like a teacher: If it's you, they're in! Dogs also like to play and have fun, and most dogs are motivated around food or a favorite toy, so you can use these prompts to encourage your dog's cooperation as well.

And thank gosh modern technology has reached the dog world! The list of helpful training tools has gone way beyond collars and leashes to head collars, clickers, and targeting sticks. These gadgets can add zip and fun to your time together as your goals come across in half the time.

Fortunately, teaching a dog is not as complicated as solving complex equations, and it's a lot more fun. As long as you remember to speak to your dog in the right way, make your position as the teacher clear and consistent, understand who your dog really is, and use the right tools, you can teach your dog all sorts of things and have fun together at the same time. Okay, so maybe that does sound complicated, but in this chapter, I unravel the mystery behind the basics of dog training.

Turning Your Dog onto Learning

Before you teach that dog of yours how to serve you breakfast in bed, you have to make sure you can get her attention. Otherwise, she'll be the one teaching you tricks — ever see the owner-chasing-the-dog routine? It's hysterical but very unsafe.

Dogs think a lot like humans in some ways. They like to learn about activities that excite them. They pay attention to routines that result in positive rewards and the people who provide them. They're willing to watch them for clues on what to do. They also have favorite things that you can offer to encourage their eagerness and cooperation. (Although a $20 bill may not get them going, wave a hot dog or a squeak toy in front of your dog's face, and you'll see what I'm talking about.) In this section, you find out how to appeal to your dog — to her desire for attention and approval, her joy of adventure, and her enjoyment of physical affection.

Dogs often perceive negative attention as confrontational play. Dogs are very keyed into what gets your attention and, like children, they don't seem to care whether the attention they're getting is negative or positive. Rather than subduing a dog, yelling or using physical correction excites them or, worse, creates a gripping sense of fear. As you flip through this book, teaching your dog skits and routines, remember the adage: You attract more dogs with praise than punishment.

Praising your pooch

Like humans, dogs will go to great lengths to please someone they love. Although I wouldn't look to this book to teach your dog how to give you a foot massage, dogs will pour themselves into tricks and adventures if it means getting to spend more time with you. When you praise your dog, you encourage her cooperation with your enthusiastic verbal coaching, and you may supplement it with other reinforcements like food and toys.

The intensity of the praise you should give your dog is a very individual thing: Too much can excite an active dog. A shy or hesitant dog can miss too little encouragement. And some dogs actually get frightened when humans bend over and pet or hug them enthusiastically. To find out what works best for your dog, offer praise and watch her response:

- If she's so thrilled with herself that she has troubling focusing again, notch it down.
- If she's hard to motivate, ratchet up your praise and find a toy or treat that gets her attention.

✔ If your dog freezes or pulls back when you bend to touch her, don't take it personally; your dog is conflicted. What is praise to you may seem to be a dominance display or a threat to her personal space. Use food and verbal praise to reward this dog.

Choosing rewards

Not sure how to reward your dog? Some people swear, "Only treats!" Others exclaim, "Only praise!" I say the best advice is to ask your dog! To discover what makes her tail wag, do this little experiment using the three different types of rewards (praise, treats, or toys) individually to see which your dog enjoys the most!

1. **Pick a well-known command like "Sit."**

2. **Do five "Sits" in a row, rewarding each success with praise only.**

3. **Three hours later, do the same thing, but reward your dog with a toy only (no praise).**

4. **The next day, do five "Sits" again, making treats your dog's only reward this time (no praise or toys).**

Your answer should be clear: Although praise is a given, if food or toys excite your dog, use those rewards, too. The following list offers you some guidelines on these reward options:

✔ **Treats:** Figure out what excites your dog. Is it food? If yours turns up her nose at dried kibble, test her with a tiny piece of hot dog or a more exciting snack.

When using food to guide or reward your dog (in dog lingo, this is called *luring*), break the snack into tiny pieces so she won't get filled up and lose interest in the lesson. It's not the size that counts; it's the gift that revs the dog up!

✔ **Toys:** Some dogs cling to their toys like a baby to a blanket. If your dog has a favorite, use this to reward her. Do what I call a *burst:* For each successful attempt, toss the toy either down on the floor or up in the air (let your dog choose which is most exciting) and shout, "Yes!"

✔ **Praise:** All dogs love attention. For some, approval alone motivates their interaction for hours. If your dog hangs on you like a noodle, turning up her nose at food and shunning toys, then you have yourself a praise junky, a rare dog indeed. Use your enthusiasm to propel her mastery of tricks and high adventure.

The million-dollar question is . . . drum roll . . . will you need to use treats forever to get your dog to respond to you? The answer is, thankfully, no.

Food and rewards are used in training to help you target the behavior that you're teaching and condition a quick response to your command words.

After your dog knows the command, you should immediately start phasing off the physical reward, using just your praise and encouragement instead. To phase off treats, don't go cold turkey, eliminating them in one day. Instead, gradually reduce your dependence — reward with food every other time your dog behaves, then every third time . . . then mix it up, giving two treats in a row, then one in three times, then every other time. The inconsistency of not knowing when the treat will come will keep your dog on her toes. Within two weeks, you can phase your dog off treat reliance entirely . . . though every once in a while, pop one in just for fun! Dogs love their treats like many people love chocolate!

Offering rewards is all about timing: Targeting your dog's success makes your intentions more clear. If you miss the moment, your dog may get the wrong message. For example, when teaching a dog to dance (see Chapter 8), you target her for standing on her two back paws; if you praise her as she's coming down, she may think dancing means the opposite.

Communicating with Your Dog

Although dogs are very similar to people in some ways, they're different, too. Recognizing what sets dogs apart can help you modify your approach to help your dog learn faster. First off, dogs don't communicate with the same language skills. Their verbal range is limited. Sentences confuse them. Warm sweet praise, while fitting when your dog is calm or you're rewarding cooperation, sounds whiny rather than supportive or directional when your dog needs a command to help her organize her thoughts.

When you teach your dog new skills, think of it as teaching English as a second language — work to translate English into Doglish! The sections that follow give you some ideas on how to make sure you're communicating with your dog in her language.

When communicating with your dog, use a creative approach and a heavy dose of patience. You need to demonstrate a lot of what you envision, and repeat the word cues again and again. Though your dog can't fully grasp the complexities of your language, she'll sure try to figure it out. When your dog finally gets it, she'll eagerly repeat the routine again and again.

Watching your dog's ears

Here's a simple way to tell what your dog is focused on: Watch her ears. They're the canine equivalent of an antenna. Unlike people's boring, stationary flaps, a dog's ears rotate to capture and locate sound. Swiveling around, they help find food and alert to danger.

When you're in charge, your dog must focus on you primarily. Ideally, the ears should be relaxed and angled toward you. When an unpredictable distraction alerts your dog, she'll likely focus on it intently. This is ok . . . for a moment — call her back to you and praise her when she reconnects. If she gets more stimulated and her ears and eyes begin to track the distraction, tug on the leash, say "Nope," and, when possible, move off in the opposite direction. As soon as your dog shifts her attention back to you, praise her calmly.

Being the one to watch

All animals respond well to authority. The member of the group who stands forward with attitude and pride and says, "I know what to do!" or "Here's the plan!" emits confidence in everything he or she does, from gathering food to playing to directing other individuals in the group. To encourage the most cooperation from your dog, you need to step forward — you need to be the one to watch.

If your dog looks to you with eyes that are trusting and eager, you're on your way. If you can't get a blink from your dog, you'll have to do some preliminary respect work by teaching some basic commands, as outlined in Chapter 4.

I have a mantra I get my clients to repeat: "The more you look at your dog, the less she'll look to you." When you're teaching your dog tricks or directing her behavior, the goal is that she watch you for signals and directions. If you're looking at her, she'll just be confused: *Why are you looking at me? I don't know what to do . . . .* Look at your dog to reward her cooperation and to confirm that everything is okay.

Using body language and hand signals

People use body language to support their words. For dogs, the opposite is true — body language is central to their communication, and their vocalization backs it up. Remember, your dog is always watching you for direction.

First of all, training calls for a relaxed and patient body posture. As you teach new tricks and skills, use one of the following positions:

- ✔ Stand upright and proud when directing your dog from a standing position.
- ✔ Kneel down or use a chair if an exercise calls for you to be at the same level as your dog.

If you hunch over or get frustrated, your dog will think something is distressing in the environment, not in her behavior. Because dogs can't reason that way, an angry reaction from you will only cause hesitation in your dog.

To capitalize on your dog's attention to body language, use hand signals, choosing one for each new direction you teach your dog. Throughout the text, I suggest a hand signal for each trick, though you can modify each if you choose — just be consistent. To direct your dog in front of a crowd without saying a word is rather impressive!

Paying attention to vocal tones

With dogs, how you sound is more important than what you're saying. When you yell at your dog, you either freak her out or look like a fool, depending on your dog's personality type. If you speak sweetly, you encourage playfulness.

When giving commands, use a clear, direct, and nonthreatening tone — think of it as a *set-the-table tone*. Use your regular voice with an ounce of over-enunciation, as though you were speaking to a toddler or directing a foreign tourist to the nearest gas station. After your dog learns a particular behavior, you can use hand signals or whisper commands. But in the beginning, speak clearly.

You can use your voice to both steady and direct your dog. Think of each command as a short bark. Powerful (not whiny or questioning) verbal directions give your dog confidence in you and the situation at hand. When your dog is unsteady, distracted, or anxious, use familiar words to direct her. A recognized word cue can steady a dog, which quickly organizes a chaotic scene, modifies mischief, and, with tricks, lightens all interactions!

Outfitting Your Dog for Training

The goal of tricks, agility, and other sporting adventures is to direct your dog off-leash, encouraging her to focus on your hand signals and verbal commands. If the thought of having your dog off-leash makes you nervous, take a deep breath. You don't have to unclip your dog before you're ready. I cover basic training and off-leash lessons in Chapter 4. This section gives you a thorough understanding of the equipment you use toward that end.

Collars

Buckle collars are a staple. They fit like a belt around your dog's neck and carry her rabies tag, license, and name tag. Some dogs behave just fine in a buckle collar; others sense the restraint like entrapment and pull hard.

If you muscle a puller to your side, the dog learns that being near you causes her to choke, so she pulls harder. If this sounds like your situation, consider one of the following collars for your training:

- ✔ **Martingale collars:** These collars come in two types: all fabric and a fabric-chain combination. Safer than chain collars (also called *slip collars* or *choke chains*), Martingale collars circle the neck and have a slip section that offers a corrective tug when a dog pulls away. The chain version also offers a corrective zipping sound that discourages pulling and misbehavior.

    Use positive encouragement as your dog walks at your side. Reward your dog when she's walking near you with food/toy rewards and verbal encouragement. This will help her recognize and rely on you to lead her. Explore the clicker and target stick too — these tools will speed up this very basic understanding. If your dog darts off, stop calmly — when she hits the end of the leash the collar's quick tug will be enough to remind her: Walking with you is good. Darting away, not so good!

- ✔ **Head collars:** A head collar lays over a dog's nose and secures behind her ear. Although some think the head collar looks like a muzzle, head collars act more like a halter placed on a horse — you use them to guide movement, not inhibit it. The benefit of a head collar is that it can condition cooperative skills if you reward your dog for walking at your side. Gently guiding a dog instead of yanking on her neck, it can work wonders if you're trying to restrain a hyper or headstrong dog.

Harnesses

Harnesses fit over your dog's back and chest. They can be used instead of a neck collar to guide and contain a dog, though a neck collar should be used to carry a dog's identification tags. Here are two types of harnesses:

- ✔ **Traditional harness:** This basic harness can incite pulling when you're reviewing basic training, but it may be ideal for directing your dog through active or complicated exercises, such as the retrieving skills found in Chapter 7 and sporting games like agility and flyball.

✔ **No-pull harness:** A *no-pull harness* is helpful to condition basic cooperation skills such as leash-walking and household calmness. This contraption discourages forward motion by applying pressure to your dog's
shoulder blades; however, the no-pull harness must be removed when
practicing tricks and active sporting lessons. There are two types of no-
pull harnesses: One affixes over the shoulders and around the armpits
and the other crosses over the chest. You can explore either option,
though both must be fitted properly to ensure effectiveness and safety.

Leashes, short and long

Good leash skills are the basis for a happy off-leash relationship. Think of
leash-walking as holding a child's hand, not as a tug-of-war exercise to determine who's in charge. If your approach is nurturing and positive — a "here,
let's go this way" or "follow me, and I'll show you" — your dog will respond
with enthusiasm each time you're together.

Here are some leashes that can help you train and guide your dog:

✔ **Teaching Lead:** This patented leash is a little invention of mine. The difference between the Teaching Lead and garden varieties? You have the
option of wearing my leash like a belt instead of holding it. I know that
may sound funky, but it's pretty cool.

For dogs in training, this hands-free lead communicates leadership pas-
sively and allows you to teach good behavior indoors and out without
a chaotic scene. Indoors? Yes. A young dog doesn't know how to act in
everyday situations: The lead can help you guide good behavior —
especially important when formatting good habits like greeting and
sitting still for mealtimes. The leash–belt combination allows you the
freedom to engage both hands while your dog learns to walk calmly at
your side. In addition, the Teaching Lead encourages the most humane
handling techniques without a lot of jerking and constant restraint.
Designed in both leather and nylon and available with an extension for
people and dogs of any size and shape, it can be used with dogs of any
age. It has three applications:

• Leading, which encourages focus and quick responses to
commands

• Anchoring, which teaches your dog to lie next to you when you're
sitting

• Stationing, which teaches your dog her place in each room of the
house and allows you to secure her outside if the situation calls for
her to stay

Because dogs get more direction and less confinement, they love this lead, too. To get information on where you can purchase one, visit me online at www.whendogstalk.com.

✓ **Drag lead:** If you supervise your dog, she can wear a lightweight puppy leash or a thin, 4-foot nylon leash indoors so you can offer gentle guidance or redirection if she acts up or ignores a direction. As you give your dog freedom to explore with her drag leash, use the commands you've been practicing (for example, "Sit," "Down," and "Stay") and reward her with food and attention. If she ignores you, pick up the leash calmly and physically position or direct her.

✓ **Short lead:** This 8- to 12-inch lead hangs from the buckle collar for guided direction if it's needed.

Short leads are incredibly useful when teaching tricks or for other sporting adventures. The light weight on the collar helps your dog maintain her concentration (it feels like a leash is on, though nothing is dragging underfoot) and allows you to handle your dog gently without grabbing at her body or collar, a startling move that elicits an innate defensive response.

✓ **Finger lead:** This is a miniaturized short leash: a tiny loop attached to the collar for small or accomplished dogs who may still need guided direction.

✓ **Long line:** This 30- to 50-foot line gives you the freedom to let your dog run or work at a distance outside without the fear of losing control — which is especially important if you're practicing in an unconfined area. These light lines are essential for off-leash work. You can choose to let your dog drag the line provided you're able to keep track of it, or loop the end and attach your normal leash to the end of it to maintain contact at all times.

✓ **Retractable leash:** These leashes stretch and retract and are useful for exercise and trick training that calls for such controlled freedom.

Please don't use a retractable leash near a road; I've known dogs to race out in traffic and meet tragic ends.

If you've gotten into a battle of wills using your leash and find yourself having to haul your dog away from certain situations or people, reconsider both your training approach and your training collar. One good session with a respected trainer can give both you and your dog a new lease — or leash — on life!

Training with a Clicker

A *clicker* is a small, handheld, toy-like object with a metal strip inside; when you press the metal strip, it makes a sharp, very distinctive click, much like the sound of a camera. Clicker training is a clever, popular way to train dogs. It's a fun, fast, and positive approach to encouraging good behavior and teaching obedience and tricks.

Some people (like me) use the clicker when introducing a new concept, especially with distractible dogs, and then phase off its use after the dog knows the trick or movement. Others use the clicker for training their dog full time, affixing it to their body like jewelry. Other people can't master the coordination or just don't like using it.

To use this gadget, you have to figure out the best way to use the clicker, and you have to work with your dog (very briefly) to help her understand what a click means. In this section, I discuss how clicker training works, give you some examples of the training process, and suggest an alternative if clicker training just isn't right for you.

The click-then-treat approach: Associating the sound with rewards

When using a clicker, always pair the snapping sound with a tasty treat. The first time you introduce the clicker, just go one for one — click-treat, click-treat, click-treat — and before a minute passes, your dog will connect the sound with getting rewarded. After that, you're ready to train with a clicker.

What's the magic here — why do dogs learn faster with the clicker? The click sound is distinct from any other sound in the dog's world. As soon as a dog discovers that the click is followed by a goody, guess what — the dog will want to hear the sound as often as possible, and you can use the clicker to highlight good behavior. For instance, say I want to use my click sound to get a dog to sit: Each time the dog chooses to sit, I click and reward. What do you think happens? That's right: The dog starts to sit more often.

Clicker training is called inductive rather than coercive. *Inductive training* means the dog repeats behavior because she decides that doing so is in her best interest. *Coercive training* means she's being positioned, corrected, or shown a behavior by an outside force, namely the dog's owner. I'd like to give a 21-tail salute to Karen Pryor — a trainer and friend who brought clickers into the dog world and popularized the concept of inductive training. Believe it or not, the simple toy-like design of the clicker is revolutionizing the way animals (not just dogs but also dolphins, cats, horses, and farm animals) are being treated and trained.

Here are a few rules of paw for using treats in clicker training:

✔ No clicks go unrewarded! If you click, you must reward with a small treat. One click, one reward. Even if you make a mistake click, reward your dog.

✔ All treats should be small and easy to swallow, so your dog can wolf them down and not fill up.

✔ Don't treat your dog when she's not having lessons, or getting a reward won't seem as exciting.

Using a clicker effectively

Here are some tips on how to use clicker training most effectively:

✔ **Use the clicker to reinforce each step of your dog's trick progression.** Think in terms of stage-by-stage training — break the lesson into steps, and click when your dog masters each one; as you build up to the full trick, the dog will have to do increasingly more for a click.

For example, say you want to teach your dog to make a left circle. You first plan to sit with your dog and click when your dog takes one step to the left; that's stage one. Then you hold out your click for two steps, then three — then a full circle. Training this way definitely takes longer than pulling your dog in a circle, but after your dog figures out the sequence, she does a circle with far more zest and enthusiasm than if you were to tug her around and around.

✔ **Capture the exact moment your dog is doing something right with a click.** If you want to give clicker training a go, timing is everything. A poorly timed click confuses a dog and can result in naughty behavior. Once you've clicked, the treat should be given immediately afterward, before requesting another behavior.

✔ **Attach a spoken command to the behavior after your dog has figured out what's making the clicker work.** Use your command after your dog is already offering you the behavior. Initially, click and reward each time your dog sits in front of you. (You may show her a treat or reward to prompt her cooperation, but initially do not use the command.) Once your dog is sitting rapidly, attach the command to the behavior — say "Sit" as she's planting her bottom on the ground. Once you've paired the two, a couple of days later you're ready to prompt the position by saying the command ahead of time — just before you offer the reward. Command "Sit" first, then click and reward the good behavior. Soon you'll be able to say "Sit" away from clicker training exercises, and your dog will be spot on.

✔ **As your dog masters each new command, begin phasing off the use of the clicker and rewards, but always praise your dog for a job well done.** Use the clicker when introducing new concepts and behaviors to highlight their importance.

Looking at examples of clicker training

To help you understand how clicker training works, this section includes a few examples and exercises you can do with a clicker.

Consider an easy trick, teaching your dog to lick your hand on cue. Spread a dab of peanut butter on your hand and offer it to your dog. Click the second your dog licks you, and then quickly offer her favorite reward. Click the very moment your dog does what you want. Keep your clicker (and food rewards) with you, and click each time your dog offers a kiss. Once it becomes apparent that your dog gets the message, add the cue word "Kisses."

Here are just a few more examples of how to reinforce everyday behaviors — basic stuff your dog probably already knows but exercises to help you understand how the clicker works. (I sprinkle clicker-hints throughout the book for all you clicker fanatics!)

- **Housetraining:** When your dog eliminates in the right area, click and reward. After your dog associates the sequence, say "Get busy!" When she's eliminating, click the instant she finishes, treat, and praise.

- **Not jumping:** When your dog jumps on you, look away. Click, treat, and pet your dog as soon as all four paws are on the ground. You can command "Four on the floor" as soon as the dog understands the sequence.

- **Chewing on the right things:** Anytime your dog is chewing an appropriate object, click, treat, and praise warmly. Put the word "Bone" or "Toy" on the behavior as soon as the dog understands the sequence.

And here are a few more ways to apply the clicker to common commands:

- **"Sit":** Click, reward, and praise the moment your dog plants her tush on the ground. Command "Sit" as soon as the dog understands the sequence.

- **"Down":** Lure your dog into position with a toy or treat. Click, reward, and praise. Command "Down" as soon as the dog understands the sequence. Good dog!

- **"Come":** You first have to condition this command as a sensation of closeness. Throughout the day, click and reward anytime your dog stands near you. Next, encourage your dog to look up by sweeping your hands to your eyes. Click and reward. Command "Come" as soon as the dog understands. Gradually extend the distance and increase the distractions, working in a safe environment.

Checking out why it's not for everyone

If clicker training is so effective, why would anyone choose differently? Honestly, I'm not a clicker-exclusive trainer. I use a lot of methods to teach dogs, and my approaches are all upbeat and fun. People have different skills, and dogs do, too.

For people who can coordinate the timing of the clicker and remember to use it, it's a godsend. Dogs learn much faster — nearly twice as quickly — when it's used properly. That said, in some homes a clicker can fall into the wrong hands or fail to fit into the daily plan. For families with young children or people who get discouraged easily or have trouble finding their car keys, just working the device can be an unnecessary frustration. Overclicking or clicking at the wrong time confuses dogs, and a clicker in the hands of a young child can give a dog career-stress overload. Don't feel bad if the clicker doesn't work for you!

Although I can guarantee the clicker's effectiveness, it's not the only way to teach your dog. If the preceding sections leave you turned off to trick training, don't be; remember, there are many ways to teach dogs. A better option for you may be to insert a sharp word cue like "Yes!" or "Good!" each time your dog successfully completes a maneuver, and leave it at that. The take-home message here is that a sharp, declarative sound used to target breakthroughs in cooperation helps your dog understand what you want her to do.

Taking Training to Another Level with Targets

You'll flip out the first time your dog completes a rollover or waves to you; it's like getting an Oscar. But after a few days, you may wonder, "How can I get her to roll over without bending over her with a treat?" or "How can I get my dog to wave to my kids or a crowd?"

Fortunately, the answer is easy — there are some simple steps you can take to get you to the next level. This section describes some helpful gadgets you may use along the way. Because you have to train your dog to respond to these targets, I also explain how you and your dog can do that prep work together.

The tools of target training include target flags (a), target discs (b), and target sticks (c), as shown in Figure 2-1.

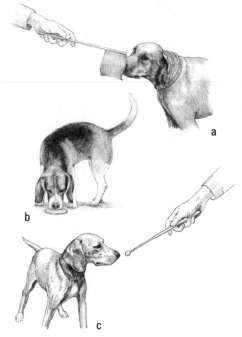

Figure 2-1:
Use target
training to
guide your
dog through
new training
exercises.

Delivering to a target flag

Target training is fun and very useful for teaching your dog how to work away from your side. You can maneuver a dog who learns to move toward a target flag in any direction. The *target flag* is simply a white strip of cloth you tie to a drumstick or dowel.

This tool is helpful in teaching dogs to deliver to a specific location, such as in the cleaning-up tricks in Chapter 10. Here's how to teach your dog this game:

1. **Hold the flag out a foot or so from your dog, and the moment she moves toward it, reward her (with a toy or treat, or a click from a clicker and a treat reward).**

   This is a fun game to practice.

2. **As she catches on, move the flag to various locations directly around your dog's body: first in front of her eyes, then to the side.**

   Add a word like "Flag" to the exercise, so you'll be able to direct her in more-complicated trick sequences.

3. **Practice placing the flag on or near an item, such as a plant or box.**

   Show your dog by moving with her how to navigate to the flag when you're not holding it.

Practice one maneuver at a time when using target training — learning them all simultaneously can get pretty confusing!

Standing on a target disc

You can teach your dog to stand on a target disc wherever you place it, enabling you to place your dog in position happily before commanding her to do a trick. You can buy a target disc, though it's just as easy to create one yourself, using something as small as a business card or the lid of a coffee can. After you choose your disc, here's how to use it:

1. **Place toys, treats, and a clicker (if you're using one) nearby, in a fanny pack or pocket for easy accessibility.**

2. **Place your chosen disc on the ground right in front of your dog's foot.**

   Watch her closely. She may sniff it, then shift it about. The moment your dog steps on the disc, click or say "Yes!" and reward her.

3. **After 20 successful steps on the disc, you may assign a word to the exercise.**

   I say "Target" as I wave my right index finger to the side.

4. **As your dog figures out the goal of this exercise, practice increasing the disc's distance from you and giving simple commands like "Sit" and "Down" immediately after your dog steps on the disc.**

Teaching your dog to navigate to a target disc may require some patience and self-control. Too much excitement can derail a dog's concentration. Some dogs pick this up quickly, whereas others take a couple of weeks to figure it out.

Pointing the way with a target stick

With a target stick, you can direct your dog from greater distances or guide her through courses and over obstacles. Sound intriguing? I find it very useful. Think of an elongated pointer directing you along a mysterious pathway. That's a good analogy of how a target stick can enlighten many of the routines in this book.

I've found that the best target stick is a tent pole or presentation pointer. Many are available in pet stores now, too. After you choose your target stick, here's what to do:

1. **Gather your rewards and/or your clicker.**

2. **Sit your dog near you and hold the end of the stick a couple of inches in front of your dog's nose.**

   The moment she reaches out to sniff it, say "Yes!" or click and reward her. Practice this no more than five to seven times per lesson.

3. **As she learns to move her head toward the tip of the target, gradually move the target greater distances from her nose.**

   Soon your dog's excitement will build each time she sees her target stick.

4. **At this point, you can use the stick to direct your dog with familiar commands, highlighting the movements as you say, "Sit," "Down," or "Follow me!"**

   Use your stick like a pointer. Gradually extend it farther away from your body as you signal with it as if it's an elongated fingertip. Sweep it just above your head to direct "Sit," drop it down between your dog's front paws for "Down," and hold it against your body (at your dog's nose level) to encourage positive walking skills.

The target stick doesn't work for every trick. For example, pointing it at your dog as you say "Speak" doesn't make much sense, but when you use it for "Roll over," "Crawl," and agility exercises, it can help you reduce your physical involvement while still maintaining your dog's enthusiasm.

Chapter 3

Understanding Your Dog's Natural Abilities and Limitations

. . . .

In This Chapter

▶ Taking age into account

▶ Considering breed characteristics

▶ Paying attention to body type

▶ Choosing tricks that fit your dog's personality

▶ Appealing to your dog's likes and talents

. . . .

Take a look at your dog. What do you have? Big or small? Active or mellow? Clueless puppy, mischievous adolescent, or full-grown set-in-his-ways dog? Before you introduce your dog to trick training, put yourself in his paws and think through the kind of activities that will get his tail wagging. Dogs are like snowflakes, thumbprints, and children — they're all unique. Each one has likes and dislikes.

No dog is going to love learning every trick in this book, but you can find enough variations in these pages to inspire your dog's particular enthusiasms. To know which tricks and activities you and your dog will enjoy the most, tip your trick-trainer's hat to his breed-driven impulses and natural-born obsessions as well as his personality type, age, and athletic ability, which I discuss throughout this chapter.

Making Your Lessons Age-Appropriate

First up, consider your dog or puppy's age. A very young puppy need not master complex skills — pottying in the right place and alerting to his name are tricks in and of themselves! You can definitely teach an old dog new tricks, and you can teach a new dog old tricks, but how you teach those tricks — and the tricks you choose — can vary according to your dog's age. This section explains how.

Beware of the aggressive reaction at any age. Some dogs have lofty impressions of themselves. If your dog growls at you as you explore any of these training routines, stop what you're doing and call a professional. Your first trick will be to smooth the communication between you and your dog (for tips on canine communication, see Chapter 2).

Puppy head start (under 6 months)

Young puppies can be delightfully sweet. Many will stick to you like glue and look to you for reassurance whenever the wind picks up.

Though seemingly open to learning about new things, a puppy can get overwhelmed by human expectations. In the earliest days of your life together, keep your "trick" routines to basic manners like where to potty and to sit before petting and rewards. You won't end up on Letterman with these tricks, but you and I know that they're truly remarkable.

As you're teaching your puppy basic routines, you can practice the skills you'll use down the road:

- ✔ **Teach as you go.** Structured lessons are too much for a young puppy. Instead, practice the teach-as-you-go method, giving direction as you walk your puppy through everyday routines. Choose your command; then say it each time you walk your puppy through the activity. Say "Outside" or "Papers" as you lead your pup to his potty area. Say "Sit" as you help him assume the dinnertime pose.

- ✔ **Avoid staring and repeating directions.** To a puppy, being stared down or repeatedly ordered feels scary. Imagine it: a giant 400-pound gorilla staring at you, giving you unintelligible orders. Would you understand him any faster if he repeated the order again and again? Say your directions clearly as you gently guide your puppy's body through the trick, or show him what you're envisioning by doing it yourself!

- ✔ **Be creative.** If your puppy isn't catching on, don't get frustrated — that only scares your puppy. Instead, ask what you can do differently. Your puppy can't read your mind, and although some pups grasp routines quickly, others need a more creative approach. For example, giving treats to puppies after they potty works for some but not for others. If your puppy is treat-obsessed, he may think that peeing anywhere is treat-worthy. As you'll discover down the road, getting a dog to perform tricks and complex routines can be a most creative process.

Your first routines should highlight puppies' natural behavior, like saying "Happy Puppy!" while they wag their tails. Young puppies, while impressionable, have short attention spans and cannot follow complex sequences.

Teenagers (about 6 to 14 months old)

Ah, the teen years. As for most animals, dog adolescence is a study in extremes: One minute, the dogs are full of enthusiasm to learn new things; the next, they're distracted, overwhelmed, and reverting to naughty behavior patterns like chewing and nipping. When introducing new tricks or routines, your adolescent dog may give you the canine version of the teenage eye roll from time to time.

If your dog knows the basics, then tricks and sporting adventures are ideal ways to have a little fun and shape his social skills. Keep these three things in mind:

- ✔ **Choose tricks that lean toward his passions.** If your dog likes to grab things, work on retrieving and carrying skills. If he's athletic or jumpy, work on tricks or agility routines that highlight those inclinations. Got a noisy or nosy companion or one who likes to bark, dig, or investigate? Find activities to encourage those skills. See the later section "Rolling with Your Dog's Natural Gifts" for details.

- ✔ **Break a trick into mini lessons to build the success rate.** Adolescent dogs get discouraged easily. Shy dogs shut down; more-energetic dogs lose interest. For instance, if your goal is to teach your dog to roll over, break the lesson into six mini lessons. Yes, six! Here they are:

  1. **Lie down.**

  2. **Lie down on his side.**

  3. **Lie down on his side and then arch his head over his neck.**

  4. **Lie down on his side, arch his head over his neck, and then roll backward.**

  5. **Lie down on his side, arch his head over his neck, and roll over.**

  6. **Lie down on his side, arch his head over his neck, roll over, and stand up!**

  Each success builds confidence, and although breaking the lesson down is more time-consuming, the extra effort can be well worth it.

- ✔ **Keep the lesson short and sweet.** Young dogs get bored and distracted easily. Keep each lesson focused, upbeat, and short: five to ten minutes maximum. Master one skill before moving on to the next, and highlight a successful routine at the beginning and end of each practice session.

Mature dogs (about 1 year and older)

As dogs age, they become less impulsive, provided they've had some basic training. Everyday distractions like the vacuum cleaner, butterflies, and the mail carrier's visit become commonplace and ho-hum.

The urge to be the center of your attention, however, never gets old. Spicing up your maturing dog's routine with some new tricks and adventures is easy. You can keep his tail wagging and the chuckles rolling year after year. Here are some things to keep in mind:

- ✔ **Give lessons before meals.** Older dogs get set in their routines and can predict meal times with uncanny accuracy. Use this ability to your trick-training advantage. An ideal time for lessons is right before a meal: hungry and alert, your dog will be eager to learn new activities — especially those that earn food rewards!

- ✔ **Factor in your dog's attention span.** Mature dogs have better concentration and will enjoy having your complete attention. Depending on your dog's personality type (which I discuss later in "Tagging Your Dog's Personality"), vary lessons from two to five minutes.

- ✔ **Account for aging.** Dogs age much too quickly. Although a 3-year-old dog can perform dazzling jumping feats or course an agility field ten times over, at some point he'll slow down. His knees will ache. He'll lose his youthful spark and drive. He'll need longer rest and recovery periods. Don't despair — we're all growing old. Work with your dog and pace his routines to his comfort and enthusiasm levels.

Sorting by Breed Characteristics

Open any dog book, and you'll see lots of different dogs. Big dogs. Small dogs. All-sizes-in-between dogs. Dogs with short hair. Dogs with long hair. Dogs with no hair! All these different dogs belong to different breeds. A *breed* is a group of dogs that share similar physical traits — they're all the same size, have the same hairstyle, and act pretty much the same.

In America, breeds are categorized into seven groups: Sporting, Hound, Working, Terrier, Non-Sporting, Toy, and Herding. The American Kennel Club (AKC) organizes these groups, according to shared characteristics. One thing's for sure — different breeds do different things.

To know which tricks and activities you and your dog will get the most out of, take a look at his breed. Certain breeds have character traits that naturally lend themselves to specific tricks and activities. In this section, I discuss the seven breed groups as well as mixed breeds and tell you which tricks may work best for them.

In the United States, the AKC recognizes more than 150 breeds (www.akc.org/breeds). The AKC is in charge of assigning a number to and counting every single purebred puppy born in America. What a job! When I try to make sense of it, I think it's a lot like a school: You have seven different classes and one principal's office — the AKC — that keeps everything organized.

Sporting group

Retrieving breeds, Spaniels, Pointing breeds, and others in this group were originally bred to spend entire days running in the fields seeking out and collecting land and waterfowl for their masters. The Sporting group is still pretty hung up on the retrieving thing. They're an energetic, loyal, happy lot who thrive on interaction. Trusting, friendly, and eager to please, they take to training (both trick and agility) well and generally view each new exercise as an adventure.

Here are some favorite tricks and activities your Sporting dog will excel in:

- ✔ Finding the keys (Chapter 7)
- ✔ Balancing acts (Chapter 10)
- ✔ Frisbee and flyball (Chapter 17), hunting trials (Chapter 18), and agility (Part IV)

An overdisciplined or untrained Sporting dog, on the other hand, will use all his retrieving skills against you. Instead of bringing you objects, he'll play "Keep Away." Call him, and he'll stay just out of reach. Ignore him, and he'll bark at you. Trained or untrained, helpful or bothersome, endearing or annoying — it's up to you.

Hound group

These guys, including Beagles, Basset Hounds, and Greyhounds, were bred to course fast-moving game, with hunters in quick pursuit. Dogs with a mission! Active, lively, and rugged, the Hound group has been domesticated into fun-loving, gentle pets with a high spirit for adventure. Here are some activities your hound dog may enjoy:

- ✔ Howling and barking on cue (Chapter 9)
- ✔ Fetching a ball (Chapter 7)
- ✔ Breed-specific adventures like hound trailing and coursing (Chapter 18)

Not bred to look to humans for direction, members of the Hound group usually don't. Consequently, obedience training can be slow and challenging; Hounds would rather trail a rabbit than hang out doing "Sit–Stays."

Trick training, however, with its use of food and toy lures, takes on a whole new meaning. Hounds excel in activities that require their nose, and if you put them in the spotlight, these guys are real hams. Although independent and somewhat distractible when their instincts call, they're still a lot of fun.

A leash or enclosure is required when Hounds are outside.

Working group

The Working group, breeds such as Bernese Mountain Dogs, Boxers, and Samoyeds, is the most diversified group in terms of their breed functions. Some members of the Working group pull sleds, others guard flocks, and others protect the homestead. They do, however, have one common thread: They've all worked in the past to serve people. Here are some activities you may want to consider with your working dog:

- ✔ Sniffing and finding (Chapter 7)
- ✔ Bang, Bang! Playing dead (Chapter 10)
- ✔ Sledding and carting (Chapter 19), *Schutzhund* or German police dog tests (Chapter 18), or agility (Part IV)

You can't ignore a dog with a history like that of the Working group. Obedience training is a must, though after the dog masters those skills, trick and activity training is a natural adjunct. Not quick to embarrass themselves doing circus routines, however, these dogs prefer more-complex, multi-step tasks that put their minds to work.

Though more patience may be required with certain routines, these guys can learn anything.

An untrained Working dog is lost. Unemployment leaves them bored, nervous, and in some cases, territorial and aggressive.

Terrier group

These guys come in two varieties: rodent and pest hunters, like the Cairn Terrier, Lakeland Terrier, and Kerry Blue, and bull baiting/fighting terriers like the American Staffordshire and the Bull Terrier. Originally bred for their tenacity in many European countries (especially on the British Isles), their popularity has spread worldwide. Terriers are a self-assured, spirited, and lively bunch. Agile and independent, they don't excel in off-leash obedience training and need to be leashed outdoors.

Trick training, however, is a different story. Terriers love the spotlight. As happy on two legs as they are on four, they'll dazzle you with their athletic feats. Great candidates for this trick and activity book, they'll leave you in a fit of hysterics marveling at their spunk, quick-mindedness, and good humor.

Here are some activities your Terrier and you may enjoy:

- ✔ "Chase your tail!" (Chapter 10)
- ✔ Combat crawling (Chapter 10)
- ✔ Flyball (Chapter 17), agility (Part IV), and earthdog trials (Chapter 18)

 Untrained or isolated, Terriers can become chronic barkers, destructive chewers, or urine markers, and they may develop aggression over objects, over food, and with other animals.

Toy group

Dogs in the Toy group (such as the Maltese, Yorkshire Terrier, and Chihuahua) were bred for one thing and one thing only: to be companions. In keeping with their ancestors, they continue to perfect the art of being adorable. Playful and affectionate, Toys love the spotlight, and if the end result of a trick session is more attention, they'll be happy to cooperate. Don't get your little handful confused with a Working breed, however. If the task is too difficult or you're not praising them enough, Toy dogs just might go on strike.

Anyone who's ever shared his or her life with a small dog will tell you they're adorable, especially when they're puppies. Spoiling them almost seems to go with the territory. Their behavior is so miniaturized that it's rarely a problem; however, living the unstructured life, being doted on night and day, is just as harmful for their psyche. The result? What I call Small Dog Syndrome, recognized by excessive barking (I'm in charge — hear me roar!), nipping (I may be small but watch out when I'm mad!), and, at the other extreme, excessive clinging (I can't cope on my own). Sound familiar?

If obedience is too structured for you, try trick training. Little dogs take to it like a fish to water, and seeing them perform is a real hoot. Here are some tricks your Toy breed may enjoy:

- ✔ Jumping into your arms (Chapter 8)
- ✔ Saying his prayers (Chapters 10)
- ✔ Freestyle (Chapter 17), obedience trials (Chapter 18), and agility (Part IV)

It's easy to neglect any type of training with Toy dogs, but owner beware! Without direction, they can become quite tyrannical, ruling the house with constant barking and snapping. To get the most from these little guys, train them to do some useful tricks, endearing them to one and all.

Non-Sporting group

Unlike other groups, there is little consistency in personalities here because the Non-Sporting dogs were all bred for different tasks. One thing is consistent though — they're all lovable! Some take to trick-training better than others. A Dalmatian, for example, will slide into a tutu much more readily than a Lhasa Apso. Here are some tricks to consider with your Non-Sporting breed:

- Dancing (Chapter 8)
- Rolling over (Chapter 6)
- Agility (Part IV), catching and retrieving sports (Chapter 17), and obedience trials (Chapter 18)

Many of the Non-Sporting breeds were originally bred for specific work, but because work is hard to come by these days, they've become companions. If you have a dog from this category, consult breed-specific books to figure out what yours likes to do.

Herding group

Dogs in the Herding group, such as the German Shepherd Dog, Australian Shepherd, and Border Collie, were bred to move flocks and herds. Agile and alert, they're quick to figure out whether the people they live with are smart enough to be considered shepherds or passive sheep. If you're a sheep, your herder will run circles around you; if you're his shepherd, training will come quickly and easily.

Ready to master anything new, Herders make great trick dogs and excel in agility games. Herding dogs take to many activities with natural style and grace. Some they naturally master include the following:

- The name game (Chapter 5)
- "Hide and Seek" (Chapter 5)
- Agility (Part IV), herding trials (Chapter 18), and flyball (Chapter 17)

Isolated or ignored, dogs in the Herding group may develop timidity, barking, or pacing habits.

Mixed breeds

If you have a mixed breed dog, don't despair! Your job is twice the fun. First, see whether you can identify the mix. If you're not sure, get a professional opinion. After you have a rough sketch, read over each group your dog may belong to. Then on to the fun part: the observational experiment. Study your dog's behavior and decide where he fits in. I know a Shepherd-Retriever mix, Charley, who's the spitting image of Rin Tin Tin but who'd retrieve a ball for you until the cows came home.

Hybrid vigor is a theory that states that mixed-breed dogs, due to their larger and more diverse gene pools, are superior in health and temperament to purebred dogs. Do I agree with this theory? A qualified *partly*. You see a lot of inherited health problems, such as hip dysplasia, in certain breeds, that may or may not show up in a mixed breed dog. There are no guarantees. Regarding temperament, much depends on environment, upbringing, and training. I've loved just as many purebreds as mixes. The choice is up to you.

Considering Body Type

Your dog's body type affects which tricks and adventures he'll be drawn to. Although your Basset Hound may have the enthusiasm of ten Border Collies, coaching him through complex agility courses may not be in his best interest; instead, teach him to find keys or to round up the kids for dinner. Which body type category does your dog fit into?

 ✔ **Balanced proportions:** Dogs who have balanced proportions, such as English Springer Spaniels, Airedales, and Bichon Frises, are generally comfortable moving into various poses and thus can excel at trick-training and sporting activities. These dogs are controlled by their breed drives, age, and personality, so read the earlier sections in this chapter for guidance on where to get started.

 ✔ **Leggy and light:** Slender, long-legged dogs such as Whippets, Vizslas, and Border Collies, often excel in fast-moving activities and tricks that utilize their agile frames. They're not built for contemplation and still-ness, so save tricks that demand these skills until after you have them hooked on performing.

✔ **Short-legged, big-boned:** Dogs with this body type, such as Bulldogs or Basset Hounds, may be high on enthusiasm, but due to their frames, they're low on flexibility skills. Although your dog may not be bred for tricks or activities that demand speed and agility, you dog can excel at plenty of clever tricks such as fetching a ball (Chapter 7) and combat crawling (Chapter 10) that will most definitely wow the crowds!

✔ **Stocky and solid:** Dogs who have solid builds, such as Rotweillers and Mastiffs, are less agile and more inclined to process their motions rather than act impulsively. Choose tricks and activities that highlight their problem-solving capacities, such as playing the role of pet detective (see Chapter 10) and participating in the breed-specific/mixed-breed hobbies in Chapter 18.

✔ **Handicapped dogs:** If you're the owner of a handicapped dog, either by accident or birth defect, I commend you for picking up this book. It says that you accept your dog's physical limitations, that you recognize that he's mentally competent and eager to learn — like every other dog in the world — and that you love him with abandon. Set your sights on tricks and other activities that your dog can easily master and perform in front of visitors or a crowd. Having your three-legged dog sit back on his haunches and wave will certainly shift others' expressions from sadness to delight!

Tagging Your Dog's Personality

After you understand your dog's ancestry (see the earlier sections on breed and body type), you need to take an individual look at his personality. Like people, each dog is different, and how dogs relate to the world directly affects how they'll relate to you, the teacher. Dogs have distinct personalities, and some are definitely more into learning than others. Fortunately, every dog has a weak spot. Whether it's cheese or liver or a toy, your job is to find something your dog is head over heels for and use it to reward his efforts and encourage his cheerful cooperation. Sure dogs could work for nothing, but that would be like forcing you to work for no pay. Dogs aren't prisoners, so reward them — the payoff is great!

I've identified six character types of dogs that I refer to throughout the rest of the book. Read them over and identify yours:

✔ **Eager Beaver:** As trick dogs, these creatures will do whatever it takes to make you happy, although they can be difficult and manic if you ignore them. Presented with new material, it's almost as if they're racing the clock to figure out what you want.

You'll notice they excel in tricks that approximate what their particular breed was designed to do. With this dog, all you have to do is decide what's next, and it's done. Though enthusiasm and staying power are a must, harsh techniques will crush their spirit.

- **Joe Cool:** These fellows are laid back and relaxed, and they're not terribly interested in organized activities. Obedience puts them to sleep, and when it comes to tricks, you may get a teenager-style eye roll when you request "Paw."

  But every dog — even the coolest of the cool — has a soft spot for something. Maybe it's cheese; maybe it's dried liver. But after you discover it, you'll be amazed at how quickly your mellow fellow will come to life. Lessons must be kept short and your enthusiasm high to keep these guys awake and interested.

- **Comedian:** These guys are the Jerry Seinfelds of the dog world. They live for a laugh. These wonder dogs will figure out a routine before you've had a chance to learn it yourself. Quick-minded perfectionists, comedians will get into a lot of trouble if they're not directed.

- **Bully:** These dogs take themselves far too seriously. In a group of dogs, they'd be destined to lead, and your home is no different. Unless you're an experienced trainer, dogs with this nature can be difficult to work with.

  Obedience training is a must, and although bullies are often turned off by lighthearted tricks, they excel in organized activities such as tracking or agility. If your bully dog threatens you, seek the advice of a professional trainer, and don't delay.

- **Sweetie Pie:** Docile and mild, these dogs like to observe situations rather than control them. Whereas obedience training makes them feel more secure about situations, tricks and organized activities help build their confidence. They adore the people they love and train best under a soft, patient hand. Yelling or hitting frightens them terribly, even when it's not directed at them.

- **Nervous Nellie:** These dogs like to view their world from behind your legs. Be patient and forgiving when teaching new maneuvers, and you'll notice how eager your dog is to please you. Training is essential to help these dogs feel more secure and to build their confidence.

Rolling with Your Dog's Natural Gifts

All dogs have natural talents: activities they live for and things they love to do. Whether you appreciate them, well, that's another story. Fortunately, trick and adventure training can channel your dog's passions into skills that put a smile on your face. Sound too good to be true? It's not. Read through this section to get a quick gauge on what sort of tricks to start with, depending on your dog's strengths.

Carrying: The Retrieving Rover

The Retrieving Rover likes to put everything in his mouth. Toys, shoes, paper towels — they're all the same in this fellow's eyes. Correcting this behavior is pointless. When you yell, it's perceived as prize envy: You want what he has, so it must be worth keeping! Chasing him only increases the obvious value of what he has, and the frustration level ratchets up. Now your dog is training you.

Turn these frustrations on their tail by working on the retrieving and carrying skills in Chapter 7. Because you can't turn off the mouthing gene, you may as well get some help carrying in the mail and collecting the dirty laundry.

You can get a head start on retrieval skills with a *treat-cup game*. Because your dog considers all his finds to be treasures (from his bone or favorite dog toy to the TV remote), encourage him to bring them by rewarding him with a treat from the treat cup. You may think you're rewarding delinquent chewing, but in fact, chewing won't become a problem because your dog is now showing you — and sharing — his treasures.

All dogs love treat cups. To make your own, get a few disposable plastic cups or deli containers (cut a hole in the lid of the container for easy access). Fill the cups halfway with small treats or a light breakfast cereal such as Cheerios. Each time you pass a treat cup, shake it and call out your dog's name. Soon he'll pay attention every time you call him, treat cup or not.

Entertaining: The Enthusiastic Acrobat

Enthusiastic Acrobats are peppy, bright creatures who are as happy on two paws as they are on four. Alert and inquisitive, they want to be in on everything and are drawn to laughter. Needless to say, their forwardness can be quite annoying if you don't redirect their energy. Fortunately, they love to learn, and you can start teaching a lot of natural routines from the start. You can find a trick in nearly every chapter that lauds their eagerness — finally, a hobby that rewards their enthusiasm!

Teach good dancing skills (Chapter 8), explore jumping and agility routines (Chapter 8 and Part IV), and turn their aggravating play bows and catch-me-if-you-can prances on their heels with commands like "Take a bow" (Chapter 6).

Problem-solving: The A+ Academic

A+ Academics are the engineers of the dog world. They're clever, smart, and keenly mindful of life's natural sequences, so you need to keep one step ahead of this dog's learning curve. These dogs love multi-step tasks, sporting adventures, and tricks.

As you work on your chosen routines, lighten up these somewhat serious souls with rewards and praise. These dogs can frustrate more easily if they're not encouraged. A simple game like "Hide and Seek" (Chapter 5) can help to keep their tails wagging and their minds sharp. You can find other appropriate activities like balancing acts, agility, and flyball in Chapters 10, 14, and 17, respectively.

Moving: The Agile Athlete

Is your puppy into everything? Are your houseplants being uprooted? Lamps overturned? Do you feel like your home has been turned into a racetrack, adventure park, and canine gymnasium rolled into one? Agile Athletes end up in the darndest places, and correcting them only increases their enthusiasm and mischief. Although not getting mad can be hard, you can channel their enthusiasm with the tricks throughout the book. Leaping skills in Chapter 8, high five and rolling over in Chapter 6, and fetching tricks in Chapter 7 can direct his energy and problem-solving skills and turn your four-legged nightmare into a dream dog.

If you have an Agile Athlete, you'll want to explore the agility chapters in Part IV, but why wait? Setting up a mini obstacle course in your house or backyard today can absorb your dog's energy level and tone down his curious streak. Be creative — brooms or logs to hurdle, a tunnel to zip through, or an old tire to climb on. If your house and yard are too small, use what you can find at a local park.

If you have a young dog, make sure your jumps are no higher than your dog's elbows. Jumping too high can damage growing muscles and joints.

Chapter 4

Encouraging Self-Control before You Launch into Lessons

- -

- -

*M*y clients always want to know how often they need to practice in order to have a well-behaved dog. My answer? You don't need to practice — you need to apply! Apply what you discover to everyday life. Basic skills like sitting before a meal or meeting company are the building blocks your dog needs to know before she can start picking up the laundry (Chapter 10) or navigating an agility course (Part IV).

Teaching tricks requires that you set some time aside, but first you need to review the basics, and that's what this chapter is all about. This chapter teaches or refreshes the skills that you and your dog may already know, like "Sit" before a meal or "Stay" while you chop the vegetables. To help you make sure your dog has these skills down pat, I also tell you how to introduce distractions, apply the skills outside your home, and work toward unleashing your dog.

Reviewing Basic Commands

Think of basic training as the backbone of trick and adventure training. From "Sit" to "Stay" and "Come," these commands are a must before you proceed to anything fancier. Just as kids need to know their alphabet before they can spell, you and your dog need to know and use these basic commands to have the proper foundation to build from. In this section, I introduce 11 commands — or sets of commands — that form the foundation of trick training.

As you teach your dog basic commands, remember that the biggest motivating factor in training is you. To be a good teacher, remember the three *c*'s:

✓ **Consistency:** Use a familiar command in similar situations, like "Sit" for greetings. Encourage everyone to do the same. If two people give different directions, your dog won't know who or what to follow.

✓ **Clarity:** Be clear in your communication. Remember that dogs are not little people. Bent postures invite playful interaction, not respect. Soft tones sound wishy-washy. When directing your dog, stand tall and speak clearly. Be the one to watch!

✓ **Compassion:** Be compassionate and praise a lot. Remember that you attract more dogs with dog biscuits and good cheer than with discipline and frustration. A cheerful attitude inspires a dedicated learner.

Think of each command as an interactive communication rather than a complex request. Your dog can't break down complex sentences, but a short, clear word cue helps your dog recognize what you'd like her to do in all situations that require that behavior. The shorter your word cue, the better. Think of a bark. "Molly, sweetie-pie, can you sit down for Mama?" is not bark-like; "Sit" is. Use this command anytime you need your dog to sit. For more tips on communicating with your dog, see Chapter 2.

Calling your dog

Three commands are associated with summoning your dog to your side: her name, "Follow," and "Come." First you want to make your dog's association with her name a positive one. Then you can get her to follow you wherever you may lead and come at your bidding. The following sections show you how.

Name

What do you do when people you respect call your name? Do you ignore them? Or do you look up, expectant and excited that an adventure may follow? You want your dog to be interested and excited, too. To create positive associations with your dog's name, remember the following:

✓ **Use your dog's name for happy interaction.** If you need to medicate, isolate, or otherwise commiserate about something (a chewed shoe perhaps), go and get your dog; don't call her by name.

✓ **When you call your dog, have something fun in store.** Shake a cup full of treats, bounce or toss a toy, or pretend you've found something in the grass. Be enthusiastic when your dog responds to you.

✓ **Don't overuse her name.** No one likes to check in constantly. Give your dog some freedom to explore. (See the later section "Working toward Off-Leash Control.")

"Follow"

Think of the "Follow" direction as the politically correct version of "Heel." When you say "Follow," you're basically saying, "We're going on a mission. . . . Follow me!" After you get your dog to focus on her name, you're ready to teach her proper following-manners. With your dog on-leash, or with the leash secure around your waist if you're using the Teaching Lead method (which I mention in Chapter 2), do the following:

1. **Take some treats in a cup or a favorite toy.**

2. **Walk forward, cheerfully calling out your dog's name.**

3. **If she darts ahead, shake the treat cup or offer the toy as you encourage her to follow you with the cue word "Follow."**

Start teaching "Follow" in nondistracting areas and praise/reward your dog for each turn she makes with you. If she doesn't want to follow, keep going . . . soon she'll get the idea that staying with you is good; moving away, not so good.

After your dog catches on to the sequence, try walking forward confidently. The second your dog forges ahead call, "[Name], follow" and turn away from her promptly without thought or encouragement. The second she races to your side, by choice or leash encouragement, praise/reward her confidently. Continue to do this each time your dog's focus wanders from you until your dog figures out that you're the one to watch. Work in increasingly more-distracting areas, following the same sequence of rewards and encouragement.

"Follow" is an ideal clicker exercise — click and reward each time your dog chooses to stay at your side. (For tips on using a clicker, see Chapter 2.)

"Come"

You should first teach the "Come" command as a sensation of closeness. Here's how the process works:

1. **Throughout the day, reward your dog anytime she chooses to reconnect with you.**

   Say "Come" as you reach out to pet or reward her, encouraging your dog to look up by sweeping your hands to your eyes. If you're using a clicker, highlight this moment of togetherness: Click and treat.

2. **After the dog understands that the word means closeness, command "Come" to get your dog to come to you.**

   Gradually extend the distance and increase the distractions, working in a safe environment.

Think of the command "Come" like the human phrase "Huddle!" You're the captain, calling your player in to come up with a new, exciting plan.

Getting your dog in position

Sometimes you need to restrict your dog's movement, and the commands that follow enable you to do just that. Teach your dog to sit, lie down, stand still, get back, or stay put under your legs or chair when you're sitting, and not only will your dog have impeccable manners, but she'll also understand the appropriate starting points for learning many tricks.

"Sit"

Think of the "Sit" command as the "Say please" direction of the dog world. Encourage it before anything your dog perceives as positive, such as meals, treats or toys, pats, or greetings at the door. Dogs learn manners at home, just like kids, so be cool when you come in; don't pay attention to your dog until she's composed enough to "Sit–Stay."

To signal "Sit," do the following:

1. **Swing a pointed finger from your dog's nose to your eyes, as if you're scooping her attention toward you as you command "Sit."**

2. **If your dog doesn't respond, use either a treat or a toy to encourage her cooperation, or position her.**

    To encourage cooperation, do the following:

    • Say a happy marker word like "Yes!" each time her bottom hits the floor.

    • If you're using the clicker (see Chapter 2), click and reward cooperative efforts.

    You can position your dog by gently squeezing her waist (the midsection just below her ribs).

Luring is an effective way to encourage cooperation. Use a toy or treat to lure your dog into position, holding the bait just so as you guide your dog into position. Then command "Sit" as your dog is doing the action. If she doesn't listen, give the "Sit" command once as you gently position your dog. Avoid repeating yourself — repeating isn't cool in any language.

"Down"

The "Down" command encourages your dog to lie flat on the floor. It's essentially for getting dogs to relax, but it's also a necessary cue for trick-training as a first step for tricks like rolling over (Chapter 6), crawling (Chapter 10), and playing dead (Chapter 10). Initially this exercise can be a real bear to teach, so here are some steps to follow if your dog doesn't know this one:

1. **Give the command "Sit" and then either kneel or stand at your dog's side. Hold a favorite toy or treat on the ground slightly in front of your dog.**

   Let your dog puzzle over the predicament, but don't release the prize or say anything until her elbows touch the floor.

2. **As she lowers herself, say "Down" and then praise, reward, and release her.**

   Continue this exchange for anything your dog treasures, from treats to toys and attention. Work on Steps 1 and 2 for three days.

   Some dogs want nothing to do with the "Down" command; they consider lowering themselves too stressful, a loss of face, or just plain not fun! To encourage the proper motion, you can press your left thumb gently between your dog's shoulder blades as you lift a front paw out gently.

3. **Starting on the fourth day, say "Down" as you stand calmly at your dog's side, adding your hand signal, which is a downward point of your left hand.**

4. **Continue the reward exchange for another three days, and then begin to phase out the object reward, relying solely on your verbal praise.**

"Stand"

Asking your dog to stand still is an essential. For everything from brushing to getting your dog to carry a book on her head to getting a good start in an agility trial, this direction is a must for your training toolbox.

Here's a quick refresher course, in case your dog has forgotten the art of standing still:

1. **Kneel down on the floor next to your dog.**

2. **Command "Stand" as you lure your dog into a stand or gently prop her into a standing position.**

   Use either a treat or a toy to lure your dog into a stand, or prop her there with your right hand, palm out, under your dog's buckle collar as you slide your left hand under your dog's belly.

3. **Relax your right hand and slide your left to rest on your dog's thigh.**

4. **Pause and later release with an "Okay."**

   When you're first starting out, count to five between the pause and the release. Slowly increase the time to one minute.

5. **Now repeat Steps 1–4, but this time do it from a standing position.**

6. **Begin to let go with your left hand and then your right as you steady your dog with calm "Stay" commands and a relaxed posture.**

   I discuss the "Stay" command in the next section.

The hand signal for "Stand" is a level hand, arm extended, palm down.

"Back" and "Under"

The "Back" and "Under" cues reassure your dog that you're in control. Each command signals a position near your body:

✔ **"Back":** This command reminds your dog to get back to your side and behind you. Think of it like calling a child back to your side who is overwhelmed, overexcited, or afraid. This command reassures your dog that you know what's happening and you'll protect her. To teach your dog this cue, help her learn to back up when you direct her.

Stepping backward feels awkward for your dog at first, so use treats or toys to teach your dog to back up: Lure your dog back by holding a treat directly under her chin. Praise her for each little step back until she's comfortable with the motion. If she sits down, gently hold her hindquarters up with your other hand.

When first teaching your dog to back up, create a channel by lining up chairs 2 feet from a wall or using broomsticks balanced on cereal boxes.

Once she's learned how to step back, here's how to teach and use this command:

1. **Place your dog on-leash, slap your side, and call your dog to your side. You may also wave a toy or a treat to get your dog's attention.**

2. **If necessary, guide your dog to your side with the leash.**

3. **Encourage your dog to sit at your side.**

✔ **"Under":** If your dog is planted out in front of you, she'll think that you expect her to protect you; however, if you direct your dog under your legs (or under the table or chair) when you're sitting, you can get her to relax by providing a little den. Use the "Under" command while you have visitors in your home or if you're enjoying a curbside latte, or use it to calm your dog before competitions and shows.

When you sit down, say "Under" and direct your dog behind your legs or under your table or chair; do not let her sit on your lap or feet.

Teaching patience

Being able to exercise self-control is always a good thing. The "Stay" and "Wait" commands help your dog to do just that.

"Stay"

After your dog understands "Stand," introduce the "Stay" command. At first, say "Stay" while standing at your dog's side; then pause and release with "Okay!"

Now tell your dog to "Stay," and pivot directly in front of her; the separation challenges a dog's impulses. Return to her side and release with "Okay!" As your dog catches on, increase your distance and add some distractions (you can hop around or make funny sounds — make it fun for both of you). If your dog stands up, reposition calmly and remind, "Stay." Slowly, as your dog improves, move farther out in front.

Remember to always return to your dog's side before releasing her to ensure that she doesn't get up while you're apart.

"Wait" and "Okay"

The "Wait" and "Okay" commands tell your dog to stop in her tracks, check in with you, and wait to be released at "Okay." It's a self-control thing like "Stay," but it's more in the moment. You teach it like this:

1. **Holding your dog to your side on-leash, walk to any threshold (doorway) in your home.**

2. **Stop abruptly as you reach the threshold and say "Wait" as you distract your dog with a toy or treats.**

   If she bolts anyway, pull her back behind your heels and repeat, "Wait," as you continue to show her the positive distraction. Repeat the pull back as often as necessary until she pauses and looks to you.

3. **The moment your dog is still, say "Okay" as you lead her forward and reward her.**

4. **Try using the "Wait" command at the front door.**

   Now you're ready for the big time! Go to your main doorway. Prepare yourself as previously, holding the leash and carrying a favorite toy/food distraction. Command "Wait" just before you open the door. If your dog bolts, be ready. Pull her back to your feet and remind, "Wait." When she does, say "Okay" as you reward her and lead her through.

5. **After you've mastered the front door, try the car.**

   Take your dog to your car and instruct her to "Wait" as you open the door. If she lunges, snap her back, refusing to let her in until she looks to you for permission.

By now your dog should perk up every time she hears you say "Wait." Start using the command whenever you want your dog to stand still: when talking to friends, crossing the street, visiting the veterinarian, or as a preliminary step to more advanced training.

A flat palm flashed quickly in front of your dog's nose is the hand signal for "Wait," and I use an upbeat flash outward for "Okay."

Saying no

Your dog won't always make the right choices — that unattended slice of sausage pizza on the coffee table may be too hard to resist. At times like these, your dog can benefit from a little guidance from you — this is where the "Nope" command comes in handy. Other times your dog may be blocking your way, intentionally or inadvertently. Either way, "Excuse me" commands the respect and behavior you want.

"Nope" (or "Wrong")

"Nope" (or "Wrong") sends a simple, clear message that what your dog is doing isn't appropriate. Use "Nope" to teach your dog to back off from temptations, whether the temptations are food, moving objects, or other distractions. Or to try a different approach, use "Nope" when a trick cue brings on the wrong behavior.

Always follow a negative command with a direction that tells the dog what to do instead. Your dog wasn't born with an instruction manual on how to live with you; you need to show and teach her what's appropriate. "Nope" says that's not the right thing to do; a follow-up direction says, "Do this instead!"

To help your dog learn better impulse control with "Nope," you must first teach her what this direction means. Here's how:

1. **With your dog in the next room, place something tempting, like a plate of cookies, on the floor.**

2. **Put your dog on a leash and say "Follow" as you bring her into the room and approach the plate.**

3. **The very second your dog notices the temptation, pull on the leash and say "Nope."**

   Say "Nope" conversationally, as you would other commands.

   Initially say "Nope" as a command, then if your dog still darts ahead, pull the leash back abruptly. Though pulling your dog back may work to discourage her, if you forget to say "Nope," your dog will have no idea what you're talking about when she's off-leash.

4. **Walk by the plate.**

   Does she stay focused on you? Good dog — say "Yes!" or click, and then offer a reward. Redirect her with a command like "Follow" or "Get your bone."

   If your dog shows any interest in the plate, tug and say "Nope." After your dog turns her attention back to you, redirect and praise her.

   Focus your correction on the object and the impulse, not your dog. Growl at the object — your dog will grow wary of the item rather than you. Timing is everything, so give corrections the second your dog starts to contemplate a mischievous deed, not after the fact. If she's already downed the cookies, you're too late!

5. **Repeat this routine the next day with a similar temptation, gradually exposing her to more tempting objects later in the week.**

Pretty soon your dog will see something tempting on the floor and turn her nose toward the sky, as if to say, "I don't see anything." Now you can practice with cars, kids, small creatures, and any other distractions. Make a huge fuss when your dog focuses on you. (For more on dealing with distractions, see the later section "Introducing Temptations.")

Next you can use the "Nope" command when directing your dog or encouraging her cooperation with tricks and other adventures. If she knows that "Nope" is about what she's doing — not a confrontation between you — she'll use her head to figure out a different approach or look to you for a clue.

"Excuse me"

Dogs, mindful creatures that they are, often use body posturing to define authority. If your dog blocks, leans, or ignores you, the message is clear: You've got no respect! This attitude can put a real crimp in your trick-training aspirations. However, saying "Excuse me" with an ounce of attitude can get you far. Here's an easy remedy for a dog who likes to get in your way or invade your personal space:

✔ **If your dog is in your way, say "Excuse me" and then shuffle through until your dog moves to one side.** If she won't move, shimmy your feet beneath her or nudge her aside with your knees. You don't have to get bossy, just nudge her aside.

Bump your dog away using your legs, not your arms. Arms are perceived as interaction and may excite play or defensiveness.

✔ **Don't allow leaning unless it's mutual and you've invited it.** Crowding is a sign of dominance or insecurity, and neither is good for long-term relationships.

A dog must learn the 3-inch exclusion zone: Unless invited in for a hug, she must respect this space between you and her. If your dog disrespects this, bump her away with your leg and say "Excuse me." You may need to do this several times before your dog takes you seriously.

✔ **If you give your dog a recognized direction and she ignores it, ask first what you might be doing wrong.** Are you mumbling, shouting too loud, or repeating yourself? Give your dog an attention-getting leash tug and say "Excuse me." Before repeating yourself, encourage your dog to listen to your first direction.

If your dog growls at you for any reason, call a professional: This signal is serious, and your dog may bite you if you push her.

Regaining control of your car from your dog

Ever hear of the fishbowl effect? It happens when bossy dogs are confined in a car. They naturally assume the car is part of their territory. The resulting jumping and barking can be a real nuisance, not to mention a true danger. If this sounds too familiar, you must regain control of your car. If your dog controls the car, she controls you, making trick-training difficult, if not impossible. This is the remedy:

1. **Create a dog station in your car.**

   Either set up a car crate or secure a doggie-style seat belt in the back seat or the cargo area of your car. Place a blanket and some toys there, and instruct your dog to settle down.

2. **Take your dog to your car on-lead, instruct "Wait" after opening the door, and permit** your dog to enter after varying durations of time by saying "Okay."

3. **Secure your dog in the crate or by leash in the dog station if your dog is over-protective or fidgety.**

4. **Before you let your dog out of the car, release the restraint and instruct "Wait" again.**

   If your dog's hyper, wait it out. Don't release your dog from the car until she's calm.

5. **Say "Okay" to release her.**

This "Wait" and "Okay" routine reminds your dog that you're the responsible person in the car.

Nailing routine directions

Your dog doesn't need a 300-word vocabulary to lead a happy life, but she will appreciate a few recognizable words to direct her throughout the day. Imagine you live in a foreign country — how comforting to hear a familiar word or phrase!

Think through your day and write down routines you repeat often. Pin a word to each activity and use it like a command to direct your dog. Now watch that tail wag each time you use it.

For instance, in my house, the whole family seems to love rousing me. Each morning I hear my husband say to both the dogs and kids, "Let's go wake up Mommy!" This trick couldn't be easier to teach: With eagerness in your voice, repeat the command as you join your dog in the chosen activity. Soon she'll do it on her own.

The following table gives some more examples of routine directions from my home to yours. These are just a handful of the commands I use to highlight our routines. Think through your day and make up your own list.

Command	*Use*
Car	We use this one each time we go for a ride.
Upstairs	Since puppyhood, this word has highlighted a trip up to the next floor.
Down we go	This highlights our descent.
Inside	I prefer this word instead of "Come" when reentering the home. This way, the dog doesn't associate "Come" with the end of fun outdoor time.
Outside	This one teaches the dog to go to the door. It's always a big hit.
Daddy	You can teach your dog everyone's name. Each time you walk toward a friend or family member, say his or her name. Like magic, your dog will be able to identify different people.

Introducing Temptations

While working on tricks or doing other activities with your dog, you'll encounter distractions. Unless you limit your performances to solitary stints in your living room, something — somewhere — will vie for your attention. Instead of waiting for that day, introduce temptations in a controlled way so your dog will know that no matter what, the show must go on. Do this before you launch into tricks and other adventures, and you won't have to waste your lessons calming or capturing a runaway dog. This section explains how.

Calming your dog with vocal cues

Going new places and learning new things can be so exciting for dogs. And sometimes, getting excited can lead to getting really excited — even really, *really* excited. These next two commands, "Easy" (or "Shhh") and "Wait," can ratchet down your dog's excitability levels when her behavior is nearing — or has rocketed right over — the top.

✔ **"Easy" or "Shhh":** Use these cues to calm a dog who is in the middle of an activity or sequence. If your dog is racing up the stairs, overstepping a trick, or blowing out of a course, use "Shhh" or "Easy" to slow her down.

✔ **"Wait":** I introduce this command in the earlier section "Reviewing Basic

Commands." Its human phrase equivalent is the word *freeze*. It's extremely useful when encouraging your dog to stop whatever she's doing. Think of it as getting a wild child to be still for 30 seconds; use it whenever your dog is acting too wound up.

When first using these calming cues, say them clearly and praise your dog if she calms down. If she doesn't, reinforce the commands with a tug on a leash. Your dog can't read your mind, so you need the leash to discourage unwanted behavior and show the proper response to each signal.

Sounds

Unfamiliar sounds are so . . . unfamiliar. Some direction from someone who knows what's going on would help — hey, that's you!

Introduce your dog to various environments and sounds. Look for weed whackers, car horns, playground noises — anything out of the ordinary. Direct your dog with recognized commands so she feels safe and relaxed no matter what's happening around her. Later, when your tricks have been well-rehearsed or you're competing in specialty events, your dog will be able to focus on you above all the other sounds going on around her.

Motion

Zippy, unpredictable motion elicits the predatory response in even the smallest of dogs. They must give chase and bring that mighty caribou to its knees! Even if it is on the small side — and looks a little bit like a chipmunk. Although a little backyard bunny-chasing is okay, racing off an agility course or running after a pack of children while performing tricks is not.

To teach your dog to focus on you above all else, praise her cooperative skills and reward her attention when working together. Then rig a scenario to elicit her chasing impulse by asking some helpers to run around you while you're proofing basic training skills. If you see your dog's chase impulse kicking in, say "Nope" (or "Wrong") and tug the leash back sharply. When your dog passes the run-by test, graduate to bike-riding and food-waving. Practice — carefully — around moving cars. Praise her when she's focused on you, and remind her to "Stay" or "Follow."

People

Good news, bad news: Everybody loves a well-mannered dog, so be prepared. Most people will ask before they approach, but some people don't. Kids and toddlers can't resist — some rush right in for the teddy bear hug before their parents can intercede. Bring your dog to a park, and you'll discover she's a kid magnet. If your dog starts doing some tricks, the swings, the ice-cream concession stand, and the pool will empty out in no time.

Prepare your dog to meet people by practicing at home. Slowly, start to encourage interaction in unfamiliar locations. Here's how:

- Shake a cup of treats and teach your dog to sit each time she hears it rattle.
- Put the cup by the front door. Each time someone enters, shake the cup, command "Sit," and reward your dog when she's sitting.
- Take the cup wherever you go and encourage the same manners you've taught at home.

If your dog is excitable, you can brace her for greetings. Hook your thumb over your dog's buckle collar with your fingers facing the ground. Hold your other hand on her waist and encourage her to "Stay."

To improve your dog's focus around children, practice with your dog on-leash. Find a location where kids congregate, and practice basics at a distance your dog can tolerate.

If children or other distractions unnerve your dog, determine how far away you need to be to keep your dog's attention focused on you. This is called your *Red Zone*. If you notice your dog getting anxious when children are within 20 yards, then work at 21 yards to start. Soon it will be 18 yards, then 12, then 6. One day, you'll be right in the middle of a foot-stamping, snack-waving, eardrum-splitting group of 6-year-olds, and your dog won't miss a beat.

Off-lead or untrained dogs

Leashes add an interesting — and not always good — dynamic to dog-dog interactions. Because the leash causes your dog to strain forward to greet a new dog, she may look assertive even if she's submissive. It creates an aggressive body posture when her mind may not be. When an off-lead dog approaches, he may misunderstand the posture and get assertive in response.

The best thing to do when an off-lead dog approaches is to discourage your dog's interaction and walk quickly away from the other dog. Most often, off-lead dogs are curious and just want to say hello, but some are aggressive, protecting what they perceive as their territory: If you leave it, they'll quickly lose interest.

If you have a small dog or encounter off-lead dogs regularly, you can buy a spray deterrent to defend yourself and/or your dog if another dog or animal charges at you. This nontoxic spray is useful to stop most animals in their tracks. I recently saw a product called Spray Shield, by Premier, which you can find online at Amazon.com.

If you're in town and approached by an on-leash but poorly trained dog, tell your dog to "Wait" at your side. You can roll with the chaotic greeting — or do what I do: Just look the dog's owner in the eye and say, "This isn't a good time now," and walk away.

Out and About: Putting Training to the Test

The best way to test your dog's knowledge of the basics is to take your show on the road. Your dog may be a living room champion who behaves beautifully in the quiet of your home, but if she can't concentrate around distractions, you'll have trouble getting her to behave when it really counts.

In your home — the den — there are few distractions, and your dog feels safe. In town or on a trail, nearly every distraction will test her focus. It's here in the real world that you can provide reinforcement. Only here will you be able to teach her focus first, gauge her distractibility, and teach her to hold still and pay attention. This section tells you how to apply basic training in fields or on trails, and in town.

Going on field trips

When you bring your dog into an open expanse, such as a field or trail, she'll be on sensory overload. Because all dogs see with their noses, not their eyes, hers will be twitching from the moment you leave the car.

Yes, you should be the primary focus, but before you start drilling her on the basics, have some compassion when you visit a field or trail: Give your dog some time to take a sniff or two. Let your dog have a supervised five-minute tour, allowing her to put her nose to the ground and orient herself before you ask her cooperation.

After she's settled, review your basic directions. Command "Sit," "Down," "Stay," and "Come." Vary the command sequences so your outings don't get stale.

As soon as your dog is focused, give her freedom on a long line or retractable leash. Every five minutes, give her a command or play a training game like "Hide and Seek" (see Chapter 5).

Hitting the town

Be it a big city or small village, trips into town can be a little disorienting for your dog at first. Dogs prefer predictability to chaos, and getting a handle on all the sights, sounds, and smells that a town or city offers is hard. The silver lining? You look authoritative and worldly to your dog as you navigate the stimulating streets.

In town, use familiar commands to anchor your dog at your side. Imagine you're the pilot on a turbulent flight: Don't run down the aisle, flailing your arms; use your grown-up voice to put everyone at ease. Work with the following commands (which I introduce earlier in this chapter):

- Ground your dog before you let her out of the car. Use "Wait" and insist that she hold still. Use "Okay" to release her.
- Tell your dog to "Follow." You're letting her know "I'm the leader. Just follow me!" Remember, you're the pilot.
- Use "Wait" and "Okay" at all curbs or thresholds.
- Command "Back" or "Under" if you sit down.
- Use "Back" to direct your dog to your side if she pulls ahead of you.

You may add to this command list, but keep it simple, straightforward, and brief. Your initial trips to town should be 10 to 15 minutes. After your dog is used to going out, you'll both enjoy your outings together and you can extend your time.

Working toward Off-Leash Control

Using a leash is a little like holding a child's hand when he's anxious or unsure: You hold the leash to show your dog what to do. You repeat exercises until your dog understands your vision.

Of course, the highest achievement in training — the big test — is how your dog acts when the leash comes off. Many of the tricks and activities that follow work best without a leash, so for those of you who are still leash-dependent, pull up a chair. If the thought of your dog's freedom keeps you up at night, hope is right here. This section explains how you can gradually increase your dog's freedom and eventually cut the cord, so to speak.

When you feel your dog is cooperating and understands your basic directions, let her drag a lightweight leash behind her: a short 4-foot leash for inside and a 25- to 50-foot leash for outside. The drag lead lets you reinforce your directions calmly. Here's how to use the drag lead:

✔ If your dog ignores a command, walk calmly to the end of the line and direct her through the exercise. Put her in a "Sit" or "Down" position or, if you commanded "Come," direct her to your side.

✔ If your dog blatantly disobeys you or races off, pick up the end of the line and tug her firmly, saying "Nope!" Then repeat your command and follow through.

Do this over and over, and you'll see the glimmer of understanding shining through. Your dog will not simply obey — she'll choose to listen because you're making good sense.

If you use a leash to pull or jerk a dog around unnecessarily, the dog will resist learning and cooperate only begrudgingly. Unclip the leash from this dog, and she'll be off and away in a flash. If you feel like I'm talking about you and your dog, get a professional to help you with the basics before you try weaning your dog off the leash.

Part II
Teaching Tricks with Positive Reinforcement

The 5th Wave   By Rich Tennant

"Watch — I can make him ring that bell just by drooling a little bit."

In this part . . .

There isn't a dog alive who would resist learning some fun tricks if it meant more one-on-one time with her favorite person and included treats and other favorite goodies and toys. In this part we cover everything from encouraging good manners to happy tricks like tail-wagging and favorites like offering a paw, rolling over, and fetching the paper. If teaching your dog to retrieve is your game, this part has it — and you'll even learn how to build on this simple skill to get your dog to fetch you a tissue or bring you a drink!

Chapter 5

Minding Manners and Trying Out Some Tricks

▶ Setting up places for your dog to relax

▶ Working on bathroom skills

▶ Redirecting barking, chewing, and jumping tendencies

▶ Doing tricks that show happiness and affection

▶ Playing games together

I have a confession to make: When people first meet my dogs, they never say, "Wow! What phenomenally well-trained dogs!" What they do notice is the good cheer and happy responsiveness of my dogs.

I don't believe in harsh methods or electronic collars to get dogs to behave or perform like programmed robots. My dogs — and the dogs I train — become regular members of the family: well-trained, respectful, and sometimes a bit exuberant — but in a good way.

Like people, every dog has different likes and dislikes, games they enjoy and routines that they count on. When your training comes from a consistent, patient, and understanding place that takes these canine preferences into consideration, your dog will master tricks and activities quickly and enthusiastically.

Teaching these everyday interactive skills is your first trick. And as you'll see, it isn't complicated at all. In this chapter, you find out how to help your dog relax by setting up a comfort zone for him. You also find some tips on improving bathroom manners, some tricks you can teach so your dog uses those barking, chewing, and jumping instincts in a socially acceptable way, and some simple tricks and games you can play together.

Giving Your Dog a Place to Settle Down

Consider a routine: You wake up in the morning and eat breakfast. You busy yourself with a few interesting, fun, and familiar activities, and then it's time for dinner. After one or two traditional nighttime rituals, it's time for bed. Repeat this every day. That may sound repetitive and a little boring to you, but to a dog, routines are wonderfully comforting. Dogs like predictable patterns, and your dog will cooperate more willingly when he knows what to expect.

One way to help your dog get into a routine — and mind his manners — is to give him a place of his own to settle down and relax. In this section, I discuss setting up and using canine comfort stations in your home, and I also explain how you can give your dog a taste of the familiar when you go on the road.

Creating comfort stations at home

Getting your dog to settle down in one spot is one of those lessons that you appreciate for the rest of your life. Pick an area for your dog in each room you share. I advise a spot that's to the side or in a quiet corner. In the TV room or the bedroom, consider positioning a permanent doggy spot near your couch or bed, because dogs love being close.

I sometimes call this dedicated dog place a *comfort station*. Adorn your dog's station with the following:

- **Bedding:** Place a flat towel, a fluffy pillow, or a special bed on the periphery of well-trafficked rooms or near the table, chair, or couch where you sit. Pick a mat or bed that your dog loves to lounge on.

- **Chews/toys:** Place your dog's chews and/or toys on his bedding. He'll know where to go to find his things — and have something to do when he goes to his area!

If you have small kids, or if your dog's still a pup, you can attach your dog's toy to a piece of rope and tie it to something immovable near the station spot. That way it won't disappear.

Time for bed: Directing your dog to his place

Teaching your dog to go to his comfort station on cue isn't hard at all. Each time you're in the room and you'd like your dog to quiet down, tell him "Settle down" as you point to his area. If he ignores you, lead him there and say "Settle" as you position him in a comfortable "Down" position and instruct "Stay." If your dog challenges his "Stay" command, secure a leash to an immovable object near the station, leaving just enough slack for your dog to lie down comfortably. Soon you can just point, and your dog will go happily — content to chew his favorite toy and stay out from underfoot.

You can turn going to the comfort station (or to his crate) into a bedtime trick. Simply choose your command, such as "Time for bed" or "Go to your room," and say it as you point toward and lead your dog to his place. If you reinforce your dog's cooperation with a treat, toy, or special bone, he'll be scurrying to the location just for the fun of it. If your dog is too distracted or ignores you, attach a drag lead (a 4-foot leash; see Chapter 2) and guide him along.

Using comfort stations when out and about

Whenever you travel, take your dog's comfort station — bedding and a toy — along for the ride. It works like a security blanket works for kids: Knowing where to go and what to do helps your dog relax, no matter what the situation. Here are some special trips that you can make more comfortable for your dog:

- ✔ **Car rides:** Car rides are jarring for many dogs. Some get anxious and bark at the sights going by, and when the scene changes, they take credit for it and bark more. Other dogs get nauseous from the motion. In either case, create a comfort station or place a crate in your car so he feels right at home. Lead him in and out the same door, and secure him with a suitable leash. The consistency is comforting.

- ✔ **Overnights:** Like young children, dogs have consistent patterns, and they prefer familiar surroundings. If you're planning an overnight, pack and put down your comfort stations as soon as you arrive at your destination.

- ✔ **At the veterinarian, dog school, café, and so on:** Short trips confuse dogs. When dogs are thrust into new situations with unfamiliar people and/or dogs, familiar directions and objects help them feel secure. Place your dog's comfort station at your side or under your legs and encourage him to "Stay" if you're forced to wait.

Party Time . . . 1 Mean, Potty Time

The most important routine your dog has to learn in leaving your home (also known as his den) is where to go to the bathroom. Think of it like teaching a toddler to go on the potty — but your dog's toilet will be a place in your yard or well-organized papers in a corner of the house.

A polite request: Adding a bell to get your attention

If you teach your dog the bell trick, you can rely on him to tell you when he needs to go out to do his business. Some dogs even use the bell to remind their people when they're hungry or thirsty, too. People either love this trick or they hate it.

When a dog needs to go to the bathroom, he'll navigate to wherever you've coached him to potty. If a door blocks his way, hang a bell next to the door at his nose level. Here's how to teach him to ring it:

1. **Tap the bell with your fingers as you lead your dog through the door.**

   Be very relaxed about ringing them, staring at the bells — not your dog — and opening the door as if the two depended on each other.

2. **Walk directly to your dog's bathroom area.**

   Your dog should begin to ring the bell on his own within a week.

Some dogs ring the bell by nosing it, others by pawing it. Let your dog do what comes naturally to him. Avoid forcing him into the bell, or he'll refuse to cooperate.

If your dog isn't ringing the bell himself after a week's time, rub a dab of butter on it before you bring him to the door; then encourage his interest and open the door the moment he sounds the bell.

Teaching your dog to potty in one place

Having a dog who eliminates in a designated place is a real advantage. No yellow stains marking up the lawn, no standing outside for hours waiting for your dog to go, a handy travel cue to take with you on trips — the benefits are endless!

You can teach this trick whether or not your dog is fully housetrained. And when you succeed, you'll consider it no small miracle. Just follow these steps:

1. **Select a "sacred bathroom area" in your yard and use white clothesline to create a 6- to 12-foot-wide circle to designate this area.**

   If you live in the city, modify the circle to encompass the curb.

2. **Take your dog to this area on lead when you're sure he has to go.**

   If your dog decides to play with the rope, soak it overnight in Bitter Apple spray (available at local pet supply stores), a nontoxic substance with a taste dogs find unpleasant.

3. **If your dog goes potty in the circle, say "Get busy" as he's peeing. Within a week you'll be able to prompt the action with these very words. Cool!**

4. **When he's finished, click (if you're using a clicker) and treat, saying "Good dog!"**

   If he misses your mark, praise warmly but offer no treat. Have faith! Soon your dog will be as potty-trained as a 6-year-old. You can remove the circle once your dog is reliably going potty in the right place.

5. **Pick up after your dog.**

   No dog will go where he's gone 20 times before without cleanup. Would you? Though there are designer pooper-scoopers on the market, I've found it very tidy to cover my hand with a plastic bag, pick up the poop, and then turn the bag inside out to surround the deposit.

Do you have an indoor dog? The circle trick may not be necessary because your dog will usually go wherever you place the paper (or indoor potty). If you and your dog are seasoned travelers, however, a portable rope outlining the paper can help ease the travel transition for your dog.

For more tips on housetraining, check out *Housetraining For Dummies,* by Susan McCullough (Wiley).

Fending off Frustrating Habits with Fun

Your dog loves you, and he ate your favorite slippers just to show how much. It's hard to understand dog thinking sometimes, but know that he chose something that carried the scent he holds most dear — your feet.

Dogs don't frustrate the same way people do. From a dog's point of view, wild barking, chewed shoes, and slobbery, overeager greetings are natural expressions of canine-centric respect and camaraderie. Your dog isn't trying to frustrate you with bad behavior; he's trying to bond with you: *We're all dogs here! Let's sniff butts, dig up the begonias, and pee-mark all our stuff! Good times!* Of course, the canine perspective isn't always well-received in the two-legged world. You need to teach your dog the manners he needs to participate in the human world.

The first step in teaching your dog better manners is to understand and accept your dog's perceptions (I discuss some of them in Chapter 2). Frustrations clearly depend on who you're speaking about. What may be utter aggravation to you — a barking dog, a destroyed shoe, an overeager greeting — is considered natural, dare I say *respectful* behavior from your dog's perspective:

- Barking dogs often perceive their noise-making to be in high demand.
- Chewing a carefully selected item that has your scent on it is actually just a dog missing the one he loves.
- An enthusiastic jump angled toward the face of the visitor is a very normal canine greeting.

When discouraging one behavior, you must encourage another. So after you think about why your dog is doing what he does, make a discourage/encourage chart, like the one in Table 5-1. List all your frustrations in one column. Then write down alternative behaviors that could satisfy your dog's impulses (without raising your blood pressure into the danger zone), and think about ways to encourage those replacement behaviors.

The upcoming subsections look at three ill-mannered behaviors — barking, jumping, and chewing — and tell you how to help your dog find more-polite ways to express himself.

Table 5-1	A Discourage/Encourage Chart	
Behavior to Discourage	**Behavior to Encourage Instead**	**How to Do So**
Jumping at the door	Sitting or fetching a toy	When you first come home, ask your dog to sit or get a toy before you greet him.
Jumping on the furniture	Relaxing in a comfort station on the floor	Provide comfort stations with toys near the couch (for info on comfort stations, see the earlier section "Giving Your Dog a Place to Settle Down").
Chewing on shoes	Chewing on toys	Place appropriate chew toys at each comfort station.
Barking at noises outside	Barking on command	Teach "Speak," "Shhh," and "Come tell me!" (see "Rehabilitating the incessant barker" in this chapter, and Chapter 9).

Rehabilitating the incessant barker

Most dogs bark, but some are more sworn to it than others — their breed impulses insist they alert you to every noise and motion. Other dogs are protective, and they assume this role if you don't take it yourself. Regardless, if your dog's a barker, you can find positive outlets for his gift in Chapter 9. But in the meantime, take a moment to curb his intensity by teaching him to bark on cue. You read that right — by teaching him to bark on command, you'll be able to turn it off.

To teach your dog to bark on command, you need to use the following:

- **Eye contact:** Look at your dog alertly when you want him to bark. Break your stare when you want him to quiet down.
- **Voice commands:** You need two voice commands: "Speak" and "Shhh." Enunciate clearly when you give your commands.
- **Hand signals:** You use snappy signals to both encourage barking and discourage it. To signal "Speak," try snapping your fingers near your mouth. To signal "Shhh," put your index finger to your lips as if shushing a child.

You can train your dog to "Speak" and "Shhh" in these four lessons:

1. **Lesson One:** Get something your dog lives for, a ball or a treat for example. Secure him to a post or tree and hold his prized object just out of reach while you encourage "Speak" and look at him intensely. When he does bark, reward him with the object immediately and cheerfully. Begin to add the hand signal to your voice and eye cues. Repeat this procedure until your dog reacts quickly to the "Speak" command.

   When you're ready to stop say "Shhh" and turn your attention to something else. If you're using a clicker, click when he is quiet, and reward and praise him. Repeat this process until your dog responds to both "Speak" and "Shhh."

2. **Lesson Two:** Encourage your dog to speak throughout the day for positive things, such as a meal or a walk. If he speaks out of turn, just ignore him.

3. **Lesson Three:** Now it's time to turn your dog's focus to "Shhh." Secure your dog and stand in front of him with something tasty or fun. Say "Speak!" After a few barks, say "Shhh."

4. **Lesson Four:** Practice your commands throughout the day, varying which ones you reinforce. Sometimes reward the "Speak," sometimes the "Shhh." Have your dog "Speak" and "Shhh" two or three times before rewarding him. He'll be so proud of his new trick, and so will you!

Reconditioning the jumper

Everybody knows a jumper — a knock-you-over-when-you-come-in jumper, a muddy-paw-prints-on-the-couch jumper, a counter cruiser. So what can you do? The first step in solving your problem is to remember the chief motivation for your dog's jumping: attention. Jumping is a surefire attention-getter. Your dog will die for it. And if he jumps up and you yell at him, he's getting attention. That makes jumping a guaranteed rewarding activity, so why should he stop?

To resolve any jumping problem, you need to remove the reward and let your dog do the math himself. This section offers some solutions to the most typical jumping situations.

Calming a homecoming jumper

You have two choices when you come home and your dog jumps on you:

- ✔ **Ignore your dog, cross your arms, and look up.** Encourage everyone in the house to do the same.

- ✔ **Very discretely use a spray mist (such as a mouth spray or commercial concoction) to create an invisible boundary between you and your dog.** Ignore your dog as you do this; the moment he stops leaping skyward give him a command like "Sit," "Dance," or "Roll over," or direct him to a play toy, as you encourage a more appropriate alternative for his enthusiasm.

  If you choose to spray, look away as you do it (so your dog won't take it as a personal attack) and don't ever spray your dog directly. Always redirect your dog the moment he stops jumping at you.

After your dog catches on to the correction, you can use it to keep him away from company. Using the same principles of an invisible boundary and no attention, you can discourage your dog's two-pawed greeting without making a fuss. Make sure your guests know not to greet the dog until he has settled down.

Have a basket of balls or a squeaky toy by the door and toss one down when you come in or when you're welcoming a visitor. This teaches your dog to focus his energy on his toy, not you.

Dogs mimic your energy level. If you come home to an excited dog, or if your dog flips out when the doorbell rings, stay calm. If you get excited in your attempts to calm your dog, you'll actually be getting your dog supercharged.

Correcting a counter cruiser

Do you have a *counter cruiser?* This dog jumps on the kitchen counter to look for crumbs or sneaks a paw to steal a tidbit. It's a nasty little habit that's hard to break.

First of all, realize that as soon as your dog is on the counter or has successfully stolen a bite, you can't correct him. Let it go. Any corrections after the fact will come across as envy — your dog will think that because you're interested in what he's doing or what he has stolen, the object must be truly valuable.

To discourage a counter cruiser, you need to correct the thought process. Each time you see your dog sniffing the counter, say "Don't think about it!" in a no-nonsense tone. Because you're smarter than he is, you may try setting up situations (say, a piece of pizza on the kitchen counter) where you can catch your dog contemplating a theft and administer the correction. (See the section on teaching your dog "Nope" in Chapter 4.)

Keep counter visits unappealing by making sure there's nothing there your dog will want. Whenever you're not in the room to teach him right from wrong, anything on the counter is fair game.

Reclaiming your seat on the furniture

Most people invite their puppies on the furniture, only to regret it later. To discourage your dog from getting onto the furniture, attach a short lead (8 to 12 inches) to his buckle collar and pull him off each time he puts even one paw on the furniture, saying "Excuse me!" in a very lofty tone.

To give your dog a place to go instead, set up doggy comfort stations on the floor, as I explain in the earlier section, "Giving Your Dog a Place to Settle Down."

Rehabilitating the chewer

The chewer likes to put everything in his mouth. Toys, shoes, paper towels — it's all the same in his eyes. Correcting a dog is like yelling at an infant: It doesn't register. In fact, yelling at a dog when he grabs a sock is perceived as prize envy (you want what he has), and that's what results in destructive chewing.

Instead, encourage your dog to show you his prize by praising him every time he picks something up, and reward every delivery with a treat from a treat cup. You may think you're rewarding delinquent chewing, but in fact, chewing itself won't become a problem because your dog will be happy to show you his treasure.

Of course, you need to teach your dog that he just can't chew certain items, fair in his mind or not. It's similar to teaching 5-year-old kids they can't sip your coffee or wine. Shoes, toilet paper, and kids' action figures are all off-limits, even though they're often lying about on the floor. Here are some tips to help you teach your dog this lesson:

- ✔ **In each room you share, arrange a comfort station.** Place your dog's favorite chews and toys in this area so he reliably finds them there when the need to nibble strikes. I describe comfort stations earlier in the section "Giving Your Dog a Place to Settle Down."

- ✔ **Direct your dog to an approved chewable.** Each time you notice your dog start to fidget, direct him to his bone or toy with a command such as "Bone" or "Toy."

- ✔ **Keep a spray deterrent near areas he likes to nosh.** If you notice your dog chewing on an immovable object, approach him calmly, spray the object with a taste deterrent such as Bitter Apple as he's chewing it (be careful to avoid spraying his face) while saying "Nope" (or "Wrong"), and then direct him to his bone or toy with a cue.

You can spray your valuables ahead of time to discourage any test chewing before it happens!

Starting with Some Simple Moves: Tricks for a Happy, Loving Dog

Whenever I listen to clients complain about their dog, I turn to the dog and say, "Well aren't you the naughtiest, most terrible little monster! What a nuisance you've become." I say it, however, in such a sweet, loving voice that it causes every dog to squirm with delight. The owners can't help but fall in love with their adoring doggie all over again.

One of the fastest ways for you to get addicted to trick training is to teach your dog some easy tricks that showcase that puppy love. And dogs, like people, love to succeed, so the surest way to get your dog addicted to trick training is to start with a few surefire winners. Here are a few tricks that everyone can master — people and dogs of all ages!

A tail-wagging trick: Are you happy?

If you're happy and you know it, wag your tail! Teaching your dog how to wag his tail on command is so easy. If a tennis ball brings the tail into action, hold up a ball; if food gets the tail to wag, use that. Catch your dog wagging, praise him for it, and think of a clever cue word to command each time (like "Wag"). Use your cue word in a positive, inviting tone, and watch your dog come alive.

Now add a hand signal like waving your right hand back and forth. Start out with a pronounced sweep, and then phase off until you can make small motions with your index finger.

If you're in front of a crowd, you can ask really difficult questions and tell your dog that if he agrees, all he has to do is wag his tail. It goes like this: "I'm going to ask you a hard question and if you agree, all you have to do is wag your tail. Ready? Would you like everyone to give you a hug?" Signal your dog and voilà! A surefire crowd pleaser!

"Give Me a Hug"

"Give Me a Hug" is a breed-selective exercise. If your dog is injured, has dysplasia, or is skeletally challenged (like a Basset, a Bulldog, or a giant breed), avoid this trick. And don't forget — if your dog refuses, move on.

You can teach this command in several ways. If your dog loves to wrap his paws around you, you can reinforce this behavior when it's happening by using a clicker (as I explain in Chapter 2), or you can cue your dog by luring him and pairing his cooperation with a word like "Hug." Reward your dog when he's in the hug position — this method works best for calm dogs who are not prone to excessive jumping.

For jumpy dogs, try a more sedate method. I taught my wild-child dog Shayna to hug by first ignoring the behavior when she was jumping all over me and then sitting with her and organizing it this way:

1. **Kneel down on the floor or sit in a chair and give your dog the "Sit" command.**

   Check to make sure your dog is sitting square on the floor, not leaning to either side.

2. **Lift your dog's front paws gently and place them on your shoulders as you say "Hug."**

   Give your dog a thorough pet and/or a reward.

3. **Say "Okay" and help him down.**

Do Steps 1 through 3 only three times per session, and stop if your dog becomes too energetic or starts to nip. Leave the leash on and give a tug on the leash as you say "Shhh!" if your dog gets too excited while on two paws. Also, try practicing "Hug" when your dog has less energy.

The silent signal for "Hug" is to cross your arms over your chest and tap your shoulders with your fingers. You can demonstrate the signal each time you say "Hug." Be patient while teaching this sign language — it may take a while for your dog to make the connection.

"Kisses!"

Getting your dog to give you kisses is a real delight — unless you hate dog kisses. You can teach this trick quickly by association, simply saying "Kisses" whenever you're getting a licking.

If your dog is licking out of control, make it more of a two-step process:

1. **First teach your dog "Enough" to signal him to stop licking.**

   Keep a short (8- to 12-inch) leash on your dog and say "Enough" in a pleasant but serious tone. If your dog doesn't listen, tug the leash as you withdraw your attention.

   When discouraging licking, look away and not at your dog. If you look at your dog, you're essentially saying, "Do it again!"

2. **Teach your dog to lick on cue.**

   To teach your dog to lick you, take a frozen stick of butter and rub it on the back of your hand. During a period when your dog is calm, go to him, extend your hand, and command "Kisses" as he licks your hand. When you've had enough, just say so — "Enough!"

   To teach your dog to give someone else a kiss, such as the next-door neighbor or a member of your audience, use a stick of butter during the teaching phase. Ask a few people to help you out, and rub the backs of their hands with butter before you instruct your dog to give them a kiss. Have them extend their hands to your dog and say "Kisses" as you point to the buttered hand. Soon your dog will be seeking out hands to kiss, butter-coated or not. This trick is handy if you have kids over; putting butter on their hands encourages licks, not jumping.

When your dog knows the trick, you can add a hand signal: Rub your right index finger on the back of your left hand, as though your finger is your dog's tongue.

Introducing Interactive Play

Dogs love to play. The more you can let go and roll with their enthusiasm, the more fun you'll have. Some games, like tug-of-war and wrestling, inspire confrontation, so use the games in this section instead to format your fun. Interactive activities like "Catch Me" and "Hide and Seek" can build your bond and inspire respect.

"Hide and Seek"

"Hide and Seek" is a great game and also reinforces that indispensable "Come" command. You need one to four players and a treat cup, and your dog needs to know his name and the "Come" command. "Stay" also comes in handy (see Chapter 4).

Start with this game inside, one-on-one:

1. **While your dog is occupied, go into an adjoining room with a treat cup; call out his name and shake the cup.**

   Use a disposable plastic cup filled halfway with small treats, such as Cheerios.

2. **When you hear him running, say "Come" clearly.**

   Praise him, offer a treat, and let him return to whatever he was doing, putting the treat cup away — or he may never leave your side!

3. **Increase the level of difficulty by calling him from two rooms away.**

   You should still be in sight, not hard to find.

4. **After a couple of days of hiding in plain sight around the house and calling from room to room, go into the adjoining room and hide behind a chair.**

After your dog catches on to this game, you can increase the difficulty of your hiding places and add another teammate. Eventually, your two-legged geniuses can play a game to see who gets found first and who gets found last. Gradually phase off using your treat cups.

The name game: Where's Sally?

Teaching your dog everyone's name couldn't be easier. Pick one person at a time and have the person sit across the room with a treat cup. Instruct your dog to find that person by name. For example, say "Where's Sally?" and have Sally shake the cup the moment she hears her name. Progressively ask Sally to distance herself from you, having her in various rooms of the house so your dog will always be curious to find her location.

After your dog is eager to track Sally (and her treat cup), reintroduce her nearby — but phase off using treats. Sally can call and encourage your dog with praise instead. Soon just her name will inspire enthusiasm.

The shell game

Dogs love to be included in the shell game. Whether you're sitting at home or on an adventure, you can use shells, cups, or even sand piles to hide your dog's treat or toy under one of three stacks. After you shift the stacks about, ask your dog, "Where's your bone?" or "Where's your toy?" If your dog's confused, pretend to sniff each pile — he'll copy your example and find the bone or toy soon enough.

"Catch Me"

I've always hated games that involve people chasing dogs, especially when that game involves a coveted laundry item. Games that encourage your dog to focus on and follow you, however, are a real prize when it comes to training and having fun. These games also reinforce the extinction of bad habits, such as nipping and jumping.

To play "Catch Me," a variation of the children's game "Red Light, Green Light," you need one or two players and a dog toy. Your dog needs to know "Sit," "Wait," "Down," "Stay," "Okay," and "Nope." (See Chapter 4 for details on these commands.)

1. **Turn and face your dog from about 3 to 6 feet away; say "Catch me" and then turn and run.**

2. **After a few feet, pop back to face your dog and command "Wait!"**

3. **Treat your dog when he stops, then say "Okay, catch me," and run again.**

4. **Now that he'll stop, try another quick command like "Sit" or "Down," luring your dog into position if he's confused by the excitement.**

5. **Follow each stationary command with "Okay, catch me" to continue the game.**

6. **When you're through, tell your dog "Okay" and give him a favorite toy.**

   Keep the game short, just one or two minutes.

Some dogs get too excited or overwhelmed by this game. If yours isn't cooperating, try a different game. If he goes wild, racing in a big circle playing hard to get, guess what? — this isn't the game for you!

I know I'll catch some flak for writing about "Catch Me." People are always asking whether high-energy games encourage mouthing and jumping. My response? If it escalates the dog's bad behavior uncontrollably, leave it out. If your dog enjoys the game and you can curb naughtiness with a sharp "Nope" or "Wrong" (see Chapter 4), then go for it. "Catch Me" is a fun activity and sharpens your dog's impulses, teaching him to follow — but not jump or nip at you.

A treasure hunt game: "Digging for China"

Have you considered hiring your dog out to the local excavating company? The prerequisite, of course, is to teach him to dig on command. Equip yourself with a clicker, garden gloves, and treats, and then follow these directions to play "Digging for China":

1. **Find a private area in your yard to teach your dog to dig; bury some treats 1 inch under the ground to pique his interest.**

2. **Start blissfully digging yourself, unearthing the treats as you go and handing them to your dog.**

3. **Reward your dog for joining in, saying "Go dig!"**

4. **Now try hiding a few treats or a toy before bringing your dog to his digging spot; then give the command "Go dig."**

   Like an archeologist discovering treasures, he'll unearth them with obvious delight.

I can already feel the page trembling; you may be worried that without your approval, your dog will unearth your shrubbery and carpets. Though I won't promise you a rose garden (no pun intended), most dogs who are reinforced for digging in one area usually stick to it. By teaching your dog to dig in specific locations, you're able to discourage him from digging in other places.

Chapter 6

Engaging Favorites

- -

In This Chapter

▶ Teaching paw tricks

▶ Getting your dog to roll

▶ Teaching begging tricks

▶ Encouraging stretches

- -

T his chapter highlights the building-block approach: using a simple trick as your foundation and then building on it to produce fancy variations. This approach takes a lot of the mystery out of complex training sequences, breaking down complicated routines into easy-to-master chunks. So in this chapter, not only do you find all the old-school favorites like "Paw," "Roll over," and "Beg," but you also find out how to update and expand on them with crowd-pleasing special effects.

But before you dive into the dog tricks in this chapter, keep the following tips in mind:

✔ **Know when to practice.** Some games are designed to burn energy. Play these when your dog is full of beans. Other tricks are just for fun; when your dog catches on, she'll want to practice as much as you.

✔ **Keep the sessions short and sweet — no more than five to ten minutes.** Several short lessons are better than one long one. With a positive attitude and the building-block approach, your dog can master these techniques in no time.

✔ **Try a clicker.** In Chapter 2, I discuss the use of a clicker. The sharp sound paired with a tasty food reward helps your dog know exactly which behavior you're after.

✔ **Avoid forcing your dog to do certain tricks.** Tricks like rolling over and begging are very entertaining, but don't force your dog if she's not into it. If your dog naturally rolls around or easily sits back on her haunches, you have the green light! If rolling on the floor is beneath her standards or physical capabilities, don't force it.

Playing with the Plain Ol' Paw

Nothing like starting with a classic: giving a paw. Some dogs are naturally predisposed to giving a paw, so much so that you're probably wondering how to teach "No paw" — but I get to that later in the sidebar "Getting dogs to keep their paws to themselves."

After your dog masters "Paw," you can really start being creative, teaching her to wave, give high fives, and turn out the lights. But everyone's got to get started somewhere — after you master the basic "Paw," the sky's the limit.

Doing the basic "Paw"

To teach the basic "Paw," first get your dog (on a leash if she's antsy) and some favorite treats, and go into a quiet room. Then do the following:

1. **Kneel or sit in front of your dog.**

2. **Command "Sit," position your dog's hindquarters if necessary, and offer praise.**

3. **You can try two methods at this point:**

   • **Physical:** Using a thumb, press your dog's shoulder muscle gently until her front leg lifts, as shown in Figure 6-1. Then lay your hand under her foot pad as you say "Paw."

Figure 6-1: Pressing the shoulder to get your dog to lift a paw.

- **Treat-based:** Hold a treat in a closed hand a couple of inches in front of your dog's foot. When she paws it, open your hand to reward her. With each repetition of this step, gradually raise your hand to your dog's elbow. Now add the "Paw" step. Keep the treat in your other hand, as you extend your closed hand. As she hits your hand, say "Paw" and gently grasp her paw with an opened palm. Treat her the moment your palm connects to her paw.

4. **Now signal and command "Paw."**

   Is she catching on? If not, help her complete the "Paw" by pressing her shoulder blade gently. Praise her warmly, whether she caught on or needed your help.

The hand signal for "Paw" is to stretch out your hand, as if to shake hands.

Paw variations: Shaking things up

Shaking paws is great, but you can easily teach a few variations that will delight you, your pup, and any onlookers. In this section, you find some new cue words and variations on the basic "Paw."

"Say thank you"

Hold out your hand as if to shake hands. At first, say "Paw–Thank you." Fairly soon she'll respond to both your signal and your new directional cue. Praise your dog for placing her paw in your hand and give her a treat.

Now get a human pal to help you out. As your human pal extends a hand, command "Paw–Say thank you" and encourage your dog to offer her paw to your friend. You're ready to spread your dog's good manners everywhere!

The hand signal for "Say thank you" is the same as for the "Paw" trick — extend your hand to the dog with your palm up.

"Wave"

A dog who knows how to wave hello and goodbye — miraculous, you say? Fortunately, it's not hard to teach at all. Here's how:

1. **Place your dog in a "Sit–Stay" and show her that you have a treat in your left hand.**

2. **Standing in front of her, say "Paw" and signal with your right hand (as if you were going to shake hands).**

3. **As she lifts her paw, wave your signal hand and say "Paw–Wave" as you reward her with the treat.**

4. **Repeat this, slowly weaning off the initial "Paw" signal in place of a wave signal — simply waving to your dog while saying, "Wave hello" or "Wave bye-bye!"**

You can use the target disc to teach your dog to wave at distances away from you. Teach your dog to stand on a target disc as described in Chapter 2. After your dog has mastered both targeting and the wave, combine the two tricks. First place the target disc next to you. Direct your dog to the disc and tell her to stay. When she's settled, encourage her to "Wave" and reward her. Gradually move the target disc away from you — now you can ask her to wave to various people or to an audience.

"Other one"

As your dog gets into the "Paw" trick, you may notice that she favors either her left or right paw. To prevent having a one-dimensional dog, teach the cue "Other one." Here's how:

1. **Say "Paw" and lovingly praise your dog when she raises her paw.**

2. **Extend your hand to the other paw and say, "Other one," using the treat-in-your-hand trick or shoulder press to inspire her cooperation.**

   Hold the treat in a closed hand a couple of inches in front of your dog's foot until she paws it, or press the shoulder muscle gently with your thumb until she lifts her paw, as I describe earlier in the section "Doing the basic 'Paw.'"

3. **If your dog lifts her favored paw, use a sound such as "Nope" and repeat your original request while you put pressure on the shoulder muscle of the other leg.**

   When your dog lifts the other paw, praise, treat, and give her a big hug (if your dog likes that sort of thing)!

The hand signal for "Other one" is to stretch out your hand to the specified paw.

"Right paw," "Left paw"

By using "Other one" to get your dog to pay attention to which hand you extend, you can pull off a trick that makes it seem as if your dog can tell her right paw from her left, the little genius!

While in a quiet room, decide which paw your dog gives most frequently. For this example, say it's the right paw. Exaggerate the "Paw" hand signal as you hold your right hand to her right side and say, "Right paw." Praise and offer a treat. Have your dog do this right three times in a row so she gets plenty of positive reinforcement. If by chance your dog swaps and offers a left paw, say "Nope" and wait to reward until she offers the right paw.

Now for the other paw. Exaggerate your hand signal toward the left side and say "Left paw." Your dog will probably try the right paw. If she does, say "Nope–Other one." Show her physically if you have to. Practice three lefts, and then stop.

The next time you go to practice, start with "Right paw," accentuating your signal. Help your dog out if you must. Do three rights, then three lefts, accentuating the left signal. Soon your dog will catch on, and you can mix it up: two rights, two lefts, two rights, one left, one right, and so on. Vary the pattern each time and keep these mind-puzzler sessions short. As your dog catches on to your body language, you can exaggerate the hand signal less.

Celebrating success: "High five" and "Go for ten"

Okay, hot shot, gimme five! Getting your dog to give you five — or ten — is easy to teach, and dogs love it. Afterward, you'll both have something to celebrate. Here's how these tricks work:

- ✔ **"High five":** To teach "High five," simply hold your hand, palm out, at the same height you normally do when you say "Paw." If the command "High five" gets a puzzled look, then say "Paw" to request the action and say "High five" as the dog's paw makes contact with your hand. Drop the "Paw" command when your dog makes the connection. Slowly lift your hand higher to accentuate the "High five."

    When asking for the "High five," stay within your dog's height capabilities. If you hold your hand too high, your dog will leap up to try to please you, but you don't want to encourage jumping. "High five" is a three-paws-on-the-floor trick.

- ✔ **"Go for ten":** This trick involves two hands and two paws. When saying "Go for ten," keep your hands at about the level of your dog's head. Any higher will encourage jumping. At first your dog may only reach up to hit you with one paw . . . after all, that's what she's used to. Reaching up will encourage her to stretch up and bring her other paw off the floor — at this point, tuck your free hand under her paw and praise her the moment both paws connect with your hands.

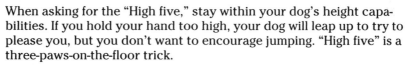

"Hit it!": Targeting paw tricks with lights, doors, and music

After your dog knows how to "Paw," you can teach her to target a disc and then use the disc's placement to help her learn to play music, close doors, and work the light fixtures . . . before you know it, your dog will be saving you a bundle in electric bills!

After your dog knows "Paw" (see the earlier section "Doing the basic 'Paw'"), create a target disc with a small container lid or a business card. Then do the following to teach your dog to strike it with her paw:

1. **Present the target disc in the palm of your hand and command "Paw."**

2. **The moment your dog hits the disc, say "Hit it"; give your dog a treat (or click and treat) and offer praise!**

3. **Phase off holding the disc flat in your hand, holding it at the same level but pinched between your thumb and forefinger.**

   Repeat this until you're able to hold the disc out and your dog will paw it when directed with the "Hit it" command.

Your next goal is to place the disc in various locations to encourage your dog to do things like turn out the lights and close doors. This section includes three tricks that do just that.

Closing the door or cabinet

Once your dog learns how to "Hit it," you can parlay that one behavior into a whole host of cool, helpful, and unique tricks, such as closing the cabinet, turning out the lights, and playing the piano! Though these tricks might sound like magic, it all boils down to the placement of the target disc.

When teaching your dog to close cabinets and doors, she may be initially startled by the sound the door makes as it shuts. Before asking her to tidy up for you, place her in a "Sit–Stay" next to the hinge and give her a treat as you open and shut the door gently. She'll then get used to the sound.

At first, hold the target disc near a cabinet door at what would be a normal "Paw" level for your dog — about her elbow. Do a couple of "Paws" (see the earlier section "Doing the basic 'Paw'"), holding your hand near the door. Next, encourage her to paw the disc by saying "Hit it." If she has a light touch, encourage her to really whack the disc by egging her on and withholding the reward until she does.

Next, tape the disc to the outside of the opened cabinet door. Kneel close to your dog and point to the disc. Reward each attempt to strike the door with her paw. After two days, withhold the reward until a successful closing.

Over the course of four days, gradually start combining the familiar cue with a new command: "Hit it–Close it." Phase out the "Hit it" command so "Close it" will mean just that.

Turning the lights on and off

Teaching your dog to turn out the lights requires blending the "Hit it" command with a jumping sequence. If your dog is tall and agile enough to reach the switch, she'll be more than happy to oblige you. (If your dog doesn't know the "Up" command, flip to Chapter 8 for a quick lesson.)

Getting dogs to keep their paws to themselves

Is your dog too paw-expressive? It happens to the best of them. If your dog constantly paws, you have two options: Ignore her, or use a mild correction. Ignoring is self-explanatory; you may simply walk away. If that doesn't work, try one of the following corrections:

✔ Keep a short *tab* (a very short loop of leash) on your dog and snap it downward while saying, "Not now." (You can buy a short lead — 8 to 12 inches — at a pet supply store or from my Web site store at www. whendogstalk.com.)

✔ Say "Nope" or "Wrong" and command "Sit." (See Chapter 4 for more on these commands.)

Remember that dogs usually paw because they want something: a treat, a toy, or attention. Avoid giving in to your dog's pestering! You're just teaching her that it works. Wait for more mannerly behavior, such as sitting quietly or lying down, before you give your dog what she wants.

To begin, get a light switch like the ones on your wall. Use your target disc to teach your dog to paw it and to get comfortable with its feel. Tape the disc above the fixture and hold the fixture in your hand initially.

At first, hold the switch at a normal "Paw" level — about your dog's elbow — and pair the command "Hit it" with "Lights" as you encourage her cooperation with praise and rewards. This will seem awkward at first; your dog isn't used to things moving when she paws them. Use praise to encourage her and rewards to emphasize the moment her paw connects with the switch.

Separately teach your dog to jump up on the wall by the switch. Pat the wall and teach "Up, up" (see Chapter 8), guiding your dog there with a treat if necessary. At first, all your dog needs to do to earn a reward is jump up and stand against the wall.

Gradually lift your practice switch higher and higher until it's at the height of the real switch. Each time, prompt your dog with the command "Hit it–Lights!" At first, reward and praise your dog if she touches the switch. After four days of practice, reward her only if she activates the switch. Once she's got it down pat, phase off the "Hit it" command and emphasize "Lights!"

Now that you've connected the dots, try this trick in the real world. Move to other switches in your home, using the pretend switch step if your dog acts confused.

Playing the piano

All you need to teach your dog to play the piano is a keyboard, a target disc, and the command "Paw." Here's how it works:

1. **Teach your dog to paw a target disc.**

   I explain how to do this earlier in the intro to the section "'Hit it!': Targeting paw tricks with lights, doors, and music."

2. **Place the keyboard on the ground and place your disc on it.**

3. **Pair the command "Hit it" with "Piano": "Hit it–Piano!"**

4. **Move the disc to various spots on the piano.**

The hand signal for this trick is to pretend your fingers are tapping an imaginary keyboard.

Going on a Roll

Dogs who are as comfortable on their backs as they are on their paws really groove with these rolling tricks. How will you know whether your dog qualifies? She'll roll anywhere, anytime, and often of her own volition. She'll sleep on her back. She'll scratch her back by rolling on the carpet. She'll come in with a grass-stained coat from rolling in the yard.

The good news? "Roll over" isn't just a one-time trick. Once your dog learns to roll, you've got lots of trick training in store, from impersonations to pup-in-a-blanket. Pup-in-a-blanket, you ask? Read on!

"Roll over"

"Roll over" always brings a smile to my face. Although teaching it requires some patience, it demonstrates the importance of *sequencing* — breaking the sum of a trick into parts and then linking the parts to perform the trick.

Before you begin, bring your dog into a quiet room and place treats on a nearby table. Find your clicker if you're using one (see Chapter 2 for more on clickers). Here are the three training sequences:

1. **First sequence:** Call your dog to you and put her in a "Down–Stay." Kneel next to your dog and scratch her belly until she lies on one side. As she does so, say "Roll"; then reward and praise her. Repeat this sequence 10 to 20 times until your dog responds comfortably to this direction.

2. **Second sequence:** Repeat the preceding steps. Then take a treat and circle it from under your dog's chin to just behind her ear (see Figure 6-2). As her head twists to follow the treat, her body will rock to the side. Say "Roll," offer a treat, and praise her. Repeat this sequence 10 to 20 times until your dog responds quickly.

3. **Final sequence:** Repeat the preceding steps. Now circle the treat slowly backward over the back of your dog's head as you say "Roll over."

When your dog is first learning to roll over, she may need some help. Guide her over by gently pushing her top front leg to the other side as you say the command.

Click (or say "Yes!") and give your dog a treat whenever she does a full roll, whether you helped your dog or not.

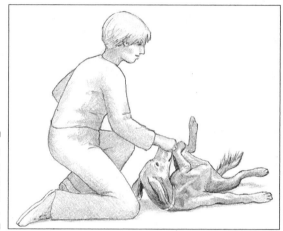

Figure 6-2:
Using a treat to lure a dog to roll over.

As soon as your dog gets the full roll sequence, practice a few times, and then quit on a high note.

Rolling over with a hand signal

Once your dog is comfortable rolling over, you can teach a simple hand signal to prompt this trick:

1. **Continue to kneel next to her when commanding "Roll over," but lean backward in the direction you want her to roll.**

2. **Hold your index finger parallel to the floor, and draw small circles in the air as you give your verbal command.**

3. **Help your dog initially if she seems confused, praising her as you assist and jumping up with her to end the trick.**

4. **As soon as she responds to the cue without your help, stand up and give the command and the hand signal, always accentuating your hand signal.**

Your end goal is to direct your dog from a standing position. Gradually move up from a kneeling position to a one-knee bend to eventually standing up, as you over-accentuate your hand signal.

After your dog seems to be able to follow the command, you can teach her to keep on rolling or to jump up after the first roll. Using enthusiastic body language, you can easily communicate when you want your dog to jump up. Toss your arms in the air and jump like a bunny when you're encouraging your dog to leap up.

If you want your dog to continue rolling, lean in the direction she's rolling and exaggerate your signal initially.

Pump your clenched fist in an enthusiastic hooray to signal your finishing roll!

Rolling over from a distance

When your dog knows the hand signal — drawing circles in the air with your index finger — you're ready for control at a distance. Here's how to cue your dog to roll from farther away:

1. **Place your dog in a "Down–Stay" and stand back 3 feet.**

2. **Use your hand signal, leaning your body in the direction you're sending your dog, as you command "Roll over."**

   If your dog looks confused, go to her calmly and help out, getting back into your starting position as she finishes the trick.

   When she performs on her own, give her a jackpot — a whole fistful — of treats and end with a fun game.

3. **Back up 2 feet at a time during your subsequent practice sessions, until your dog will roll over at a reasonable distance from you.**

Visualization helps you teach a trick, so create a picture in your mind of your dog performing the trick flawlessly. Can dogs read minds? I think so!

"Pup-in-a-Blanket"

"Pup-in-a-Blanket" is a fun trick that bridges two trick sequences into one cool trick. For this one, you need a large blanket (twice the size of your dog). You also need the commands "Roll over," "Take it," and "Hold it" (the latter two are taught in Chapter 7), and the knowledge of which side your dog generally rolls to. Here's how to get your pal to roll up inside a blanket:

1. **First get your dog accustomed to holding the blanket by practicing simple "Take it" exercises (as I describe in Chapter 7).**

2. **In the same quiet room where you initially practiced "Roll over," place the blanket so that the majority of it is on the side that your dog generally rolls to.**

Adding variety to the roll-over performance

To add some flavor to your dog's performance, consider setting up the trick in the following fun ways:

✔ **Dolphin imitation:** Who hasn't seen a dolphin do a perfect water roll at an aquarium or a water park? Your dog, though not as fluid in her movements, can still do a pretty fair likeness. Once your dog knows the signal for "Roll over," you can signal this exercise as you pair it with funny questions like "Who's the happiest fish in the sea?" or "What does a dolphin do when she's really happy?" Or you can do impersonations and ask your audience to guess . . . or better still, buy a costume and dress her up!

✔ **Dizzy dog:** When performing, it's fun to ask silly questions or riddles and have your dog's answer come in the form of a cleverly choreographed trick, prompted by a subtle hand signal. You can say something

as simple as "Heard you stayed out a little late last night. How are you feeling today?"; then pair "Roll over" with the spinning trick from Chapter 8 — you'll give the impression of a really dizzy dog and leave your audience in stitches!

✔ **Rolling down the hill:** If your dog belongs to kids, there's no better fun than to climb a hill and have everyone roll down it. When first teaching your dog to roll in the open grass, work on a level surface; then move up to low-grade hills. Graduate up to the type of hills that everyone — whether they have two paws or four — can accelerate on!

Remember: As you take this trick on the road, your dog may get performance anxiety. If this happens, just backtrack to the beginning stages of the "Roll over" trick to help jar her memory: She'll ground herself and be wowing the crowds before you know it!

3. **Encourage your dog to "Take" the blanket and "Hold it" in her mouth.**

   Praise and reward this sequence 10 times or until your dog seems eager and comfortable with this step.

4. **Next, signal and guide (if necessary) your dog to roll over while she's still holding onto the blanket.**

5. **After your dog cooperates, work on standing up and stepping back, using your target disc to teach your dog to stand on the disc and take direction from a distance (see Chapter 2). Then you can do this fun little crowd pleaser anywhere, anytime!**

Sitting Up: Ain't Too Proud to Beg

"Beg," "Ask nicely," "Put up your paws" — take your pick of a verbal command — they all mean the same thing! Getting your dog to sit up on her back legs (also called *haunches*) is a real charmer. Some dogs come by this trick fairly easily. Others aren't as coordinated and need help up. Either way, this section explains how to teach your dog to beg.

The naturals: Teaching the art of begging

Some dogs are born beggars. Your dog may have even discovered the begging trick by herself during one of her more-successful ploys to get attention. If your dog is a natural beggar, praise her each time she offers you the begging behavior. Soon you'll have a smart aleck on your hands who sits up at every opportunity, and you'll have no trouble getting her to beg on cue.

Here's how to teach the begging trick:

1. **Instruct "Sit" and make sure the dog is sitting squarely (not leaning to either side).**

   If your dog is relatively coordinated but often gets a little too excited about food rewards — she's jumping, turning inside out, and basically unable to sit still — make her part of the "Corner Crew": Start the dog out in a corner of the room to help her feel more secure. Tuck her back end toward the wall. The walls on either side help limit and guide her movements. If she's super-excited, practice when her energy is lower, such as late in the evening or after a good romp.

2. **Take a treat and hold it an inch above her nose.**

3. **As she stretches to sniff the treat, bring it back slowly between her ears as you command, "Ask nicely."**

   The dog should rise up to follow the path of the treat.

4. **Click (or say "Yes!") and reward the dog's split-second attempt to sit up.**

   After she catches on, hold out on rewarding treats for performances that are more balanced.

The hand signal for this trick is to move your palm upward, facing the sky. Start your hand at your hip and move it to your chest level.

Bowser bracers: Begging for a little help

If your dog is less than coordinated, you need to be a more active participant in the learning phase of begging. Try this approach:

1. **Sit your dog squarely (not leaning to either side) and instruct "Stay."**

   Stand directly behind her tail with your heels together and your toes out to either side of her spine.

2. **Hold a treat above her nose and bring it upward and back toward her ear (see Figure 6-3a).**

3. **Give the command "Ask nicely," and as your dog begins to rise, brace her back with your legs for support (see Figure 6-3b).**

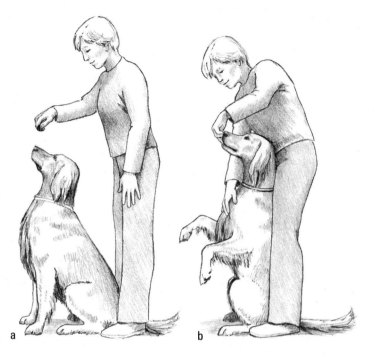

Figure 6-3:
Help your
dog learn
to beg for
a treat by
letting her
use you for
support at
first.

a   b

4. **Click (or say "Yes!") and reward the slightest lift.**

   Gradually, hold out for routines that are more balanced (though still supported).

5. **When you see that she can balance well with your help, try supporting the dog with just your knees.**

   Eventually, she'll perfect a steady balance while supported by your knees.

6. **Withdraw your support in increments until you're just standing there cheering your pal on.**

   Fairly soon, you can begin to step away. See how she shines!

Expanding Your Repertoire with Stretching Tricks

Stretching is a simple trick to teach because you can reinforce it simply by catching your dog in the act. Of course, you can build on the simple stretch technique that I explain in this section and get your dog to even take a bow after she's done performing.

Super stretching

Certain tricks don't involve more than catching your dog acting normally and attaching a cue word to the behavior. The stretch trick is no exception. To teach your dog the "Stretch" command, just follow these easy steps:

1. **Watch your dog as she wakes up, is excited in play, or is preparing to rest.**

2. **Use the command word "Stretch" as she stretches forward.**

3. **Praise and reward her enthusiastically.**

Taking a bow

Of course, no performance would be complete without a bow. To teach your dog to bow, utilize all three of the following approaches. Soon all of them will meld together and your dog will be dazzling her audience to the very end of the act!

- ✔ **Caught in the act:** Whenever you catch your dog stretching her front paws with her bum in the air, command "Bow" as you flip twirl your arm out for a signal. Praise enthusiastically.

  Or if your dog's feeling spunky and playful and crouches on her front legs with her bottom in the air, take a bow as you command "Bow." Praise enthusiastically and reward her with her favorite game.

- ✔ **Jury-rigged:** Take your dog aside into a quiet room with some favorite treats and a clicker if you have one. Hold her belly up as you hold the treat to the ground, just in front of her paws, and command "Bow." Slowly fade off the belly hold, simply using the cue word "Bow."

- ✔ **Smush face:** In a quiet room, take a treat and hold it against your dog's nose. Press the treat gently back and downward, thus encouraging your dog to bend forward on her elbows to get the reward. As she does, say "Bow" and reward her!

Other cue words besides "Bow" fit the stretching behavior just as well. Your dog can learn multiple words for the same behavior. Just make sure you start with one command cue before adding others, and always use the same hand signal.

Chapter 7

Go Fetch! Finding and Retrieving Tricks

*H*aving a dog who'll retrieve in your home has many perks: the fun of fetch, a helper to carry in the groceries, a drink delivered to you. Few things in life are more astounding. On the other hand, nothing may be more frustrating than the retriever turned inside out — the comic fellow who runs away from you or brings things back to you but taunts you with them just out of reach.

In reality, there isn't too much distance between the cooperative retriever and the ham. Both are thinking of their owner when they have something in their mouth. The Good Retriever has been taught to share. Mister Comedian has been taught that treasures are best kept to oneself. Of course, not everybody loves a comedian.

The tricks in this chapter go from the basic fetch to more complex variations on the theme — not to worry though, because if you're game, I'll walk you through each step. For some of the tricks, like picking up the trash and fetching the laundry, your dog should know the touch and target exercises I cover in Chapter 2. These exercises and commands make it easier for your dog to understand your directions, especially when you're working on sequence tricks. Clickers are also useful and can really help your dog put it all together. Check out Chapter 2 for more on clickers and target training.

Fetching: It's a gene thing

The impulse to retrieve is natural for some dogs, while others don't show much interest in fetching. Most of the sporting breeds instinctively like to carry objects and can easily be taught to share. Dogs who were bred to work with their humans take well to the lessons if taught with patience and positive reinforcement. If you're sitting across from a dog who won't fetch your ball, don't feel bad. Some dogs were called for other wonders. In truth, while I could have used unnatural or harsh methods to train my husky-mix Kyia to retrieve, I chose not to. In her lifetime, I've never forced Kyia to do anything that didn't agree with her natural instincts.

Of course every rule has its exceptions: There are huskies who would put most retrievers to shame and retrievers who won't give the ball back to you. Many have elevated the game of "Keep Away" to an art. If this type of dog is your pal, there's hope. To teach a full retrieve — go out, bring it back, and give it up — each of the steps must be taught individually before they're brought together.

Snoop Doggy Dog: Training a Canine Detective

Calling all dogs! Your dog doesn't need to be a miraculous retriever or double-jointed to succeed in Doggy Detective School. The only prerequisites are a curious nose and an enthusiastic heart. Believe it or not, by the end of this section, your dog (of any size, shape, or color) will be helping you locate your mislaid keys, the missing TV remote, and anything else you choose to designate. Don't think it's possible? Read on!

Although your dog won't be able to find you a refund on your taxes, he can learn to find just about anything you can lose. Dogs are capable of associating plenty of objects and words. Just follow the basic framework for the tricks in this section, and initially rely on treats to reinforce his success. Other everyday things you may want to teach your dog to scout out include your slippers, the cat (you know the cat is going to love this one!), your other mitten — even your wayward children! You can have your private eye retrieve the object once he has found it, as I explain in the upcoming section "Fun Fetching Tricks." Praise the "Find," and then encourage "Bring."

If he can't actually "retrieve" what you send him off to find (like the cat or the kids), encourage him to find a way to let you know, such as barking (see Chapter 5) or standing near them.

The basics: "Sniff" and "Find"

To train a good detective, you must start with the basics: "Sniff" and "Find." What better way to get that sniffer going than with some tasty treats? I've divided this foundational skill into three, easy-to-master stages. Make sure your dog feels confident and successful at every stage.

Stage 1

1. **Gather some good-smelling treats, go to a large room or hallway, and place your dog in a "Sit–Stay" on-leash.**

2. **Say "Sniff" as you hold a treat in front of your dog's nose.**

   Discourage any taste-testing with "Ep, ep."

3. **Remind "Stay," and toss the treat no more than 3 feet in front of you. If your dog moves, snap the leash and remind "Stay."**

4. **Release with "Okay, find."**

   Praise your dog for locating and gobbling the treat.

5. **Gradually extend your toss to not more than 10 feet.**

   Once your dog perfects this part of the trick, move on to the next stage.

Always vary the amount of time you pause before releasing your dog so that he won't jump the gun. Pause 3, 10, 14, or 20 seconds — mix it up. The pauses encourage your dog to concentrate on your commands.

Stage 2

1. **Command "Sniff" and "Stay" as before, but leave your dog's side and place the treat inches in front of him.**

2. **Return to your dog's side, pause, and release him with "Okay– Find."**

3. **Gradually extend your distance to not more than 15 feet.**

   At this point, your dog may lose sight of the treat and have to rely on his sniffer to find it.

Unlike humans, dogs have better peripheral vision than they do distance vision. That's why when you see something in front of you, your dog may not.

Stage 3

Now you're ready to put your four-footed detective to the test:

1. **Place your dog on a "Stay" about 4 feet from the entrance to the room.**

2. **Instruct "Sniff," remind "Stay," and place your treat out of sight around the corner.**

3. **Return to your dog, pause, and then send him off with "Okay– Find."**

   Cheer him on if he seems confused. You may have to get on all fours yourself and sniff around, though you should praise him enthusiastically regardless of how he locates the treat.

Once your dog has the idea and is racing to put his nose to work, you can progressively hide the treat in more challenging places. And who's to say that you have to hide just one?

This game was my dog Kyia's favorite one to play. I used vegetables, hiding four or five while I was making a salad, just to keep her busy.

Finding toys

Now you can progress to something just as fun but a little less tasty: toys. For this trick, you need a clicker if you use one, some good treats, and two distinctly different toys. I use a ball and a little stuffed cow toy in this example, but you can use whatever toys your dog loves.

Place the cow in the center of a room and remove all other toys. The instant your dog approaches the cow, say "Find–Cow" and then click/praise and reward. Suddenly the cow will have great value . . . treat value, that is. Once your dog shows interest in the cow reliably, ignore simple interest, only clicking/rewarding mouthing or carrying the cow.

Also say "Find your cow" every time your dog picks up the toy on his own. Praise him enthusiastically.

Once your dog is associating a word with a toy, practice this:

1. **Hold the toy in front of your dog, clicker in the other hand and treats lined up on a nearby table.**

2. **Say "Find your cow" as you hold the toy in front of your dog. When he reaches for it, click, treat, and praise.**

3. **Repeat a few times, then tell your dog to "Stay" as you place the cow a few feet in front of him. Repeat "Find your cow" as you point to it. Click and reward any contact.**

4. **Continue to move the cow farther from him and progress to hiding it out of sight.**

That was the easy part. Now the trick gets a bit more difficult:

1. **With your dog in a "Sit–Stay," place the cow and another toy (a ball) in front of him, about 3 feet apart.**

2. **Command "Find your cow."**

   If your dog picks the ball, don't correct him or sound disappointed. Calmly take the toy, replace it, show your dog the cow, and say "Cow."

3. **When he makes contact with the cow, click/praise and reward — make a big fuss. What a genius!**

4. **Practice Steps 1–3 a few times at each session, sometimes sending the dog for the ball and sometimes for the cow.**

   Don't alternate the toys; that's too easy and your dog will quickly catch on. Progressively place the toys farther away.

Although I encourage you to use treats initially to motivate your dog, you'll be able to phase them out as soon as your dog gets a mental image of what you're expecting.

When your dog has mastered the art of association, you're ready to test his brain some more. Place one toy 3 feet from you, and the other 10 feet away. Send your dog for the closer one at first, and then send him for the one farther away. Switch the toys' locations and vary which one you send him to.

At this point, you can apply the dog's discrimination abilities to other objects, such as car keys and the remote control (see the next two sections). You can also help your dog identify other toys or bones; just follow the same routine!

Finding the keys

How much time do you spend around your house looking for your keys? Wouldn't it be great if you could just send your little genius detective after them? Here's how:

Place your keys in a small room, like a bathroom. Click/praise and reward movement toward the keys. Progressively reward greater interaction with the keys. Once your dog identifies the keys reliably, add the word "Key" as he interacts with or carries them. Onward!

1. **Line up some treats, grab the house and/or car keys, and round up the clicker if you use one.**

2. **Place your dog in a "Sit–Stay" position, and let him sniff the keys as you say "Sniff."**

3. **Toss the keys a few feet out and release your dog. If he goes for the keys, click/praise and reward. If not, ignore your dog and do more work in the bathroom.**

4. **Once your dog reliably goes to the keys, instruct "Find the keys."**

5. **Progressively extend the distance at which you place the keys in front of you. Leave your dog with a "Stay" command, walk out and place the keys, walk back, and release your dog from your side.**

6. **Once your dog really understands Step 5, you can start to hide the keys in another room.**

   When you hide the keys, place them in plain sight and follow your dog while he searches. Reinforce with a click and/or a treat the second he locates them.

When practicing this trick get a bulky key chain — something your dog can sink his teeth into and grasp easily. You definitely don't want your overly enthusiastic dog swallowing your car key by accident!

Locating the remote

"Where's the remote?" is, perhaps, the most often-asked question in U.S. households — and your doggy detective always knows the answer!

To do this trick, your dog should know "Sniff" and "Find" (see the earlier section "The basics: 'Sniff' and 'Find'"). Line up the treats and your clicker, and follow these steps:

Place the remote in the center of a small, uncluttered room, such as a bathroom. Click/praise and reward any interest. Progressively click greater interactions, saying "Remote" once your dog interacts with the remote reliably. Now progress to the next phase of training:

1. **Let your dog have a good sniff of the remote.**

   Enhance the smell of the remote control with something memorable, such as baby powder. Though you can phase off the powder after your dog has learned to find the remote, the scent will linger on it for many months. By then your remote won't need an auxiliary scent — it will smell like your dog!

2. **Leave the dog in a "Stay" and place the remote a few feet away.**

3. **Release your dog with "Find the remote," and reinforce any contact.**

   Continue to increase the distance, then begin to hide it in the usual lost-remote locations.

Fun Fetching Tricks

Before sending your dog out to fetch the paper or retrieve a tissue, you need to teach him exactly how to retrieve things. Believe it or not, dogs aren't born knowing how to do this — no matter how clever they are!

Retrieving has three tricks built into it — following and grabbing the object, returning with it, and last *but not least* — giving it up. Teaching each step separately ensures success and fun every step of the way!

Avoid overdoing it! If you toss objects all day, saying "Bring, Bring, Bring," your dog may avoid you, saying "No, No, No!" Each "Bring" lesson should be no more than three to five minutes. And no more than four lessons a day! I tell my clients less is more. If your lessons are upbeat, the dog will retain the behavior much better than if they're long and frustrating.

Mastering the basic fetching sequence

Though a well-trained retriever looks like he was born with a tennis ball in his mouth, fetching is a little more complicated than it appears. The toughest trick is teaching your dog to release the object happily: the human equivalent of sharing. The best approach in my opinion? Break this one into three, easy-to-master parts before stringing them all together in the final stage.

Stage 1: "Go get it!"

Here's where you can instill a love of fetching in your dog. Simple to master, all your dog must do to earn praise, rewards, and your attention is to chase after toys. That's it!

1. **Toss a favorite toy.**

   If your dog doesn't chase it, go after it yourself: dogs, like kids, learn by example.

2. **The moment your dog starts chasing the toy, cheer him on: "Good boy!"**

   If your praise distracts him, wait until he's reached his toy.

3. **As he plays with his toy, approach him with a treat and reward, and praise him.**

4. **As your dog catches on, command "Go get it!" as he chases after the thrown object.**

All your dog has to do is to follow and grasp his toy: *nothing else.*

Stage 2: "Bring"

Anything a dog puts in his mouth is special, at least to him. So the first step in teaching your dog to retrieve is to get him psyched to show you his "treasure." All your dog must do for this step is come back with his prize.

The focus here is on the "Bring," not the "Give."

Here's what to do:

1. **Pocket some treats or another favorite toy.**

   If your dog is too treat-focused and won't leave your side if there's a treat on the scene, leave food rewards and clickers out of the picture. In this case, your overwhelming enthusiasm will be your dog's just reward.

2. **Gently toss a toy a few feet away from you, saying "Go get it!"**

3. **Each time your dog brings the toy back, shower him with praise, but don't take the toy away. Click and/or reward him with food if it doesn't overshadow the toy; or bring out another toy to excite him to drop the one he brought back.**

   If your dog ignores you when he gets the toy, try running away from him after he has picked it up, with a different toy in hand. If he still won't bring it back, pretend to eat some of his treat.

   If your dog is a comedian and prefers playing "Keep Away," go into a small room, like a bathroom, so his freedom to run off is restricted and you can teach him the fun of the new retrieving game. Toss the toy. The second your dog picks it up, start praising/treating. Continue this game until your dog's perspective shifts.

4. **As your dog catches on and trots back to you happily, say "Bring."**

5. **Toss a different toy and repeat Steps 3 and 4.**

After your dog is bringing his toy to you on the "Bring" command, you're ready for the "Give" command.

Stage 3: "Give"

Parting is such sweet sorrow. Relinquishing an object is the trickiest part of the retrieve, especially if you've chased your dog for things in the past. Remember, when you chase a dog for an object, you're communicating "prize envy" — that whatever the dog has must have value because you want it back. Be patient. Follow the steps and be smart enough not to lose your temper if your dog tries to outsmart you. A graceful retreat is not a failure.

Start young! Fill and place cups of treats around your home (see Chapter 2). When your pup/dog is chewing or playing with his toys, shake the cup and say "Give" as he spits it out. Treat him, pet him on the head, and leave — without touching his toy. By connecting the command "Give" to the act of releasing, you get two helpful results: Your dog relaxes when people approach him, and he has a more comfortable association with the "Give" command.

Never chase your dog to get him to give up an object. Instead, teach the "Give" command and be patient! Follow these steps:

1. **Pull up a chair and line up some treats plus your dog's favorite toy.**

2. **Call your dog over, show him the toy, and praise him when he takes it.**

3. **Wave the treat in front of your dog and say "Give" as he spits out the toy. (The treat should induce him to drop the toy.)**

4. **Praise and reward your dog the second he releases the toy.**

5. **Now go to a hallway or an enclosed space. Toss the toy a short distance, saying "Go get it."**

6. **Praise your dog the moment he picks it up, and then kneel down and say "Give" as you reward the release.**

   To signal "Give," hold your open palm in front of your dog's mouth.

Some dogs are so food-obsessed that they can't think of anything else. If you're having a rough time getting your dog's attention with treats around, you need to teach him without treats. Simply replace Step 3 with an extra helping of praise, or use two toys and exchange one for the other.

You may notice that your dog releases the ball as you approach or tosses it on the ground near you. Although this is acceptable when starting out, you eventually need to be more selective with your rewards.

Deliveries are to be made mouth-to-hand. Here's how to shape this behavior:

1. **Go back to your chair. Hold your dog on-leash if he moves away.**

2. **Now give your dog the toy, praise him for having it, and then say "Give" as you extend your hand under your dog's mouth.**

   If your dog drops it on the ground, ignore him, pick up the toy, and prompt him again, this time angling your hand and bracing his body with the leash. Enthusiastically praise and reward the instant the toy drops into your hand.

3. **Click/reward the moment the toy drops into your hand.**

Do you have a clencher — a dog who just won't relax those jaws? For this guy, carry treats in your pockets and reward him every time he chooses to release a bone or toy. Also use treat cups to approach the dog while he plays, and lay the treats in front of him whether he has released the object or not. In all likelihood, he feels threatened by your approach — treating him will help shape a more cheerful association.

If your dog becomes aggressive, stop immediately and call a professional — you've got a spatial aggression problem.

Stage 4: All together now

After your dog learns that when you say "Bring," you want the object you point to and when you say "Give," you're looking for a hand delivery, then you're ready to help him connect the two talents.

1. **Go to a hallway or small room, like the bathroom.**

2. **Give the toy a short toss and instruct "Go get it!"**

3. **Say "Bring" and cheer your dog back to you when he grabs the toy.**

4. **Extend your hand to retrieve the object, and say "Give."**

5. **When he releases the toy, reward him with praise and/or treats for a job well done!**

6. **Repeat Steps 2 through 5 twice, and then stop.**

If your dog gets so excited that he can't hold onto the toy, you might be rushing it. Try teaching the last step first: praising your dog for releasing the toy. This should help him feel clever and calm down. Encourage him to "Hold it" by picking up the toy and playing "Keep Away": when he grabs it, he'll be more eager to "Hold it." Last but not least, you can work on "Go get it."

Getting the paper

Once you've taught your dog a cheerful retrieve, he'll be happy to apply these skills to improve your life together. So happy, in fact, that as you're staying inside, cozy in your pajamas while your best furry friend happily braves the morning cold to fetch your paper, you may want to be careful what you wish for! A dog who's trained to fetch the paper won't discriminate. You may end up with 20 newspapers on your stoop and 20 angry neighbors!

Here's how to get your dog to do your bidding:

1. **Fold a section of your newspaper over and tape it securely.**

2. **Tempt your dog with it, praising any interest.**

3. **When your dog lights up at the sight of the paper, begin to blend a known command with a new one, "Paper–Go get it," and let the dog take it in his mouth.**

4. **If your newspaper comes in a plastic bag, place the folded (and worn) paper in its plastic bag and repeat Steps 1–3.**

Now you can take your show outside. The next morning, have a big treat waiting inside, and then take your dog outside with you on-leash. When you come across the paper (which should be similar to the one you've been practicing with indoors), act surprised and point to it, saying "Go get it–Fetch the paper." When your dog seizes the opportunity, command "Hold" and trot back to the house. Reward him with the treat and enthusiastic praise.

Concerned your dog will gather all the papers in the neighborhood? He may if you leave him outside all day! If you notice your dog racing off toward the neighbor's drive, put him on a long line and discourage him with a quick tug and "Nope!" (see Chapter 4).

When your dog carries the paper back for you, you're ready to start sending him from the door:

1. **Initially, walk within 3 feet of the paper and say "Fetch the paper."**

2. **If your dog looks confused, run forward, shake the paper playfully, run back, and repeat the command.**

3. **Progressively increase your distance from the paper.**

Each time your dog returns the paper to you, make a big fuss!

Whether sending your dog out to get the paper or signaling him to deliver a message (as in "Fetching a fax: A four-footed delivery option," coming up), send him off with a happy point in the direction you want him to go!

Fetching whatever you need

Whatever your life pattern, involve your dog whenever you can! Personally, my family is in the midst of raising young kids, so "Fetch the diaper" was a no-brainer. The fact that my dog (like yours) actually enjoys helping out is like icing on the cake.

1. **First, introduce your dog to the household object you want him to retrieve.**

2. **Practice the steps in the earlier section "Mastering the basic fetching sequence," substituting the new object for the toy.**

   • Toss the object, say "Go get it," and praise any interest.

   • Encourage your dog to mouth it, and don't take it away immediately.

   • Teach "Give" separately once he's willing to hold it; then unite the steps as you did in Stage 4 of the "Mastering the basic fetching sequence" section.

3. **Now place the object in its normal location. If your dog must stand up to reach it, review "Up, up" in Chapter 8 and practice that step separately.**

4. **Send your dog to get the object from a distance of no more than 3 feet.**

5. **Gradually extend your distance until you're able to send your dog from another room.**

Always reward and praise a proper delivery . . . it can't get much better than this!

Fetching a fax: A four-footed delivery option

My big brother, John, showed me the "Four-Footed Fax" trick when I was but a pup myself. He and his wife had an English Springer Spaniel named Chelsea who would deliver notes to anyone in the house. You'd just write out the note, fold it up, tell Chelsea who it was meant for, and off she'd go, note in mouth.

This trick is actually a more advanced version of "Hide and Seek" (see Chapter 5 for details on that trick). To teach your dog to give the FedEx courier a run for his money, just follow these steps:

1. **Play "Hide and Seek" with two or more people in your house. Equip everyone with a treat cup.**

   When first playing "Hide and Seek," have everyone in visual range. Slowly start to spread out until everyone is hiding in different areas of the house.

2. **Tell your dog to "Go find Mom" and have Mom call out.**

   When the dog gets to Mom, have her give the dog a treat (or simply praise if treats are overwhelming).

3. **Next, tell him to find another family member, for example, "Go find Lindsay," and have that person give a yell.**

4. **Repeat the routine with different family members' names, changing the hiding places from time to time to keep the game fresh and fun.**

   Once your dog learns who everyone is, you can phase out the yell from the person being found. Soon your dog will know everyone by name!

Now for the delivery! Start with one delivery, ending on a successful note. Within sight of your intended recipient, place a note in the dog's mouth and send him off: for example, say, "Go find Frank!" Upon delivery, the recipient must instruct "Give," and then praise plentifully!

Once your dog will deliver a note, you can develop this trick in three ways:

✔ Increase the distance of the retrieve.

✔ Introduce different family members and friends.

✔ Vary the objects delivered: socks, sodas, a soup spoon!

Carrying This and That

Every Sunday my daughter and I walk to the corner bakery for bagels with our dog, a Labrador Retriever named Whoopsie. On the way home, it's a common spectacle to see Whoopsie trotting next to us carrying breakfast in a bright white bag.

Once your dog has learned the retrieving exercises in the previous sections of this chapter, you can teach him to carry things for you. Like fetch, it's a three-part exercise, but these three go faster once you've mastered the retrieve. Once the basics are mastered, you can get your dog to help you carry just about anything.

Mastering the fine art of "Carry"

Like many of the other retrieving skills, "Carry" can and should be broken down and taught step by step. To carry anything, your dog will need to know to take it calmly and hold it in his mouth, and then, finally, to release it on command. If you've shaped the retrieve, this is an easy adaptation.

Stage 1: "Take it"

Put your dog on a leash and go to a quiet area to practice this trick. Choose an object that's unfamiliar to your dog, like an empty paper lunch bag or a wooden dowel, and follow these steps:

1. **Place the object in front of your dog's mouth and say "Take it."**

   If he seems unimpressed, you can try a variety of enticements to encourage him to open his mouth: jiggling the object around, using a treat, or tickling his whiskers below his nose. Remember, you attract more attention with antics than anger.

2. **When your dog takes it, click/praise and reward him.**

   Be patient.

3. **When your dog will take the object, gradually extend the distance he much reach out to grab it. At each distance, jiggle the toy and encourage him to "Take it," then click/reward his efforts.**

   Practice holding it increasingly farther from you until you have it lying on the floor.

   Remember what I just said about patience? This step alone may take 5–10 practice sessions.

Stage 2: "Hold it"

Your next goal is to teach your dog to hold the object. Follow these steps:

1. **Present the object and scratch your dog's chin, putting a little upward pressure on it to keep the object in place.**

   At first he'll probably spit it out; ignore that and present the object again.

2. **Command "Hold it–Stay" and pause for two to five seconds.**

   When your dog starts to roll the object in his mouth and chew, gently discourage him with "Nope." If that doesn't impress him, tug his collar gently, say "Nope–Stay," and don't reward him until he does. Keep your cool, however, or you'll discourage your dog from ever retrieving for you again.

3. **Next, command "Give," and click/praise and reward.**

4. **Slowly progress until your dog holds the object for 30 seconds.**

   Don't worry if the seasons change while you're perfecting this exercise. I had a Collie who took almost six months to fully grasp "Hold it."

To signal "Hold it," point your finger close to his nose.

Stage 3: "Carry"

This part ties the loose ends together into a wonderful, helpful canine package. The real delight is how excited your dog is to get involved: It sure beats staring out the window all day!

1. **Put a raw potato in a lunch sack.**

2. **Put your dog in a "Sit."**

3. **Fold the top of the bag crisply, turn to your dog, and say "Take it–Hold it," as you offer the bag.**

4. **When he grasps the bag, pause for two seconds, and then say "Give." Praise him, click, and treat.**

5. **Next, ask your dog to "Hold it" again, and walk forward as you encourage your dog to follow you.**

6. **When he takes a step, say "Carry." After a few steps, reward and praise your dog.**

7. **Repeat Steps 5 and 6 three times.**

   Keep these lessons short — 3–5 minutes — especially in the beginning. If you notice your dog getting antsy or clamping on the objects destructively whereas before he was cooperative, take a break. Practice these short sessions 2–4 times each day when time allows.

8. **Next, put your dog on a leash and go to a hallway or open area in your house or garage. Present the bag as you command "Take–Carry," and increase your steps as you encourage your dog to follow you.**

   If your dog drops the bag, ignore it and quit. Busy yourself and ignore your dog for 15 minutes. Next time, lower your goal — reward two steps.

   Once your dog reliably carries the bag, you can discourage a distracted drop by saying "Nope," and then pointing to the bag. Stay upbeat and positive. No dog wants to carry things for a grump.

9. **Continue to increase the number of steps until your dog follows you around the house.**

Now you're ready to take this show on the road. Repeat the preceding process, praising your dog a few steps at a time.

Creating variations on the theme

When your dog has learned this trick with a bag, he'll want to carry other things, too. He'll insist on helping with the groceries; just give him a cereal box or the buns, tell him "Carry," and off to the kitchen he'll go with you. When it's time to clean house, ask your dog to carry the rag or the paper towels. You'll both be happy. Here are four of my favorite variations — be sure to add your own to the list:

✔ **Helping me with the groceries:** I'm not a huge fan of grocery shopping — a task born of necessity. But unpacking the groceries . . . that's a different story! Not only does my dog help, she gets so excited about it that the kids come down to help too. At first I started with easy-to-hold objects like a box of raisins or plastic storage bags. Now she'll happily carry anything she can fit her mouth around.

✔ **Carrying a kid's toy:** Though I'm a minimalist by nature, I've been forced to relax my standards since the birth of my two kids. Every outing has its own checklist: diaper bag, check; sippy cup, check; toys, check . . . oops, that's one too many things to hold. Whoopsie to the rescue. Our dog is more than happy to help out!

✔ **Bringing a log to the fire:** One of my favorite pastimes is hanging out by the fireplace with my family. Whether we're gathering to read, play games, or toast s'mores, the first step in having a fire is to build it, and nothing could please my dog more than carrying a few logs in from the wood stack!

✔ **Getting the leash:** All dogs love an adventure! To teach your dog to bring you his leash, hang/place it in a consistent location and fold it over until it's no longer than 2 feet, depending on the size of your dog.

Once your dog knows where his leash is, teach him to retrieve his leash: "Get your leash." Send him from no more than 3 feet, gradually increasing the distance until you're able to direct him from another room.

Never ask your dog to carry hazardous things like cleaning products, paints, or paint remover. If you wouldn't ask a 5-year-old to handle something, don't ask your dog! Also be mindful of size. Though a dog wouldn't go out of his way to swallow a key, in the enthusiasm of the retrieve there might be an inadvertent gulp. Not good!

Advancing with Fetching Skills: Pulling Out Tissues and Raiding the Fridge

Has your dog mastered his finding, fetching, and carrying skills? More clever tricks await you. . . . While I've listed a couple cool tricks in this section, you're sure to come up with a few favorites of your own to enhance and brighten up your everyday life! Be sure to share your favorites with me: E-mail me your version via www.whendogstalk.com or send it via snail-mail to When Dogs Talk, P.O. Box 802, Katonah, NY 10536, and attach a picture of your dog in action to boot!

Achoo! Getting a tissue

You have two options with the tissue trick, which basically involves fetching a tissue from the tissue box:

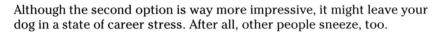 When you say "Tissue," your dog runs and gets you one.

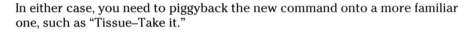 When you sneeze, your dog gets you a tissue.

Although the second option is way more impressive, it might leave your dog in a state of career stress. After all, other people sneeze, too.

In either case, you need to piggyback the new command onto a more familiar one, such as "Tissue–Take it."

For props, you need a box of tissues and a low table that your dog can reach without jumping aboard with all four. Also, go to your local discount store and get one of those fancy plastic tissue box containers, so the box will have some resistance when your dog fetches the tissue. (You can also weigh down a regular box.) Fasten the tissue box to the table with tape initially. And for the training phase, the tissues should be pulled out and lightly re-stuffed into the box.

Stage 1: Fetch me a tissue, please

The first part is a classic retrieve:

1. **Kneel on the floor next to your tissue box. Entice your dog to take the tissue; when he is reliably taking it, pair the behavior with a command, like "Tissue!" If your aim is to have your dog fetch the tissue on an actual sneeze, follow your tissue command with a very theatrical sneeze.**

   Ruffle the top tissue as you sneeze, to pique your dog's interest and to entice him to take the tissue.

2. **Reward him for taking the tissue.**

   Now your dog has the tissue. Not much help if you need to wipe your nose! But you both know about retrieving.

3. **When your dog takes tissues, encourage "Bring" and "Give."**

4. **Reward your dog the instant he drops the tissue in your hand.**

Stage 2: Retrieving off the table

The next phase of this trick is to teach your dog to put his front paws on the table. If the idea is abhorrent to you, place the tissues on the ground or on a low coffee table. Otherwise, pat the table and give the "Up" command (see Chapter 8). Click and reward the instant your dog's front paws hit the table. Be patient; just getting your dog to believe you're inviting him to come up on the table may take awhile.

Make sure your dog understands that it's front paws only on the table. You can discourage him from bringing the rest of his doggy self along with a gentle "Nope" or even a mild restraint at first.

Though I recommend using a low table, even that may not be low enough for a very small trickster. Use a low stool or chair, or even a pillow, to help your little dog reach the table. Place the stool between you and your dog, facing him. With treats in hand, command "Up" and pat the stool. If your dog jumps up with two paws, reward him immediately. Soon you can say "Up" and point without patting the chair. Then simply follow the preceding steps to teach him to put his paws on the table.

Stage 3: Putting the whole act together

Now to unify the acts . . . soon your dog will automatically fetch you a tissue each time you sneeze!

1. **Sit down and place the tissue box between your knees.**

2. **Tell your dog "Get me a tissue," or sneeze your most wonderful sneeze, and hold out the box.**

3. **Reward him the instant he grasps the tissue, the little genius!**

   Progressively reward only proper tissue pulls, where he pulls the tissue all the way out of the box and drops it in your hand.

4. **Set the box on the corner of the table (the place it will always be when you do this trick) and repeat Steps 1–3.**

   Your dog may need a gentle reminder of "Up," but you can soon phase out that command.

5. **Move a little bit away from the table, and then request "Get me a tissue."**

   Repeat the command, moving farther from the table each time. Eventually, stand and sit in various places in the room when you make the request. Be sure to reward — and say "Thank you" — each time he brings you a tissue.

Bringing you a drink

I saved the hardest trick for last. It's a personal favorite. My dog Shayna could tell the difference between a soda can, a water bottle, and a can of beer.

In this trick, your long-range goal is to be able to say — from anywhere in the house — "Get me a soda!" and have your dog run to the refrigerator, open the door, remove a can of soda, close the refrigerator, and bring the soda to you. Sound impossible? It's not so tough — just a lot of steps to master before you put it all together.

Stage 1: Carrying the can or bottle

Part one of the trick is to teach your dog to carry a can or bottle. This is a basic retrieving exercise.

1. **If your dog is uncomfortable holding a bottle or can in his mouth, wrap it in a light rag initially.**

2. **Show the can to your dog and say "Take it–Drink."**

3. **Using the skills I discuss earlier in the "Carrying This and That" section, teach your dog to hold the can, carry it, and then bring it to you from a distance — in that order.**

4. **When your dog is comfortable with the wrapped can in his mouth, repeat Step 3, but begin to fold the width of the cloth down so your dog gets used to the bottle or can.**

Stage 2: Opening the fridge

Opening the refrigerator sounds trickier than it is. I've broken it down into easy steps:

1. Cut a piece of rope long enough so that when it's hung in a loop from the refrigerator door handle, it hangs at the level of your dog's chin.

   If you have small children in the home, don't leave the rope hanging from the door. Devise a rope system that can be easily removed after training time.

2. Let your dog sniff the rope to get familiar with it. Offer the rope to your dog and encourage, "Tug it." Pull against your dog for 5 seconds and then instruct your dog to release the rope.

3. Secure the rope to the handle. (I use industrial-strength Velcro to affix my rope to the refrigerator door.)

4. Jiggle the rope in front of your dog's nose and command "Tug it."

5. Using praise or a click, reward your dog the instant he grasps the rope.

6. Once he's grabbing the rope on cue, encourage and reward only a solid tug on the door.

If you have a very clever dog, remove the rope or handle to discourage between-meal snacking or other incidents.

Don't let your dog swing from the rope or shake it like a stubborn rat. If you do, you may ask for a soda and end up with the refrigerator door. Reward only gentle pulls. Correct hard yanks with a "Nope!"

Stage 3: Removing the drink from the fridge

Now it's time to teach your dog to remove the can from the fridge.

1. Wrap the same can you've used for practice back up in the original unfolded cloth. Place the can on an empty shelf that's the right height for your dog to comfortably retrieve the can in his mouth.

2. Prop the refrigerator door open and lead your dog into the kitchen.

3. Act truly surprised and happy to find the can in the fridge and say "Drink" in a clear, enthusiastic voice. Point it out if your dog doesn't see the can right away.

4. Reward your dog even if his attempts to retrieve the drink are less than perfect. If he drops the can on the floor, encourage him to pick it up.

5. Continue to practice until your dog is successful at each attempt to get the soda off the shelf.

Stage 4: Retrieving the drink and bringing it to you

Now you and your little genius are ready to put together what he's learned so far. Drum roll, please!

1. **Approach the refrigerator with your dog.**

2. **Jiggle the rope and slowly say "Get Me a . . .–Tug it"**

3. **Wait until your dog is pulling the door open to say "Drink."**

4. **If he seems confused, show him the can and say "Drink."**

5. **Click and reward the instant your dog gives you the drink.**

This is the time for jackpot treats. Mission accomplished!

Always place the drink in the same place. Moving it around makes it difficult or impossible for your dog to retrieve for you. Also, if you buy a six-pack, remove the plastic rings that hold the cans together. Cut up the plastic before you throw it out. (The animals of the world will thank you. Very often, the plastic rings end up around the necks of birds and small animals, causing them to choke or become unable to swallow.)

Stage 5: Closing the refrigerator door

No task is complete without teaching your dog to close the door. Though some of you may be so impressed with the retrieve that you're tempted to leave out this stage, I don't recommend it. You may come in and find the contents of your fridge have disappeared . . . and the only clue will be your very satiated canine, licking his chops. Either get up and close the door yourself, or teach this last sequence with the help of Chapter 6 and the trick sequence for turning out the lights.

1. **Hold your target disc directly in front of your refrigerator door.**

2. **Tell your dog "Target–Close" and praise him for even the slightest bump.**

3. **Now tape the disc onto the door and point to it as you say "Target–Close," once again rewarding and praising even the slightest bump.**

   If your dog doesn't hit the door hard enough to close it, begin to withhold the treat until he does.

Stage 6: Putting it all together

Now that your dog has figured out all the steps, it's time to test his English comprehension. Stand at the fridge and command "Get me a drink!" Is he confused? Not sure what all the words mean when they're squashed together? Don't get frustrated. Enunciate each word slowly, and walk your dog through the process. Continue to work through this procedure until he masters it. When the drink is in hand, send him back to "Close" the door.

Progressively extend your distance from the fridge until you can ask your dog from another room. Now imagine lying on the couch, watching the game. You call out "Get me a drink," and here comes your dog, drink in mouth.

Part III
Tackling More Advanced Tricks

The 5th Wave   By Rich Tennant

"You know, you're never going to get
that dog to do its business in your
remote control dump truck."

In this part . . .

Ready to tackle some more complicated moves? Here you'll find many dramatic routines and complicated tricks, from doing the combat crawl and leaping through a hoop of fire to sounding an alarm and showing emotions! Of course, none of these tricks is life threatening — or even poses a safety hazard. Once you teach your dog to dance, bark, or retrieve, only a few more learning steps are needed to master these more complicated maneuvers.

Chapter 8

Jumping and Dancing for Joy

*I*t's no secret: Dogs love to jump — on guests, counters, family members, each other — it's all one big game. But for those of you who are less than delighted at your dog's enthusiasm for standing on two paws, read closely: Your jumper is simply trying to get a little face time. If she could get her paws on some kind of magic device that conveyed her through the world at eye-level to humans, she'd never need to jump again. She'd be face-to-face with her pack members, seeing what they see and doing what they do.

Well great, you say. I've got an emotionally healthy dog. She's still driving me nuts. That's why I push her off! And off. And off again. But here's the difference between dogs and people: When you nudge her off the couch or attempt to repel her two-legged embrace, she likes it. It's interactive and exciting. You're encouraging her. While this sounds like quite a predicament, help is only pages away.

The best way to teach your dog when not to jump is to teach her when she *can* jump. Redirect that enthusiasm, and put it on cue. Jumping tricks give her an appropriate expressive outlet for her in-your-face enthusiasm. Have fun with your dog when she's jumping, and you'll see your relationship leap to a whole new level — almost overnight! This chapter shows you how.

Dancing Dog and Other Two-Legged Tricks

Is your dog just as happy on two paws as she is on four? Is she a ham who likes to jump around on her hind legs? A showoff? If you're answering "Yes, yes, yes," have I got some tricks for you!

Dancing or standing on two legs is not a trick for growing pups. It can wreak havoc on their growth plates. Wait until your dog is at least 12 months old before starting on this trick.

Basic steps: Getting your dog on two legs

The "Dance" trick can help you in the greeting department, too. When your dog learns to dance on her hind legs on command, you can call up the routine whenever you open your door to guests. Here's how to teach this trick:

1. **Gather some treats and a clicker, if you're using one.**

   Give your dog a hearty scratch and lots of praise to loosen her up.

2. **Hold a treat at arm's length just inches above your dog's nose.**

3. **The moment she stands on her hind legs, click/praise and reward.**

   Do this five times, and then stop for the day. Once she connects this sequence, add the cue word "Dance."

4. **Increase the time your dog must balance on her hind legs before you reward her, but don't go overboard!**

   Three seconds is a long time for a dog to balance. It takes a while for your dog to build the muscles necessary to stand on two legs.

5. **Now you can get fancy: Moving the treat slightly to the left or right will encourage athletic dancers to spin in a circle; bringing the treat forward an inch will encourage your dog to step forward like a human!**

As your dog gets familiar with the routine, think up clever sayings to add to your fun, and repeat them whenever you're practicing. Soon these word cues will prompt your dog into action! Here are a few tricks to try:

- **Walk like a lady (or a gentleman):** For this sequence, back up slowly as you lure your dog to follow you. As your dog catches onto the word cue, you can maneuver to her side to give the impression you're walking together!

- **Twirl round and round:** To teach your dog to twirl, move the treat in slow circles. Spinning is a true balancing act, so reward quarter spins and progress slowly.

- **Bucking bronco:** Are you a rodeo fan who just can't afford the lifestyle? Well, while your dog probably won't fit into a saddle, you can get her to buck like a wild pony any time you like. Cue her with a neighing sound or a command like "Bucking bronco" and lift the treat above her head and slightly forward.

Remember this secret — if you have fun with it, your dog will be in heaven, jumping just to please you. What could be better than that?

May I have this dance? Dancing together

Personally, I love to dance. Now that I'm homebound with young kids, I often indulge my dancing feet right in my living room. It's a great way to exercise and fun for the whole family — whether they walk on two legs or four. Whatever your personal taste, nothing pleases your dog more than being invited to share your passions!

These are not tricks for impulsively excited or dominant dogs! If yours is assertive, engaging her in this way may send her the wrong message. Better skip this one!

Disco dog

If your dog loves to jam and you're into disco music, dust off your record collection and clear the floor. You'll never dance alone again (or be kidded about your Bee Gees infatuation).

As you're jammin', your dog will be getting excited and wondering what part she can play in all this fun. Take one of her treats and say "Dance–Disco," and then simply show her the direction you'd like her to move by inching the treat to the left or right. Review moves like weaving and spinning taught in the "Crazy Eights" and "Chase your Tail" tricks in Chapter 10, and put them to music! Reward even her simplest efforts. Soon you'll notice that your dog is movin' to the groovin'.

The two-step

Are you a country music buff? Well, here's the dance for you — the canine two-step. Hold a bent arm out just above your dog's head and encourage your dog to jump up and rest her front paws on it. When your dog is in the proper dancing position, up on her hind legs, ask a helper to bait your dog forward with a treat and move together paw-in-arm!

It takes a few weeks for your dog to build the muscles necessary to walk on two legs. Don't overdo it! Build her stamina gradually, and stop the moment she gets down. Think of your dog as an athlete. Work her out slowly.

If your dog's a diehard jumper who just can't seem to keep her paws off you, rethink this paw-in-arm dancing routine. Sure, it's fun, but you won't be able to get your little Casanova to stop.

Trying four-paw and no-paw dance moves

Talk about a clever canine! These next moves involve little motion, are fun to work on together, and look oh-so-groovy once they're mastered.

Doing the moon dance

In the moon dance, your dog will bow down on her two front legs and shimmy backwards. This step requires a good understanding of the "Back" and "Bow" commands (see Chapters 4 and 6).

1. **Tell your dog to "Bow" and "Stay."**

2. **Luring your dog with a biscuit, command "Back."**

   Most dogs will pop up and scoot back from a standing pose. To prevent this, hold your hand over your dog's shoulder blades.

3. **Treat your dog for the proper move.**

   If you're using a clicker, this is the perfect moment to introduce it. Click the moment she nails the motion, then reward your dog immediately.

   Soon you'll be paying respect to the late Michael Jackson in tandem!

Break dancing

A year ago, I was trying to teach Beauty, my Bulldog student, the "Down" command. Whenever she heard "Down," she'd flip over, belly up, and twist around like a silly worm. Because it was too hard to be serious with such a funny-looking dog, I started saying "Break dance" whenever she'd start her routine. Before long, dear Beauty was break dancing on command.

There's a prerequisite to teaching your dog this command: She must feel comfortable on her back, with her feet in the air. Follow these steps:

1. **Encourage your dog into the proper "Break dance" position by sitting on the floor and scratching her belly.**

   Small dogs need more security when learning to break dance, although they're able to roll around on the floor like the big guys once they learn. Initially, sit down and straighten your legs in front of you. Now place your dog belly up between your legs. Sandwich your dog between your calves, and she'll feel very safe indeed.

2. **As soon as those paws are airborne, start waving your hands above her feet and say "Break dance."**

   She won't know what you're doing at first, but stick with it. Soon she'll be imitating your movement.

3. **Immediately reinforce your dog with enthusiastic praise and treats.**

   As soon as she catches on, it will be hard to get her to stop!

4. **Now give her the "Break dance" command from a standing position, wiggling your fingers above her belly.**

Pushing a cart or carriage

While pushing a cart involves little dancing, it requires lots of coordination and excites dogs who are more comfortable on two paws than four. Sound like someone you know?

You can use a baby carriage or a shopping cart for this trick. Got a small dog? Go to your local toy store: They make these for mini people and small dogs too! The height should allow your dog to stand comfortably upright. This is a sequence trick involving "Up, up" and walking forward.

1. **Let your dog smell and sleep on a soft hand towel, and then wrap the towel around the bar she will put her front paws on to push the cart.**

   Secure it with strong tape.

2. **Secure the cart to a wall so it won't move when your dog first stands on it.**

3. **Using treats and enthusiasm, encourage your dog to place her front paws on the bar with "Up, up."**

   Repeat this until your dog is clear on your direction and excited to see the prop.

4. **Now stand in front of the prop and hold it securely; bait your dog forward with a biscuit as you command "Forward."**

   If your dog follows you, ask a friend to help and stay at your dog's side.

When teaching your dog to push the cart or carriage on her own, practice on a carpet or grassy surface — a fast-moving cart is hard to keep up with!

Place objects in the cart to weigh it down. Nothing could be scarier than having the cart tip back on your dog as she's learning to push it.

Leaping Up and Over

There's no better outlet for happy, athletic dogs than jumping. Of course, if you don't direct this activity, your dog's jumping will frustrate you, but teaching jumping tricks satisfies everyone on so many levels. You get to spend time together, collaborating and learning activities that bring a smile to your face and a wag to your dog's tail.

As you practice these tricks, remember jumping is an athletic activity. Warm up with gentle routines and watch your dog for any signs of discomfort, such as limping or refusals (unwillingness to take a jump). Dogs get thirsty too, especially when exercising, so have a bowl of water close at hand. Make sure all the jumps are lined up so that your dog can easily clear them and her landing space is level and open. Dogs should be able to take three full strides after each jump.

Clearing bars, poles, and broomsticks

Structured jumping must start somewhere, so try this: Get a broom, a bar, or a pole. In a carpeted area, balance it on two objects of equal height (paper towel rolls or cereal boxes work nicely). Make sure it's secure enough so that it can't be easily knocked over but will yield if your dog bumps into it.

To determine how high to place the pole to start, measure the height between your dog's paw and her shoulder. Divide this in half. That's how high your training jump should be.

To make sure your dog has enough runway, clear space for five strides coming up to the jump and four strides after she's cleared it. Zoom!

Now you're ready to begin:

1. **Place your dog on a short leash for control, and then let her sniff the jump.**

   Verbally discourage any test-chewing by saying "No."

2. **Bring your dog to a point several feet from the jump. Say "Over" before you move toward the jump.**

3. **Jog up lightly to the obstacle and jump just ahead of your dog.**

4. **If your dog refuses to follow you over the jump, stay calm. Walk over the jump several times while your dog watches, and then try to walk over it together.**

   When practicing your jumping tricks, don't look at your dog if she refuses to jump. Focus on and praise your dog when she's cooperating!

5. **Pick up the pace, with both of you jumping the pole.**

   Move at your dog's natural gait, not too fast and not too slow.

6. **When you see your dog taking the jump with pride, stop yourself just before the jump and let your dog jump alone.**

   Be sure to reward with a jackpot of treats and praise.

7. **Gradually train your dog to take the jump alone by stopping your own approach farther and farther back from the jump.**

   The goal is for your dog to take the jump when you merely point to the intended obstacle and say "Over."

After your dog learns how to jump properly, you can raise the jump to a height that's appropriate for your dog.

Never raise a jump higher than 1½ times your dog's height, and note that many dogs are comfortable jumping only at lower heights.

Practice your jumps whenever you come across a natural obstacle, such as a railing or a fallen branch — opportunities abound. If you and your dog are really addicted, read about agility training in Part IV of this book!

Jumping over the kids

Kids make good natural obstacles (as any parent will tell you) for the jump trick. And although children don't exactly get into the "Sit," "Stay," and "Come" exercises, they do like to join in fun tricks with their dog.

For the "Over the Kids" trick, your dog must be confident enough to take the jump solo. Have the kids sit and watch you as you practice "Over" with the broom so that the dog gets used to performing around the children. The next step depends on how many kids you have:

✔ **One kid:** Ask your child to lay face down under or alongside the broom-jump. Take your dog and let her sniff the new setup. Say "Ep, ep" if she gets too excited and lead her back five strides. Say "Over," run toward the jump, and encourage her to leap over the new obstacle. Praise lots when your dog clears your kid! Good dog!

Next, have your child raise his or her back toward the ceiling until it's at broom level. When your dog's clearing both the broom and your child confidently, remove the broom. Ta-da!

✔ **More than one kid:** Always start the "Over the Kids" jump with one child, as described in the preceding bullet. If you want to add children, first let the dog jump over them one at a time, just to get used to each child. Next, line the kids out face down next to each other, on either side of the broom jump. One at a time they should raise their backs to a height that's comfortable for your dog.

Be realistic: Don't add so many kids that your dog is forced to step over them like rocks across a stream, and if you have a big weighty dog and small kids, be realistic — a big dog can only jump so far, and you don't want an early landing!

Jump rope

Jumping rope with your dog is quite a spectacle. This takes a little doing to teach — sequencing staying, jumping up, rhythm, and awareness — but with a little patience you'll most certainly wow any crowd!

First your dog needs to get the hang of the "Jump" command. When being taught to jump up in the air, she may get confused and try to jump on you. To teach your dog the new definition — "no paws on me" — you can use the flat of your hand or a square of cardboard. While your dog's standing, hold your prop above her head. When she sniffs it curiously, reward her immediately!

As she catches on to the new game — "bump the prop with my nose" — attach a word cue such as "Jump" to direct her off your body. Now hold the prop up so that your dog must jump to hit or bump it. Jump, dog, jump!

You can use this prop in tricks like jumping rope or to shape better behavior like door greetings when your dog is über-excited — though she may still jump, at least she's not jumping on anyone!

If your dog touches your body or anyone else's while jumping, say "No," and withdraw the treat. Look up at the ceiling for 10–20 seconds (to show her the fun ends for a while); then start again.

Next, secure a piece of carpet to the floor, making sure it doesn't slip. Tell your dog to "Stand" and "Stay" on the carpet. Have her do a few practice jumps.

Then do the following:

1. **Introduce a 7-foot nylon/cotton weave jumping rope.**

   Let your dog sniff it so that it doesn't startle her. Jiggle it to familiarize her with the motion.

2. **Secure one end of the rope to a doorknob or immovable object at your hip level; encourage your dog to jump and try to sneak the rope beneath her.**

   Don't circle the rope over her head yet because this might startle her. Reward your dog for jumping whether or not she clears the rope.

3. **Now work on your timing, helping your dog get accustomed to the rope's motions. Don't swing it over her head yet!**

   As your dog's enthusiasm grows, reward only her successful jumps.

4. **Once you've got this down pat, begin full over-the-head swings encouraging one, two, then three jumps in a row.**

   To infinity and beyond!

Once your dog is a master, you can practice jumping rope together. Watch your knees and focus on the timing.

Jumping Through

Jumping through something is a natural progression from "Over" and really adds zing to any trick routine. (Make sure your dog is really comfortable with "Over" before you try "Through.") In this section, you find out how to train your dog to jump through a hoop or your arms.

Through the hoop

For humans, living your life jumping through hoops can be a drag — but for dogs, it's just fun. For this trick, dig up a hula hoop from the corner of your basement or get one from your local variety store. Though its place on the toy store aisle isn't as prominent as those of electronic pastimes, you can still find a hula hoop if you look hard enough.

If your hoop rattles when you shake it, cut a little hole in the plastic and dump the beads. This sound frightens some dogs.

Then do the following:

1. **Set up your original jumping pole across a threshold or between two pieces of furniture. Center the hoop next to the broom. Ask a helper to hold it or brace it between two heavy books.**

2. **Let your dog sniff the hoop.**

3. **Instruct your dog "Over" as you move toward the obstacle. If your dog refuses, toss food or a toy through the hoop.**

   If your dog still refuses to jump through the hoop, let her watch as you climb through cheerfully. You can also stand on one side of the hoop, toss a cherished treat through to the other side, and lead your dog through calmly.

4. **After your dog cooperates, start adding the command "Through" to "Over" as you start for the jump, like this: "Over–Through."**

5. **Hold or prop the hoop higher, so that the bottom of the hoop is even with the height of the pole positioned at a familiar, comfortable jumping height for your dog.**

   At this point, your dog might hesitate because the hoop looks, well, like a hoop, not like a level jump. If this is the case, approach the hoop slowly and let your dog walk through it a couple of times. Use food and/ or toys to encourage her.

When you feel that your dog is ready, have her try the hoop alone by following these steps:

1. **Vary your locations to get your dog used to hoop-jumping in various areas. Prop or hold the hoop securely on the floor.**

2. **Instruct "Through" as the two of you trot up to the hoop. Let your dog go through the hoop alone.**

3. **Praise her joyously and encourage her to jump back through the hoop toward you by running backward yourself.**

   Clap, sing, praise, treat — let your dog know what a star she is!

4. **Progressively raise the hoop to a height appropriate for your dog.**

Performing in front of a crowd

You and your dog will have so much fun practicing and perfecting your jumping routines that you'll want to show off. Whether you've got an audience of one or a dozen, here are some good things to remember:

✔ Warm-ups are a must. If you're going to be practicing jumps and other athletic feats, warm your dog up before you begin.

✔ Everyone gets a little nervous when variables change. Take your dog on a tour of her new surroundings before you start, letting her sniff out unfamiliar people and places.

✔ If you're using props, practice at home first. If your routine will require your dog to work away from you, review and practice with targeting discs (see Chapter 2).

Once she's comfortable with this routine in a restricted area, start working her in more open areas. Keep your praise and energy high; this display is a real crowd-pleaser.

Through your arms!

This is one trick you can take everywhere. No props required! Just create a circle with your arms and teach your dog to jump through them.

If you're truly daring, you can try the trick with a large dog, but let me warn you: Watch out for your nose. One of my brightest students, a chipper chocolate Lab, had mastered every trick I knew, so I decided to give this trick a try. Of course, once he figured out what I wanted, he was eager to give it his all. Unfortunately, one day my nose got in the way and there was blood everywhere. Poor boy — he thought he had killed me.

Approach this trick as with the hoop (see the preceding section), but use your arms instead. Here's how to work up to this trick:

1. **Start the early lessons with warm-up hoop jumps.**

2. **Place your dog in a "Stay" on one side of a doorway, and lay a broomstick across the floor (as you do for the "Over" command I describe earlier in "Clearing bars, poles, and broomsticks").**

3. **Kneel next to the doorway with one elbow on the floor. Encourage your dog to jump over your arm to reach the treat.**

   You might get some face licks, so don't be too surprised.

Lean your head and body away from your arms when practicing this trick. If your dog does bonk you by accident, don't respond; otherwise, she won't want to practice this one again.

4. **Once she's mastered this, repeat the initial steps, placing your other arm above to create a hoop shape.**

   To make your arm circle, hold a scarf or piece of rope between your hands. This trick is easier to do if you have an extra person around to lure your dog through your arms with a treat as you say "Through."

5. **Shower your dog with ecstatic and uplifting praise.**

   What a great team you make!

6. **Progressively hold your arms higher and slowly work away from the restrictions of the doorway, as shown in Figure 8-1.**

Gauge your praise. Some dogs get overly excited when concentrating on hard tricks. If your enthusiasm causes your dog to lose focus or get wild, tone it down. For your dog, just being with you may be encouragement enough.

Figure 8-1:
This dog has mastered jumping through her owner's arms.

Jumping Into

Dogs, being dogs, love to jump into things. In fact, sometimes the real trick is getting them to jump out. The hardest decision for me was where to start this section. Here, I explain how to get your dog to jump into your lap, into your arms, and into (and out of) a box.

Into your lap

Dogs love laps. Getting them to jump there, however, is a stunt that is somewhat restricted by size.

Avoid this trick if your dog weighs more than you do or weighs less than 5 pounds. Small dogs have big hearts but short legs; leaping more than twice their height could seriously injure them. Be wise.

Here's how to teach this trick:

1. **Sit on the floor with your legs extended. Wave a favorite treat or toy in your hand and pat your lap; call your dog, saying "In my lap."**

   The first time you try this, the dog may run over and stop short or put two paws up. Pat your legs again and help her onto your lap.

2. **Now raise yourself into a low chair and repeat this sequence.**

   Praise and offer a treat.

   Is your dog earthbound in disbelief? The next time she approaches, gently grasp her collar under her chin and ease her up. Reward that. Soon she'll be leaping at your invitation.

The hand signal for the lap trick is simple: Pat your lap.

Of course, once you teach your dog to jump into your lap she may never want to leave. If your dog jumps up without permission, just tell her "not now" and encourage her to settle down at your side or in her comfort station (for details on setting up comfort stations for your dog, see Chapter 5).

Into your arms

One of my favorite pals is Buddy, a large-boned Yorkshire Terrier and a champion into-your-arms jumper. Open your arms and call to him, and he'll be up giving you a kiss before you can blink. If you watch freestyle and Frisbee routines, you'll notice this move a lot — it's the ultimate canine hug for a job well done!

1. **Start out by kneeling in front of your dog.**

   If your dog is small, you can begin this trick by placing her in a chair or on a table.

2. **Encourage your dog with "Up, up" as you pat your thighs.**

3. **Either lure your dog up or scoop your dog's rear as you say "Come up!"**

   Wrapping your arms around her body, praise her warmly and highlight your closeness with a kiss!

4. **Next, leave your dog in a "Stay" and kneel 5 feet away. Call her with "Come up" as you tap your thighs and open your arms encouragingly.**

   Initially she may stand there looking at you as though you've lost your mind. Go back and practice the first directed move; then encourage her as you guide her up and say "Come up!"

   Praise like mad when she ends up in your arms — whether you had to help her or not.

5. **After your dog catches on to the run and jump, begin to rise slowly to a standing position.**

   Figure 8-2 shows the final result you're looking for. Soon your dog will jump into your arms for the sheer delight of a kiss. But if you have trouble encouraging your dog to jump toward your face, try placing a treat between your lips. It works every time!

To signal jumping into your arms, bend your knees and pat your thighs.

Figure 8-2:
You eventually want to be standing up fully when your dog jumps into your arms.

Into a box

This is a fun routine that can be the start or finish to many sequenced tricks, such as "Hide and Seek" (see Chapter 5) and "Elevator up," which I describe shortly. To teach your dog, pick a cardboard box that your dog can sit snuggly in (too small and she'll be too cramped to be comfortable; too large and she'll fidget) Cut one of the sides down so that initially your dog can step into the box without effort. Then do the following:

1. **Initially let your dog sniff the box.**

   Make sure the box is on a non-slip surface.

2. **Guide her into the box with a treat or toy. Command "Box" as you point to direct your dog where to go.**

3. **Instruct her to "Sit" and/or "Down–Stay" for ten seconds.**

   Gradually increase the time up to two minutes.

4. **Now get a similar box and cut the side down only halfway. Then use another box with just a few inches cut down and signal your dog in and out of the box with the lure.**

   Reward all cooperation.

Each time your release your dog, use a special cue such as "Out of the box."

Once your dog eagerly jumps into and out of the box, you can decorate your box or graduate to a basket or chest. Now use your box to play "Hide and Seek" or as part of a routine like "Elevator up," where you lift the dog up as she stays in the box, asking silly questions like "Is this doggy for sale?" "Where's Lassie?"

Chapter 9

Barking, Counting, and Singing on Cue

Does your dog love to make noise? Does he bark when he's happy, excited, when he doesn't get his way? Is your biggest question not how to train him to vocalize but how to turn him off? Actually, it's easier than you think. First you encourage your dog to do something he already likes to do — bark! Once he learns how to bark on cue, you can direct his passions to completing complex math equations and counting the candles on the birthday cake! Next you can teach him perhaps an even more miraculous trick — to stop barking with one cleverly positioned finger to your lips. Bark–stop barking; bark–stop barking. When your dog catches onto this "trick," you'll be in the driver's seat. Not only will you be able to shape your dog's barking habits, but the world of talking tricks will also be yours to explore!

Barking and Not Barking on Cue

Some dog breeds are prone to barking . . . a lot! Terriers bark when a sound alerts them. Hounds bark when they catch a scent. Protective breeds bark when alerted to the unfamiliar. And many dogs love to bark just to hear themselves. Dogs who bark for a cause will not be silenced, but don't despair — if you're sharing your life with a barking dog, there is hope. Once you embrace your dog's natural vocal talents, you can teach him when barking is appropriate and when it's not. Although it sounds too good to be true, conducting your one-dog band is easier than you think. After you check out a few basic tips in the upcoming list, you can dive into the following sections to figure out how to train your dog to both shout and shush on command.

To teach your dog to bark on command, use the following tips:

✔ **Make eye contact:** Look at your dog alertly when you want him to bark. Break your stare when you want him to quiet down.

✔ **Use voice commands:** You need two: "Speak" and "Shhh." Enunciate clearly when you give your commands.

✔ **Give hand signals:** Use snappy signals to both encourage barking and discourage it.

  • To signal "Speak," try snapping your fingers near your mouth.

  • To signal "Shhh," put your index finger to your lips as if shushing a child.

Getting your dog to speak up

First, you must embrace your dog's natural vocal talents. This is easy enough — just attach a command to his passion. If your dog is a little hesitant in the barking department, you'll need to be more demonstrative to egg him on, but the goal is the same. The following steps show you how to attach the "Speak" command to your dog's barking behavior:

1. **Get something your dog lives for — a ball or a treat, for example.**

2. **Secure him to a post or tree, or stand on the other side of a door.**

   Stay within your dog's sight if he's stressed by being physically separated from you.

3. **Wave his prized object just out of reach while you encourage him to get it.**

   The moment he barks, give it to him and praise, praise, praise!

4. **Begin to add the hand signal to your voice and eye cues.**

   Snap your fingers near your mouth.

5. **Repeat this procedure until your dog reacts quickly to the "Speak" command.**

   Encourage him to "Speak," using the command and hand signal, throughout the day for positive things, such as a meal or a walk. If he speaks out of turn, just ignore him.

To encourage a puzzled or submissive barker to speak up, try baiting him with an enticing toy or treat, prompting him with a sound cue like the doorbell ringing, or tossing a toy and not releasing him to chase it until after he has sounded off!

Commanding "Shhh" for peace and quiet

Now it's time to teach your dog to be quiet. Sound like an impossible dream? If you make it fun and teach it like a trick, you may be shocked to find how quickly your dog picks it up!

To link the "Shhh" command to silence, follow these steps:

1. **Return to Steps 1–3 of the "Speak" lesson in the preceding section, isolating your dog and standing in front of him with something tasty or fun. Say "Speak!"**

2. **After a few barks, say "Shhh," stamp your foot, and avert your eyes.**

   The moment your dog stops barking, reward his silence.

3. **Gradually extend the time your dog must be silent to be rewarded.**

4. **Repeat this process until your dog responds to both "Speak" and "Shhh."**

   Practice your commands throughout the day, varying which ones you reinforce based on the situation. Sometimes reward the "Speak," other times the "Shhh." Have your dog "Speak" and "Shhh" two or three times before rewarding him. He'll be so proud of his new trick, and so will you!

If your dog is not connecting the "Shhh" command to being silent, see the section on remedying problem barkers at the end of this chapter.

From Counting to Calculus

My dog Hope, a Cairn terrier mix, is a total ham. Auditorium events really knock her out! One of her favorite tricks is what I call the numbers routine. I'll give her an arithmetic problem or have her count to ten with a group of kids, and she's more than happy to oblige. Using my signal, I start her off on cue and (magically) quiet her when the stunt is complete. Ta-da! The counting trick is where your bark-training efforts really pay off. People will be thrilled to see your dog doing so well in math.

Before you start asking your dog to count anything, you must polish his "Speak" and "Shhh" skills so that he can do them with hand signals alone. If you use voice commands, some doubters may think your dog isn't really counting. Check out the earlier section, "Barking and Not Barking on Cue," for more on reinforcing the "Speak" and "Shhh" skills.

After you have the commands down pat, you can begin asking your dog some basic questions. Just follow this sequence:

1. **Give the "Speak" hand signal.**

2. **Count the barks.**

3. **Signal "Shhh" after your dog has barked the correct number of times.**

Try starting with these questions:

- How much is two plus two?

- How old are you?

- How many eggs are in a half dozen?

Work on your silent communication, making your signals progressively subtle so that no one can tell you're helping out. After your dog can answer the basics, you can proceed to more difficult math problems, such as

- How many stars make up the Big Dipper? (The answer is seven.)

- What's the square root of 64? (Hint: It comes after 7.)

Regarding how the hand signals work, if your dog's a focus freak and can't take his eyes off you, you may need a signal for each bark response. For example, if the answer is "3," you signal three bark cues, and then cut the barking off with your silencing cue. Of course, you'll be far more discreet if you can use your signals like an on–off button. Many dogs will just keep barking until they see the silence cue. See what works for your dog.

Doing a Doggone Duet

Concerned your dog's not musically inclined? Most dogs aren't, if that makes you feel any better. In fact, I've never owned a dog who knew just what to do when I brought out my guitar. The silver lining? Most dogs who love to bark can be easily cajoled into barking along to music.

Choosing your instrument

When choosing an instrument to play with your dog, think it through. If you've got a passion for playing a particular instrument — the piano, for example — think twice about inviting your dog to join you in a duet. While it's fun once in a while, his eager intrusion may wear on your nerves. Consider an instrument that's cheap to buy and a rare noise in your home, such as a harmonica or kazoo. Your dog will nearly go into convulsions when you pull it out, so be prepared — after you teach him to bark, you'll have a rough time quieting him until the instrument is safely tucked away.

Howling the blues

While few dogs will howl in unison to a melodious sax, the arctic breeds, shepherds, and hound dogs are notorious for letting out a howl when they hear music or get excited. "Monkey see, monkey do" applies here. To see whether you can get your dog to howl, follow these steps:

1. **Play some soulful music, and let out a good howl yourself.**

   Toss your head back, and hit the high notes!

2. **When your dog joins in, congratulate him and keep on howling.**

Don't worry if your dog doesn't join in during the first session. Just let yourself go, and see if he doesn't show more enthusiasm the second time around!

3. **End by playing your dog's favorite game.**

   Soon, his tail will beat the floor whenever you pass by the stereo.

Once your dog gets the hang of howling, you can signal him to howl sans music. To signal a howl, lean your head back, face to the moon, and purse those lips. Now you can think of clever questions to ask your dog. "What does a werewolf do when he sees a full moon?" "What do you say when you see your girlfriend/boyfriend?" Clever dog!

Barking to the beat

To teach your dog to bark when you sing a certain tune or play a specific instrument, first you need to teach him how to speak and quiet down on hand signals, as I explain earlier in this chapter (see "Barking and Not Barking on Cue"). After he's learned these skills, the rest is easy if you follow these steps:

1. **Get out your instrument.**

   If it's new, let your dog sniff it.

2. **Put it in your mouth and signal "Shhh" to get his attention.**

   Blow a few short warm-up notes as you continue to signal him to stay quiet.

3. **When you're ready for your dog to begin barking, signal "Speak" as you egg him on with excited sounds and body postures.**

4. **When you're done, stop playing, say and signal "Shhh," and take a bow!**

Teaching Your Dog to Sound an Alarm

Dogs can actually be taught to bark for a variety of reasons, from alerting to visitors to barking when they hear a phone ring or when they see smoke. From usefulness to entertainment, finally a barking dog has something to offer everyone! This section describes how to put that barking to good use.

Alerting you to visitors or strangers

To your dog, your entranceway is the mouth of his den. Sure, you pay good money for your home sweet home, but to your dog, your home is just an oversized den. While many dogs bark to alert to visitors, some don't. Whether your goal is to teach your dog to bark when people arrive or to stop barking on cue, practice this:

1. **Put your dog on a "Sit–Stay" and stand at the open door.**

2. **Ring the bell (or have an assistant ring it) and command "Speak."**

   Click/praise and reward the inevitable bark.

3. **Ring the bell and give the "Speak" command again, but this time, after three barks, instruct your dog to "Shhh."**

   Wait until he quiets before you reward him.

4. **Ask a neighbor to come by and ring the bell or knock when your dog isn't expecting company.**

   Reinforce "Speak" or "Shhh" — whichever happens to be your dog's weak suit.

Repeat the process in your car. While the car is parked in the driveway, have someone approach as you tell your dog to "Speak." As your dog catches on, you can gradually work up to doing this trick in parking lots and gas stations.

Warning you of fire and other dangers

Think through your day: You're likely to come up with some reasons for your dog to bark. A client of mine had trouble keeping up with her 3-year-old son. We taught her beagle mix Bea to alert us each time he got too far away: This was handy out in the yard and even indoors when her son would toddle off. Another universal barking trick is to teach your dog to bark when he sees smoke or fire. I detail how to do this in the following steps, but remember, you can use this formula to teach your dog to alert you to just about anything:

1. **Gather a book of matches, treats, and a clicker if you use one, as well as a toy for good measure.**

   See Chapter 2 for more information about using a clicker.

2. **Put your dog on a "Sit–Stay," and light a match at least 4 feet away.**

3. **When the flame rises, say and signal "Speak."**

4. **Blow the flame out when your dog barks, then quiet him with the signal and command "Shhh."**

   Reward and praise him.

5. Repeat and repeat, increasing your focus on a quick response.

You can also teach your dog to alert to smoke. Training follows the same procedure: When the smoke rises, you give the signal to speak.

If you're big into candles and fireplaces, you'll need to think through this one. You can teach your dog to differentiate between a fire that's contained in a pit or fireplace versus a fire outside such confines, but it will take some cajoling. First, work with the match as described in the preceding steps. When building a fire or lighting a match, keep your dog on a leash to hold him back from the flame as you direct him to "Stay" and remind him to "Shhh."

Turning Off the Bothersome Barker

A barking dog is a real headache. How you handle your situation depends on what's prompting your dog to bark in the first place. But whatever you do, don't yell — yelling is barking in Doglish, and instead of calming your dog, it riles him up. To solve your problem, stay cool. I break up the barkers into categories in this section to specifically target how to curb this habit.

Dogs who bark at everything often fall into one of the following categories: Some perceive themselves as your leader; others haven't been socialized well and are freaking out; still others are submissive but assume you don't have a handle on the situation and they must do their best to control it. One of the leader's duties is to guard his territory and pack from intruders. All the other training and interaction you're doing will help your dog focus on and respect you as the leader of the pack. Without that "leadership" lesson, you'll be hard-pressed to make any impression.

Silencing a door barker

Almost everyone appreciates a dog alarm at the door — a few woofs to announce new arrivals. It gets annoying, however, when the alarm can't be shut off. After all, enough is enough. The ideal situation is to have an alarm bark with an off switch. To teach this routine, you'll need a few props. Gather together a clicker and/or a treat cup, as well as a soda can filled with ten pennies and/or a spray deterrent such as a canister of mouth spray or a water sprayer. Let your dog's leash drag behind him when practicing these setups:

1. **To desensitize your dog to the sound of the bell, position someone outside the door, and ask that person to ring the bell once every 20 seconds for 3 minutes.**

2. **When your dog starts barking, say "Speak." Approach the end of his leash calmly, and pick it up. Praise him for alerting you — "Good dog!" — and click/reward.**

3. **After a round of barking (3–5 good woofs), say "Shhh."**

    If your dog ignores you, discretely shake the can behind him or spritz over his head. When he stops barking, praise/click and reward.

4. **Before opening the door, direct your dog behind you or secure him on a greeting station (see Chapter 4).**

    Don't interact or socialize with your dog until he has calmed down. Give him a toy to play with or simply ignore him until he's calm.

    Never hold your dog back while you open the door. Like holding a frantic child, doing so will only make him wilder. Also, approach the door calmly. Running to the door and screaming at your dog will create a frenzy.

5. **Repeat and repeat until your dog gets the hang of it.**

    Then you can try it with a real guest.

If your dog is too excitable at the door, work in an enclosed, distant room. Move progressively closer until your new game's the best game in town!

Dogs like to keep busy. One activity many dogs enjoy is playing the gate-keeper — watching the periphery of your home to make sure everything is safe. If you've got a barker, discourage furniture perching (sitting and keeping watch) in favor of other games like "Fetch" and "Follow Me." If your dog watches you instead of the window, you'll find the silence shattering!

Shhh-ing a motion detector

Do you have one of those dogs who barks at everything he sees and hears? This type of barking can be really rewarding for your dog, because whenever he barks at something, whether from the window or the yard, it goes away. Sure, you and I know that the letter carrier and the kids on their way to school are going to keep moving anyway, but your dog doesn't know that.

If you want to quiet your motion detector, try the following techniques:

- ✔ **Avoid leaving your dog alone outdoors for long stretches of time.** Confinement often breeds boredom and territorial behavior. Put those two together and you're likely to end up with a barkaholic.

- ✔ **Don't yell.** Screaming is barking to a dog: Instead of training him, you're egging him on.

- ✔ **Any time you see (or hear) your dog start to perk up, praise him initially ("good boy"), then quiet him by encouraging "Shhh" and calling him back to your side: "Come tell me!"**

- ✔ **Use your clicker or treat cup to encourage your dog to check in with you.** If he ignores you, leave him on a drag leash when supervised or attach a short leash (see Chapter 2) to enable calm but clear handling: "Come tell me" means just that.

If necessary, use a penny can or spray deterrent (see the preceding section) to help break your dog's focus.

✔ **If your fellow is a night watchman, station or crate him in your room.** Give him a bed and a bone, and secure his lead to something stationary. Bedtime!

✔ **Give your dog an outlet for barking by teaching the noisy tricks outlined in this chapter.**

Curbing a car barker

Being locked in a car with a barking dog is my version of purgatory. For dogs, a car is like a fishbowl, creating the ultimate territorial ego trip. They bark, and whatever is outside disappears. In the case of a moving car, it disappears even faster! Yelling at your dog isn't the thing to do. Pleading won't help either. This problem needs a good training regime. Here are some tips to get you started:

✔ Instruct "Wait" before you let your dog enter or exit the car, and give permission with "Okay." It's your car, your territory; don't let him forget that.

✔ Enforce stillness while you drive. Secure your dog in the backseat of the car with a crate or other car safety device. Give your dog a chew toy to keep him happily occupied while you drive.

✔ Ignore the barking if your car is moving. Driving is a job all by itself.

✔ Whenever your dog is quiet, reward him with your clicker and/or treats.

✔ If your dog barks at people who approach the car, ask a friend to help set up the situation by approaching the car when you're not actually driving. If your dog barks, correct him (see the earlier section, "Silencing a door barker"). When/if your dog stops barking and settles down, ask your friend to toss a piece of cheese into the car window. The idea is to give your dog a more positive association with people who approach the car.

Dealing with an attention hound

Imagine this: You're sitting reading the Sunday paper when suddenly your dog comes out of nowhere and starts barking for a pat. Cute, huh? Not really. So what should you do? Giving in makes you look like a servant. Yelling is counterproductive.

Following are three ways to remedy the situation:

- ✔ Teach your dog a good way to get your attention, such as by sitting or bringing you a toy. Whenever possible, ask your dog to "Sit" before giving him attention, and add a cue word to your fetching games, such as "Ball" or "Toy."

- ✔ If your dog has mastered the on–off trick (see the earlier section "Barking and Not Barking on Cue"), turn to your dog and instruct "Speak!" Let him bark a couple of times, then say "Shhh" and ignore him. Walk away if you need to, but don't give in and pay attention.

- ✔ If your dog barks at you for attention, ignore it. Wear your headset, use earplugs, or walk away — just don't give in. When your dog stops, ignore him another three minutes, and then ask him to sit or fetch his toy. When he cooperates, give him a pat. Otherwise, you're teaching him that barking is a very effective tool.

Quieting a protest barker

Some dogs don't like to be left alone. To tell you the truth, neither do I. If you return to soothe a protest barker before you leave, you'll end up with a really spoiled dog on your hands — one who has trained you.

On the other hand, if you ignore the protest barking, your neighbors or even your spouse may protest. Is there a happy medium? Not really, but I'll give you some suggestions:

- ✔ Ignore the barking if you can. Never yell.

- ✔ Avoid grand departures and arrivals; they're too stimulating.

- ✔ Let the dog be with you when you're home. He likes that. (See Chapters 2 and 5 for more on leading and stationing your dog.)

- ✔ Place peanut butter in a hollow rubber toy or bone, and give it to your dog as you leave. That's a tasty way to keep him busy!

- ✔ Return to your dog only after he has calmed down. If you must interfere with his barking tantrum, go to him quietly without making eye contact or comments, place him on a Teaching Lead tied around your waist (see Chapter 2 for more on this device), and ignore him for half an hour while you lead him around.

Chapter 10

Adding Drama with Clever Tricks

· ·

In This Chapter

▶ Showing emotion and acting silly

▶ Performing balancing tricks

▶ Playing housekeeper

▶ Preparing for the showdown at sunset

· ·

*T*hink your dog is clever? Here's a chapter to put her to the test! What she doesn't know yet she can learn, of course! Before long you'll be winning prizes like "Biggest Drama Queen/King," as you direct your dog to look sad or disgruntled; "Best Impersonator," as your dog slithers along the ground like a snake or balances a book on her head like Eliza Doolittle; or "Most Helpful," as you direct your dog to pick up your laundry and help you throw out the trash. Sound impossible? Broken down, many of these tricks build on skills your dog already knows, like fetching and targeting. Ready to jump right in? Time to get started!

Acting Emotional

Some people argue that dogs don't have emotions — people who obviously have never owned a dog. I know when my dog is happy, and you know when your dog is, too. There's a hearty tail wag and fun in her eyes. I can also tell when my dog's having a bad day. Her tail is lifeless; her head hangs down; she makes a feeble attempt to lick me — poor dear!

Though you and I can predict how our dogs will feel in different situations, this section is not about predictions. It's about teaching your dog mood tricks to fool people's perceptions. For example, say my friend's having a bad day and I instruct my dog Hope to act sad. When Hope lowers her head and looks up with that soulful expression, I know I've made my friend's day!

When your dog can act out each mood with style, you're really on your way to pleasing audiences everywhere. But don't tell your audience it's all an act . . . perception is reality, and what they don't know won't hurt them!

In Chapter 5, I tell you how to get your dog to show happiness by wagging her tail on cue. In this section, you discover how to help your dog act out other emotions: sadness, embarrassment, or disgust. For each mood I suggest a hand signal. This discreet direction encourages your dog to focus on you and enables you to direct your dog without saying a word!

Showing sadness

For this "Sad" trick, your dog lies down, places her head or nose between her paws, and looks up at you with a sad and soulful expression. Of course, I'm not suggesting you actually make your dog sad! It's just a trick.

First, be mindful of when your dog's doing this naturally. Perhaps it's more an expression of exhaustion — I can always count on this behavior after a long walk. Using the clicker or other food inductions, praise your dog whenever she assumes this position. Once your dog catches on to the fact that you like this head-down posture, put a cue word on it like "Tired" or "Head down." Remember, if you're using the clicker method, you must follow each click with a food reward.

Two other methods are useful in helping your dog learn this trick. Deciding which method to choose really depends on the dog you have. Try out each method, and see which one your dog jives with. I call the choices "Gentle Hold and Stay" and "Lure Lassies."

"Gentle Hold and Stay": Using a pressure point

If your dog's a real mush pie, she'll let you manipulate her head gently into position during the "Sad" trick:

1. **Get your dog into a "Down," and position her head on the floor between her paws.**

   To encourage this position, pressure your dog very gently behind her ears, which serve as pressure points for the head-down position (see Figure 10-1). *Never* force your dog into any position. Once her chin touches the floor, instruct "Stay." Check out Chapter 4 for the scoop on the "Down" and "Stay" commands.

2. **Click (if you're using a clicker), reward, and praise a three-second "Stay."**

3. **Slowly increase the "Down" time until she can hold herself in this position for ten seconds.**

4. **Introduce a word or phrase such as, "Are you depressed?" or "Are you sad?"**

   Have your dog respond by lying down and putting her head between her paws. What a heart-stopper!

The signal for "Gentle Hold and Stay" is to clasp your hands together under your chin.

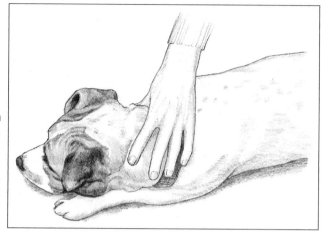

Figure 10-1:
Use pressure points for a gentle "Hold and Stay."

"Lure Lassies": Using a treat

If your dog has no interest in sitting still and truly resists having you manipulate her head, you need to be more creative in your approach to teaching her the "Sad" trick:

1. **Get your dog into a "Down" and tell her to "Stay."**

   See Chapter 4 for the "Down" and "Stay" commands.

2. **Hold her favorite treat between your thumb, index, and middle fingers so that she can smell it but not eat it.**

3. **Lure her head down between her paws by using the treat, and then instruct "Stay" once her head is resting on the floor.**

   At first, you may have to settle for a nose to the ground.

4. **Hold your hand still for three seconds, then release (good click moment if you're following that methodology — click and reward as you release your dog with "Okay") and praise.**

5. **Slowly increase the time until your dog can be still for at least 15 seconds.**

6. **Introduce your catchphrase ("Are you depressed?" or "Are you sad?") while you're practicing the trick.**

7. **Once your dog follows your verbal prompts, add a signal. Rest your chin on the back of your outstretched hand.**

8. **Slowly wean your dog away from your presence on the floor.**

Gradually stand up, treat in hand, and give her the reward the moment after you release her with "Okay." Got that? Now tell her to "Stay" and begin stepping away. Reward her the instant after you release her from her pose.

Even though you're removing the treat, praise her for a job well done.

When using food as a lure, cage it securely in your fingers and don't release it until *after* you release your dog with the command "Okay!" (See Chapter 2 for more on "Okay.")

"Sneezy": Acting offended or annoyed

You can have your dog pretend to be annoyed or offended about something by having her let out a sneeze or snort. I call this the "Sneezy" trick.

Of course, the first way to teach this command is to praise your dog when she's sneezing naturally. Anytime your dog sneezes, make a fuss — "Good girl!" It may take ten sneezes for her to catch on to what you're so happy about, but once she does, you can start using a cue word to encourage her to do it on command, "Ahhh-choo!" or "Sneeze!"

You can also encourage the behavior and reward it. Do this:

1. **Go to your dog and tell her to "Sit."**

2. **Blow into her nose gently from a distance of about 2 or 3 feet.**

   Doing so should encourage her to sneeze.

3. **When your dog sneezes, pinch your nose with two fingers and say "Ahhh-choo!"**

You may want to teach your dog to sneeze on cue for a couple of other reasons. The next time you have guests over, you can ask your dog, "Who's your favorite dwarf?" If you're a theatrical sort, you can get your dog to sneeze with you for the fun of it. A sneeze-off!

The hand signal for "Sneezy" is to bow your head and gently pinch your nose with index finger and thumb. Try to get her to sneeze using only the hand signal.

Looking embarrassed or disgusted

I've saved my toughest mood for last. But oh, how endearing to see your dog hide her face behind her paw in embarrassment. Or, you can associate this trick with the emotion of disgust by having her simply scratch her nose in disgust. Eventually your dog will respond to a hand signal only, and you can lead up to it with questions like "I heard you met a fancy Poodle the other day" (to show embarrassment), or "Would you like some beans with your dinner?" (to show disgust).

Getting your dog to do this trick takes patience and repetition. First, catch her in the act as often as possible. Anytime your dog voluntarily scratches her nose, praise her enthusiastically. If you've got a clicker handy, use it only if you can click while she's got her paw on her face. Poorly timed, the clicker can teach a dog to stop scratching her nose!

To practice these exercises, work with your dog when she's calm and co-operative. If she has too much energy, she'll quickly get frustrated and quit.

First, you must practice your "Paw" command (see Chapter 6). Then you're ready to begin:

1. **Take your dog into a quiet area and tell her to "Sit."**
2. **Practice a few "Paw" commands.**
3. **Hold a treat down low and on the opposite side of the paw your dog has been giving you.**

   If your dog has been giving you her right paw, hold the treat to her left side.
4. **When her paw and nose meet, mark the moment with a clicker or a "Yes!" and reward and praise.**

   You may need to gently hold the skin below her neck to brace her head into position as her paw comes up. If your dog lies down, place your hand along her ribcage to prevent it.
5. **Stop the instant she makes a contact and give her a healthy helping of treats (known as a "jackpot") and/or reward the session generously with a favorite game.**

Avoid overdoing this trick. It's not a common behavior like sitting or lying down, and your dog will grow frustrated with it if it's repeated excessively. Short sessions ensure fun!

The hand signal for embarrassed or disgusted is to cuff the side of your nose.

If your dog is clueless with the preceding procedure, you'll need to get more ingenious with your training techniques by using what's called the induced training method.

To teach this trick using this method, have your treat rewards and your clicker handy:

1. **Take your dog into a quiet area and instruct "Sit."**

2. **Stick a piece of cloth tape — or clip a clothespin *lightly* — to the side of your dog's nose.**

   Use only cloth tape, and stick it on lightly. You don't want to hurt your dog by pulling out her hair along with the tape.

3. **When she lifts her paw to knock off the tape or clothespin, click/ praise and reward.**

   Initially, reward your dog for any attempts to remove the tape or clothespin with her paw. Gradually reinforce only full-fledged face-pawing as you shape the behavior to what you're looking for.

4. **When your dog catches on to the game, start to introduce a command such as "Hide your face," and blatantly scratch the side of your nose as a hand signal.**

Now you're ready for showtime. Practice this trick in increasingly distracting areas before inviting an audience to witness your brilliant pal at work.

Being Zany

Are you wondering how your dog could be any zanier? Well, there's zany . . . and then there's zany on cue. If your dog is energetic and fun-loving or you can see real benefit in having her spin a few circles on a towel to wipe off her muddy feet, then these tricks are the ones for you. If your dog is a real looney-tune during greetings and other activities, these tricks are a perfect displacement for her unbridled enthusiasm!

"Chase your tail"

A dog chasing her tail is a funny thing to watch, and no one can argue that she has truly mastered the art of having fun with herself. Whether your dog's a natural for this routine or not, it's not a hard trick to teach.

If your dog chases her tail naturally, praise her while it's happening. Use the clicker method or other positive reinforcements like food or toys to let your dog know you think the behavior is cool.

Take a biscuit, hold it level with your dog's nose and command "Chase your tail" as you slowly rotate the treat around her body. I said slowly! Start slow; that's an order! Reward half-spins initially, then full spins, then two, three, four spins, and so on.

The hand signal for "Chase your tail" is to hold your index finger up and swirl it in a circle. Accentuate your hand signal, and soon you'll be sending your dog silent cues — no words needed!

This trick is great if you want your dog to wipe her feet. Just command "Chase your tail" while she's standing on a doormat!

Around the legs: "Crazy Eights"

The "Crazy Eights" trick is fun for you to teach and fun for dogs of all shapes and sizes to learn. What could possibly be better than that?

1. **Starting from the "Heel" position, take a giant step forward with your right foot only, and hold that position.**

2. **Point between your legs and use a treat to encourage your dog to come "Through."**

3. **When your dog has perfected "Through," use the treat to lead your dog once around your legs in a figure eight pattern, ending up back in the "Heel" position.**

   Obviously, you'll have to rely solely on the lure of the treat; using a leash to lead your dog would leave you both hopelessly tangled!

4. **Repeat Steps 1–3 until you're *sure* your dog knows the trick well.**

If your dog is having trouble, do one part at a time: First through the middle, then around the right leg — reward. Then through the middle again — reward, and so on. Practice this until she does it very well. Then you're ready to proceed as follows:

1. **Put all of the parts together by doing the same routine, but walk forward extremely slowly.**

2. **Each time your dog circles a leg, move the opposite leg forward.**

3. **If she doesn't get confused, pick up the pace; if she is confused, keep working on Step 2 until you've perfected that.**

After some practice, she'll be tripping you and bringing the crowds to tears with laughter.

Getting Ready for Bedtime

While these tricks set up a perfect nighttime ritual, "Say your prayers" and "Go to sleep" can be used anywhere, anytime! "Go to sleep" is a more politically correct term for the trick "Play dead" or "Bang, bang." Call it what you will, both of these are pure crowd pleasers and your dog will have fun learning them too!

"Say your prayers"

Having your dog say her prayers is a dear little trick. The goal is to get your dog to place her paws on any object and lower her head reverently. Are you laughing? I'm serious!

1. **Sit your dog squarely in front of you and show her a treat. You should sit, too.**

2. **Lift her paws gently onto your lap.**

3. **Hold the treat between her paws and under your legs so that she has to drop her head between her paws to reach for it.**

4. **Tell her "Stay" as you let her lick the treat. Say "Okay" as you give her the treat, and praise her.**

5. **After you sense that she has caught on to this sequence and can hold her head still for 10 seconds, begin to use the phrase "Say your prayers."**

6. **Practice having her rest her paws on other things, such as a bed or chair. Offer the treat over the back of a chair, for instance, always using "Say your prayers."**

"Go to sleep"

When I was growing up, the command given for this trick was "Play dead." To me the whole dead thing seems a little depressing; I prefer "Go to sleep" — so much more peaceful.

When focusing on this trick, reinforce your dog with praise each time you see her lying on her side naturally. After a day or so, add a word cue like "Sleep" when you catch your dog resting on her side, and praise your dog just because she's wonderful.

Teaching this trick isn't too difficult if your dog has mastered the "Down" and "Stay" commands that I cover in Chapter 4. Get your dog to show she's dog-tired with these steps:

1. **Instruct "Down," kneel beside your dog, and gently roll her on her side.**

2. **Rub your dog's belly until she's calm, and praise her.**

3. **After a few days of this, your dog should be comfortable rolling onto her side. Start giving the command "Sleep–Stay."**

   "Stay" should be familiar; if not, review Chapter 4. If she lifts her head, lovingly rest it back on the floor and command "Stay." Initially have her stay two to ten seconds, varying it each time but rewarding her enthusiastically!

4. **Extend the "Sleep–Stay" time until your dog is up to 30 seconds.**

5. **Now it's time to command your dog from an upright posture. Give the command from a standing position, bend to help your dog into position, stand back up, pause, and release.**

   Once you're able to stand, vary the time you pause before releasing and praising your dog.

   It may take a week or two for your dog to catch on, but soon she'll "Go to sleep" at the simplest suggestion.

6. **When your dog cooperates, introduce the trick command, "Go to sleep."**

The hand signal for "Go to sleep" is to place your palms together and raise them to the side of your face in a sleepy-time position.

Balancing Acts

Balancing tricks take a bit of coordination, but they're very impressive. In this section, you teach your dog how to balance a treat on her nose, flip it into the air, and catch it in her mouth. You also encourage your dog to practice her posture by balancing a book on her head. With these tricks, your dog will be a hit wherever she goes, whether she's joining the circus or preparing to make a good impression in polite society.

Flipping and catching a treat off the nose: The seal

In this trick, you teach your dog to balance a treat on her nose, then flip it up and catch it. Sound hard? Maybe you've seen seals do this with a fish. And surely your pup is smarter than a seal!

You need to break this trick into two parts: the balance, and the flip and catch.

Stage 1: Balancing the treat

The first part trains your dog to keep her nose still:

1. **Line up treats on a nearby table.**

2. **Put your dog on a "Sit–Stay."**

3. **Gently hold your dog's nose steady for five seconds, reminding "Stay" if she gets restless. Click and reward her steadiness.**

4. **Repeat Step 3 five times.**

   Take a break, and pick up training again later that day or the next day.

5. **Repeat Steps 1–3 above, but place a treat on your dog's nose while you steady it, reminding "Stay."**

6. **After five seconds, say "Okay," and remove the treat that's on her nose.**

7. **Reward her with a different treat, so she doesn't become obsessed with the treat that's on her nose.**

8. **Repeat this exercise four times, then stop for the day.**

Practice this balancing act until your dog is proficient at balancing the treat on her nose for at least 15 seconds with no nose-holding required.

Stage 2: Flip and catch

Teach the flip and catch only after perfecting the balance.

1. **Balance a treat on your dog's nose, and then introduce the next concept (the flip) by saying "Okay" as you slide the treat from your dog's nose to her mouth.**

   After a day or two you should notice that your dog tries to flip the treat herself. Praise her only if her flip follows your "Okay."

   If she flips prematurely, say "Ep, ep," and practice the balance alone a few times before continuing.

   To help your dog learn to wait for your "Okay" before flipping the treat, vary the balance time before sliding the treat into her mouth.

2. **Balance the treat on her nose and command "Stay."**

3. **Walk back 3 feet and pause.**

   Vary the length of your pauses as you practice.

4. **Say "Okay" for the catch and make a big fuss when she does, praising your dog with lots of love.**

Balancing books for good posture: Eliza Doolittle

One scene in the film *My Fair Lady* shows the central character, Eliza Doolittle, walking around the living room with a book balanced on her head. Okay, this isn't an animal trick, but it's still impressive — especially when your dog does it. As usual, I break down this trick into its significant parts.

Stage 1: Standing still

Here's a quick refresher course, in case your dog has forgotten the art of standing still.

1. **Kneel down on the floor next to your dog.**

2. **Place your right hand, palm out, under your dog's buckle collar.**

3. **Slide your left hand under your dog's belly.**

4. **Command "Stand–Stay" as you gently prop your dog into a standing position.**

5. **Relax your right hand and slide your left to rest on your dog's thigh.**

6. **Pause, count to five, and release with "Okay."**

7. **Slowly increase the time to one minute.**

8. **Now repeat Steps 2–7 but from a standing rather than kneeling position.**

9. **Begin to let go with your left hand; then let go with your right, as you steady your dog with calm "Stay" commands and a relaxed posture.**

The hand signal for "Stand" is a level hand, arm extended, palm down.

Once your dog catches on, you'll find a million uses for this command: wiping muddy paws, brushing, drying off, or imitating Eliza Doolittle.

Stage 2: Slowing down

Slowing down is another little trick that I'm sure you can think of a million uses for. Plus, your dog can't possibly balance a book on her head and fly across the room at the same time.

To get started, you need two people: one to lead the dog forward and one to hold her back.

1. **Position yourself in front of your dog with treats and your partner behind your dog, holding a leash attached to your dog's buckle collar.**

2. **Using your "Stay" signal, command "Stand–Stay."**

   If your dog moves, reposition her calmly and quietly.

3. **To signal your dog to move forward, slowly close your fingers, move your hand forward, and say "Slowly."**

4. **After each step, reward your dog with a treat as your assistant pulls gently back to stop the dog from taking more than one step at a time.**

   Repeat this until your dog begins to slow after each step on her own, no tug necessary.

5. **Now see if you can do it without a partner, using "Shhh" if your dog gets too excited.**

Try doing this part of the trick from a distance: Leave your dog in a "Stand–Stay" and stand 3 feet in front of her. Command and signal "Slowly," and praise your dog for moving with caution.

Stage 3: Balancing the book

This next step is a big one. If your dog's not ready for it, slow up yourself.

Consider the type of book you use. Paperbacks sag and don't balance well. Avoid books with jackets or glossy covers — too slippery. A bare, hardcover book works best. Also, use a book that doesn't weigh too much and that suits the size of your dog; your Chihuahua may only be able to handle a book of postage stamps.

To help your dog learn to balance a book on her head, do the following:

1. **Gently place the book on the dog's head, centering the book so that it rests evenly.**

2. **Steady her head by gently holding her muzzle with your right hand, giving the "Stay" signal with your left hand in front of her nose, and repeating "Stay."**

3. **Calmly remove the book, and reward your dog generously.**

   Gently hold your dog's nose as you proceed to get her comfortable with the book-on-the-head routine. Work up from 2 seconds to 30 seconds, which is likely to take a week or more.

4. **When your dog begins to learn the routine, lift your right hand off her muzzle ever so slightly as you leave the "Stay" signal in place and remind "Stay."**

5. **Slowly increase the time your dog can balance the book without your help and the distance you can move from her.**

Is your dog letting the book slide? Either you're going too fast or your dog is following you with her eyes as you step away. Help her keep her focus steady by holding the hand signal for "Stay" steady at nose level, then moving it slightly up or down if she needs re-centering.

Stage 4: Putting it all together

If I had to pick the toughest trick in the book, this would be it. So drum roll, please. Here goes:

1. **Standing close to your dog, place her in a "Stand" position and tell her to "Stay."**

2. **Place the book on her head, remind "Stay," and step away 2 feet.**

3. **Keeping your "Stay" signal level with your dog's nose, command "Slowly" and give the hand signal.**

4. **Immediately remove the book after one step, click, and reward.**

   Take a breather and stop at this point. Good job. Pick up practice the next day.

5. **Work on this step for a few days to build your dog's confidence. Progress to two steps, and then three, four, five, and so on.**

6. **Now send me a picture of your dog imitating Eliza Doolittle for the next printing of this book.**

Playing Housekeeper

If your dog has her fetching and retrieval skills down, you can get her to play the role of maid or trash collector. Fortunately, unlike your spouse or the kids, your dog won't think you're a nag when you ask her to pick up the laundry and take care of the trash. Your dog will view these chores as one big game and rush to get started.

To do these tricks, your dog should understand how to respond to target discs (from Chapter 2), how to carry objects (Chapter 7), and the "Give" and "Take it" commands (Chapter 7).

Before you get started

In Chapter 2, I introduce you to targeting. Before you can master the tricks here, you need to teach your dog how to deliver to a target:

1. **Place an 8½-x-11-inch piece of white paper in the middle of the floor.**

   The paper represents the "target."

2. **Stand next to the paper, and encourage your dog to retrieve and "Give" you the object by signaling with an open palm.**

3. **Next, teach her to drop the item on the target itself. Lower your open palm to the target and say "Deliver–Give." Gradually remove your palm and simply point to the target as you say "Deliver."**

4. **Command "Deliver–Target" as your dog stands over the paper. At first, reinforce all decent retrieves, but then address only the ones that land on the paper by praising "Good–Target!"**

5. **When your dog is reliably dropping the object on the paper when you say "Target," gradually move farther from the paper as you continue to train.**

6. **Gradually trim the target paper size until it's a palm-sized square.**

Now the target paper can be used to instruct your dog anywhere. You can carry it with you and place it anywhere you want your dog to drop something. Pretty cool!

Completing each step of target training can take a few weeks. Don't sweat it — at times you may feel like you're hitting a brick wall, and then suddenly your dog will put it all together.

Collecting the laundry

The idea of this trick is that when you say "Laundry roundup," your dog will go to each room, collect the dirty clothes, and put them in the basket. Miraculous!

If your dog is a laundry thief, you may be skeptical, but hear me out. Laundry bandits are often the top candidates for this task. After all, they're already interested. All you need to do is redirect their efforts.

Stage 1: Picking up laundry and delivering it to a target

Start this trick by teaching your dog a few new vocabulary words. Get together with a few pieces of clean laundry and a low-sided laundry basket. Proceed as follows:

1. **Place the basket on the floor of a small room (bathroom or hallway). Click/praise your dog each time she sniffs or approaches the basket. Command "Basket" as you reward her interest.**

   Continue to reinforce/command "Basket" until your dog will approach the basket on cue.

   Now you're ready to teach your dog to pick up laundry and go to the basket.

2. **Take out a dirty sock and encourage your dog to pick it up.**

   Either click each time your dog shows interest in the sock, or use your fetching command from Chapter 7: "Take it."

3. **Introduce other apparel as you add the word "Laundry" to your cue command: "Take it–Laundry."**

4. **Now get your dog to deliver the sock to the target (see the preceding section).**

5. **Advance to trying this with multiple socks; they should be lumped in a pile on top of the target paper.**

Stage 2: Putting laundry in a basket

Once you've mastered picking up the laundry and delivering it to a target, you can advance to having your dog put the laundry in a basket. Here's how to make that association:

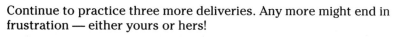

1. **Go back to your small room with both the sock and the basket.**

2. **Place the target paper in the basket, and show your dog the target and how to get to it (large dogs can just reach their head over; small dogs may have to jump on a box or climb a ramp).**

3. **Say "Take it–Laundry" as you offer your dog a sock. As she holds it, direct her to the basket using the command "Target–Roundup."**

4. **Reinforce any behavior in the direction of the basket, even if the drop is a little off.**

Continue to practice three more deliveries. Any more might end in frustration — either yours or hers!

The first few training sessions should reward any basket attempts.

5. **Once your dog is making the connection between the sock and the basket, reward/praise only successful deliveries.**

If your dog is still confused, try encouraging her by luring her head over the basket with a treat or toy, or by clapping your hands over the basket.

The first time your dog makes a successful delivery, celebrate. Quit the lesson and go have some fun. Great job!

Stage 3: Picking up and delivering laundry throughout the house

You should progressively reinforce only successful deliveries. Once that's accomplished, you're ready to start cleaning up your home:

1. **Go into a familiar room. Place the sock on the floor and instruct, "Take it–Laundry" as you point to the sock. Then say, "Target–Roundup" as you encourage your dog to follow through with the delivery.**

If your dog hesitates or seems confused, you may need more practice in the small, quiet room.

At this point you should be able to fade off the familiar cue words "Take it" and "Target," relying on "Laundry–Roundup" to get your dog going.

2. **Slowly increase the number of laundry items by spreading two, and then three, pieces around the room. Send your dog with the command "Laundry" each time. Be sure to click and praise each retrieval.**

3. **Position the laundry basket 3 feet away from you. Prompt your dog toward the basket by saying "Laundry." When she understands your direction, say "Roundup."**

You may help your dog a little by pointing to the basket.

4. **Stand across the room from the basket and send your dog, pointing at the basket and saying, "Laundry" and "Roundup."**

5. **Gradually progress to more pieces of laundry in the same room — then aim for a house-wide roundup!**

Do you have a small dog? Too small, in fact, to place her head over the roundup basket? Cut a hole large enough for your dog to slip her head through in the side of a plastic basket.

If you have a big house and rooms and rooms of dirty clothes, you can send your dog out on clothes patrol: Start introducing her to the concept one room at a time with an identical basket in each room. Eventually one basket can be placed on each floor. Start your progression in the rooms closest to the roundup basket and work your way up.

Picking up the trash

Once your dog knows how to pick something up and put it in a basket, the possibilities for turning her into a top-notch housekeeper really expand. Picking up the trash is a natural. The goal here is that when you say "Trash it," your dog will pick up whatever trash she sees and put it in a trash can.

Is this another request that leaves you speechless? Has your dog spent most of her life pulling trash out of the bin, rather than putting things in it? Once your pal has learned to retrieve properly, you can trust her around anything, including the garbage.

Trash bins are often light and flimsy. You can weigh yours down with several books or rocks in the bottom so that it doesn't tip over and frighten your dog.

For props, you need a trash bin with a flip-top that's sized for your dog. The top of the bin should be 4 inches lower than her chin, so either get a small bin or a booster box for your dog. You also need some trash that's safe for her to practice on — never ask your dog to mouth sharp edges or rancid food items.

As with all complex tricks, I break this one down and teach it in stages.

Stage 1: Getting to know the trash can and learning to open it

Start by introducing your dog to the trash can. Place it in a small room. Click/praise and reward any interest. When your dog catches on, start saying "Target–Trash," combining the new command with the old.

1. **Encourage your dog's interest in the trash can by rubbing some butter or peanut butter along the inside edge of the lid.**

2. **When your dog makes contact with the trash can, click, say "Trash," and reward.**

3. **Now for lid training. Take the lid and hold it front of your dog. Click/ praise and reward a nose touch. Add the words "Touch–Trash" as your dog grows friendly with the concept.**

4. **Put the lid on the can, and encourage your dog's interaction by instructing "Touch–Trash." Encourage and reward any interactions with the lid.**

5. **Gradually phase out rewarding all interactions and only focus on the ones that involve an upward flip of the lid.**

Stage 2: Delivering trash to a target

Now for some trash. Start with an easy-to-handle item like an old animal crackers box or, for your small fry, an empty gum package.

First practice delivering to the target as I describe earlier in the chapter. Next place the target on the lid. Reinforce initial retrieves, then place the target in the can. At first, remove the lid to ensure success, then challenge your dog by putting the lid back on. Repeat "Target–Trash it" as your dog works to get the trash to the target.

Stage 3: Placing garbage in the can

Now comes the hard part: getting your dog to place the garbage into the can.

1. **Start at the can, leaving the flip-lid off. Place the garbage into your dog's mouth and say "Trash it," leaning over the garbage with your head and using your clicker or saying "Yes!" to reward her first attempts.**

   Your dog will probably look confused. Gently help her place her head over the trash bin (just like you do with the laundry basket trick). If you find she's hopeless and frustrated after a few tries, just be patient.

2. **Click/reward every attempt initially, then fade off and reinforce only those drops that are on target.**

3. **Place items of trash around the room and send your dog out for them one at a time, pointing to each object and saying "Trash it."**

Stage 4: Opening the lid to drop in garbage

Finish this trick by getting your dog to push the lid open and drop the garbage in.

1. **Sprinkle some trash around the room (don't worry — your pal will take care of it!).**

2. **Stand next to the trash bin, this time with the flip-lid on.**

3. **Point to each piece of garbage and instruct your dog to "Trash it."**

Help her out initially, rewarding each entry. You know she'll catch on eventually.

Never move on to the next step of a trick before your dog has completely mastered the previous step. If you try to rush ahead before your dog is ready, you'll both just end up frustrated and unhappy.

A fun variation on this theme is picking up toys. Follow the preceding steps, substituting toys for trash and the toy box for the trash can.

The Action Hero: Evading the Bad Guys

Action movies often show the hero ducking, crawling, and peering around corners. In this section, your dog does a few evasive maneuvers — crawling across the floor, running for cover, and making sure the coast is clear. It all ends with a big showdown at the O.K. Corral.

Crawl, baby, crawl: The snake

In this trick, your dog crawls across the floor on her belly — perfect for when your action hero needs to sneak around out of sight. This trick always amazes me, and it's fairly easy to teach. Your dog must be proficient in "Down;" see Chapter 4 if you need to brush up on this basic skill.

1. **Find a low object like a coffee table. Gather up your treats and a clicker, if you're using one.**

2. **Give your dog the "Down" command.**

3. **Hold a treat under the table and in front of your dog's nose. Bring it forward slowly so she has to stretch. The second she stretches her body out, click/praise and reward.**

   The first few days you should reinforce one crawl step at a time.

4. **Wiggle your hand forward as if it were a mouse in the grass, gradually increasing the distance your dog crawls before you reward her.**

5. **When your dog crawls out from under the coffee table, be prepared for her to stand up.**

   Kneeling at her right side, hold your left hand above her shoulders and pressure them slightly before you reward her. (If you're using clicker training, only click for crawling behavior. If your dog pops up, no click. Pretty soon she'll catch on: Want a click? Keep crawling!) Slowly increase the distance your dog must crawl before you reward her.

6. **Gradually, progress from giving your command as you kneel close to the ground to giving the command while standing upright.**

   Tricks look coolest when the commands are given from an upright position!

If your dog's having trouble keeping her belly planted on the floor, lay your right hand across her shoulder blades and apply the least amount of pressure possible.

Think you're hot stuff? Try this crawl routine.

1. **Place your dog in a "Down–Stay" and stand 3 feet in front of her. Instead of calling her, kneel down and say "Crawl."**

2. **Release her with "Okay" the moment she gets to you, and celebrate.**

   Job well done! Now you can work at getting her to crawl to you from across the room. Good luck! Once she gets the crawl, stretching it out (literally) is fun.

Running for cover

"Run for Cover" is a two-part trick, but trust me: It's so endearing that once you and your dog put it all together, she'll be using it whenever she wants attention. First, teach your dog to crawl under an object. Use a treat to lead your dog under the object you want her to go under (I use a table covered with a drooping tablecloth). Each time you lead or lure your dog with a favorite treat or toy, command "Hide–Under." Practice this exercise five times a session, anywhere from one to three sessions per day.

Now send her under the table with "Under" and command "Stay." Release her with "Okay" and a great big hug. Gradually increase the amount of time before the release.

Now it's time for peekaboo!

1. **After sending your dog "Under" and instructing "Stay," say "Peekaboo" as you use a treat to lure just your dog's nose out from under the table.**

2. **Click/praise and reward the instant your dog's nose appears.**

   If she has her whole head out, lure her head back saying "Under" as you start again.

Although it may take a week or two of repeating this exercise to master the perfect "Peekaboo," once learned, it's never forgotten.

Bang! Shoot-out at the O.K. Corral

This trick combines two commands: "Ask nicely" (from Chapter 6) and "Go to sleep" (from the earlier section "Getting Ready for Bedtime"). Together, they create a cool stunt that will wow audiences everywhere.

First, get your dog to sit up by using the "Ask nicely" command, adding a command such as "Put 'em up." Make the shape of a gun with your thumb and index finger and point it at her. Practice that quite a few times.

The way to teach a new command for an old trick is to first link them, then phase out the old command. So when your dog starts this trick, you need to give her the commands "Ask nicely–Put 'em up." Emphasize the new hand signal, and slowly eliminate the "Ask nicely" command.

Once your dog is sitting up, it's time for the "Go to sleep" command. Link it with "Bang" as you "pull the trigger" on your hand gun. If she has trouble, gently help her over to her side. Often the dog gets so excited that she falls down anyway. Practice the two steps together several times, rewarding for each improvement and phasing out "Go to sleep."

Now, put it all together:

1. **Put your dog in a "Sit–Stay."**
2. **Stand 3 feet away and command "Put 'em up" as you take aim.**
3. **Pause a few seconds and say "Bang."**

    Mission accomplished! Now practice at progressively farther distances.

As outlined, this trick would be considered politically incorrect. You can always insert new words for the same actions to change the flavor of the routine. For example instead of "Put 'em up" you could say "Did you wash your paws?" and then "Go to Sleep," rather than "Bang, you're dead." So instead of sending your 3-year-old to bed with nightmares, you'll be encouraging her to wash up before bedtime!

Part IV
Exploring the World of Agility

The 5th Wave   By Rich Tennant

"It's not officially part of the obstacle course, but I thought as long as I'm training him how to do things..."

In this part . . .

An agility course is the canine equivalent of a jungle gym — an intertwining blend of tunnels, jumps, bridges, and A-frames. Chapters 11 and 12 provide you with an overview of the sport, introduce agility commands, and get you familiar with the tools and equipment.

If the nuts and bolts of agility have captured your enthusiasm, then you'll be excited to know how much more you have in store. In Chapters 13 and 14, you'll get up close and personal with each agility obstacle as I explain a positive approach to training, from jumps and tunnels to teeters and weave poles. Chapter 15 explains the concept of sequencing and gives you some advice for troubleshooting challenges you may encounter.

In Chapter 16, I tell you about the differences between some of the top agility organizations. Each one has its own slant, competitive emphasis, and awarded titles. Course layout is also interpreted to enable you to prepare for the variety of sequences you'll experience on the competitive circuit.

Chapter 11

Considering Agility Training

In This Chapter

▶ Finding out what's involved in agility

▶ Taking a look at course obstacles

▶ Assessing whether your dog has what it takes

*I*f you've never seen dogs performing an agility course, get ready to be amazed. It's part crazy playground game, part circus act, and part synchronized equestrian-show-style jumping. It's fun, it's fast, and it's a little bit daunting. Dogs and handlers compete for time and accuracy on a predesigned obstacle course. The dogs run free and are guided only by the handler's voice and movements. Courses are designed with standard obstacles, and competitors must run through, jump over, teeter on, and wiggle under all of them in a set order.

"Wow," you're thinking. "My dog could probably do that. He runs, jumps, teeters, and wiggles all over the place! Where do I sign up?" Before you enter the nearest competition, understand that agility requires a lot of off-leash control. And I mean a *lot* of off-leash control. If you're sure your dog is ready for agility training, be further warned: Agility is addicting. Dogs love it, and people get pumped . . . it's an athletic, competitive activity that can quickly become your obsession.

In this chapter, you find out more about exactly what agility training and competitions consist of, and I help you determine whether you and your dog are well-suited for agility.

Discovering Agility

Agility is a relatively new activity in the dog world, but it has become wildly popular in its short life. Why? Because it's fun, fun, fun. It all started in England in 1978. John Varley, a committee member serving at the Crufts Dog Show, wanted to keep the crowds entertained during breaks. He and dog trainer Peter Meanwell set up something that resembled an equestrian-show jumping course and sent a few dogs out to run, jump, and generally mesmerize the assembled guests. It was a hit.

Within months of the original demonstration, dog owners were clamoring for more organized events, and by 1980, agility was recognized as an official sport. Agility organizations were formed to provide instruction, designate rules and regulations, and create benchmarks to judge individual mastery.

Few things in life take my breath away and leave me on the verge of tears. A moss-lapped river, a sun-sparkled ocean, a lake at daybreak. I get this same feeling when I watch the synchronized movements of dogs and people working together.

Agility is a sport based on the ancient partnership between humans and dogs — a partnership that exists only rarely today. You can't perform agility without your dog, and your dog can't do it without you. One gives direction, the other follows, off-leash and free. Agility reinforces the connection between you and your dog as you work together toward a common goal.

So where can you find out more about agility? How can you decide whether it's the right sporting event for you and your dog? Agility enthusiasts are always willing to welcome new members and share their love of the sport. Attend an event, view agility online, or observe a class. Watch carefully, ask questions, and if your curiosity is piqued, consider participating in a beginner's program. Several levels are available to encourage participation in a less competitive, family-friendly format.

Agility is an amazing way to spend time with a dog. No matter the level at which you choose to participate, you will be teaching, and your dog will be learning and looking to you for direction. Together, you'll build skills and master obstacles, collecting those magical "Ah-ha!" moments when you and your dog just flow.

Agility practice takes full advantage of all the basic training skills you know — off-leash. You'll meet other people who love their dogs, just like you. So how about it?

It's All About the Obstacles

When you first look at an agility course, you'll notice a lot of different things going on — dogs leaping over several different types of jumps, climbing up ramps, and racing across bridges and teeter-totters. "Hmmm . . ." you might think, "it's all very interesting, but what exactly is the point?"

The sport of agility boils down to teaching your dog how to navigate each obstacle correctly, and, once you've mastered that, being able to direct your dog through a course of obstacles of varying sequences. If you're competitive or want to earn titles for your achievements, you can enter organized events where judges rate your performances.

The following sections explain the five categories of obstacles you'll encounter on the agility course.

Jumps

Agility dogs do a lot of jumping. There are different types of jump obstacles — some challenge a dog's ability to leap high, others test precision on jumping through, and still others see whether a dog will leap over something he can't see through.

- ✔ **Bar jumps:** A bar is spread between two poles and set at a specific height. The height is determined by the dog's size, as measured at his shoulder (also known as the *withers*). See Figure 11-1.

Figure 11-1:
A bar jump.

- ✔ **Spread jump:** Multiple bars are arranged to test a dog's ability to jump high and wide. See Figure 11-2.

- ✔ **Jump with wings:** This jump has decorative sides to instill a handler's ability to direct from a distance — the sides block the handler from getting up close to the jump itself. See Figure 11-3.

- ✔ **Panel jump:** This one looks like a solid wall. A dog must clear this jump without touching it. Hard to do — from my vantage, climbing over looks like more fun! See Figure 11-4.

Figure 11-2:
A spread
jump.

Figure 11-3:
A jump with
wings.

Figure 11-4:
A panel
jump.

✔ **Tire jump:** A tire or tire-like object is anchored in a frame. Jumping through it seems hard enough — but a lot of precision is also required to take this at full speed. See Figure 11-5.

Figure 11-5:
A tire jump.

✔ **Broad jump:** This is the only jump brought over from the obedience ring. Panels are laid out to a premeasured width to test a dog's ability to jump low and long over the width. See Figure 11-6.

Figure 11-6:
A broad jump.

Contact obstacles

These daunting obstacles are suspended in the air and would be highly dangerous if not for colored, designated zones that require a mindful approach and dismount. During a trial, a dog must touch these zones, or *contacts,* to validate his completion. You'll find three contact obstacles in the sport of agility:

> ✔ **The A-frame:** Two 4-foot panels are arranged at a climbing angle (specified according to the size of each dog in timed trials). A dog must climb up — that's the fun part — and then descend carefully. See Figure 11-7.

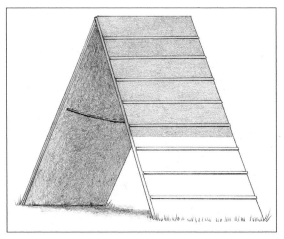

Figure 11-7:
An A-frame.

> ✔ **The dog walk:** This obstacle looks like a cross between a balance beam and a bridge. Suspended 3 to 4 feet above the ground, balance is everything — jumping off early is a big no-no. Geared for the finish, a dog who has learned to run through the obstacle safely running through the colored zones, is a master of self-control. See Figure 11-8.

> ✔ **The teeter:** This one looks like a seesaw from a school playground. The teeter's 1-foot width tests a dog's balance and self-control. He must run up the teeter in a controlled fashion, pause as the obstacle shifts downward, and then run off — running through the colored zones as he goes! See Figure 11-9.

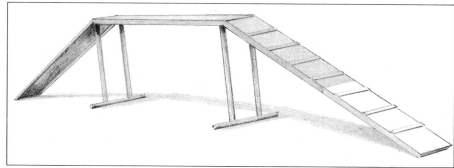

Figure 11-8:
A dog walk.

Figure 11-9:
The teeter.

Tunnels

Two kinds of tunnels are used in agility: open and closed. Both types are secured to the ground to prevent shifting or movement.

- ✔ **Open tunnels:** This type of tunnel is open at either end and can be arranged as a straight-line run-through or angled to test a dog's processing skills as he's running at top speed. See Figure 11-10.

- ✔ **Closed tunnels:** These tunnels sport a wide, barreled opening with an attached draping fabric section, or *chute,* that a dog must tunnel through to emerge. See Figure 11-11.

Perhaps the most comical term in agility is *tunnel sucker.* This dog has a fetish for tunnels and will routinely break from other activities for a quick run through a tunnel!

Agility UKC-style

The United Kennel Club (UKC) has some unique obstacles that aren't seen in events sponsored by other agility clubs. The UKC's crawl tunnel simulates the movements of a typical tunnel, but it looks more like a ribcage than a closed chute. The swing plank and sway bridge simulate the moves of the dog walk, but these obstacles differ slightly in that they swing. Whether you compete in UKC events or not, you gain diversity practicing on these obstacles if you can find them! For more information on these UKC obstacles, visit their Web site at www.ukcdogs.com.

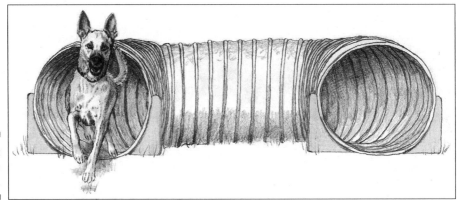

Figure 11-10:
An open tunnel.

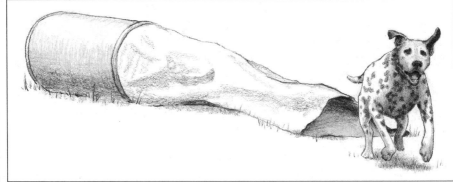

Figure 11-11:
A closed tunnel.

Weave poles

This obstacle sports 6 to 12 upright poles that a dog must weave through. It sounds easy, and maybe even a little fun. But people who love agility will tell you that this is one of the biggest challenges on the course!

Calling all dogs

One thing I love about agility is that there's a venue for everyone — even at the competitive level. Purebreds and mixed breeds mingle, testing both the course and the clock. Jumps and contact obstacles are adjusted for dogs of different heights and ages. True, you may not win the highest score with your 12-year-old mini Dachshund, but you two can get out there and run — or waddle if necessary — with the best of them. There are classes for junior, senior, or disabled handlers as well.

Admit it — it sounds like fun, doesn't it? If you've got the gumption — and a fit and agile dog — read on. See if the agility bug bites you!

Table

This 3-x-3-foot table tests a dog's self-control. In the midst of tunneling, weaving, and jumping, a dog must leap on the table, assume a stationary pose ("Sit" or "Down"), hold it for five seconds, and then blast off at top speed!

Deciding Whether Your Dog Has What It Takes

I'm not a singer. Don't get me wrong — I can pick up the hairbrush microphone and belt out a pretty credible version of "I Will Survive," but that doesn't mean I want to be the next American Idol.

The same can be said for dogs. All dogs can run, climb, and jump. But competitively? Repeatedly? With lots of noises and limited snacks? Not all dogs want to sign up for that.

On the other hand, if you've got a thrill-seeker on your hands — a natural athlete who really *does* want to be the next canine American Idol — chances are good that he'll love agility.

I've shared my life with both types of dogs. I've had "Eveready" dogs, who would urgently wake me in the predawn hours so we could get the day started. A bright, expectant gaze would fix on me: *Sleeping? Why are you sleeping? No more sleeping!* Agile and alert, these dogs took to agility like fish to water. But I've loved the opposite, too: sweet, tolerant types who preferred more solitary activities like the "joring" activities explained in Chapter 19 or sedentary activities like pet therapy, discussed in Chapter 18.

Agility as a confidence booster

In my work as a trainer, I often run into dogs who "act like wild animals" according to their frustrated caregivers. They jump and nip and pull uncontrollably on the leash. Very often, it turns out that these dogs are acting up because they've never been taught how to behave. Mishandled and misunderstood, many of these "unmanageable" dogs come around quickly with some basic training skills and become wonderful, eager-to-please companions. I often recommend a sport like agility to refocus their energy and reward their drive to please — and play.

Consider your dog: If he hasn't been trained and behaves wildly, it may simply mean that he doesn't know what you expect. Work on the foundations of good behavior, and your dog just might surprise you. You could have a diamond in the rough — an agility master in the making.

I took my first agility class with a mixed-breed Terrier rescue named Hope. Feisty and disgruntled, Hope had been tossed a few lemons in life. Jumps weren't Hope's thing, and she wouldn't set foot on the bridge. But the A-frame! Hope came to *life* on the A-frame. On the way up, she would concentrate, her head bent low and her expression deadly serious. Coming down the other side, she'd open up, head and tail held high for all to see. Hope, Queen of the A-Frame! Those two sections of scratched-up wood gave her so much joy; I would look forward to our class work all week long. While we never entered an event, we still had a great time together, and it did wonders for her attitude and confidence.

Personality traits suited to agility

How can you tell whether your dog is agility-eager? Consider these five personality traits:

- ✔ **Gumption:** Agility dogs have gumption. They see a new object and want to investigate it. They get energized when they see other people and dogs. They like new adventures. Sound familiar? Does your dog do back flips when you jingle your keys? That's gumption: an adventurous spirit.

- ✔ **Focus:** This sport requires attention to details and an ability to filter out distractions and stay completely focused on the task at hand. In order to excel in agility, a dog needs to be addicted to action, attentive to verbal direction, and mindful of subtle body cues.

- ✔ **Determination:** Agility is a "can-do" sport — one that requires a fall-down-and-get-back-up attitude. Why walk if you can run? Why hurdle a jump when you can sail over it? A dog who is willing to try something new and repeat it again and again until it feels natural will enjoy the rigors of agility.

- ✔ **Cooperation:** Agility is a team sport. Dogs who are motivated to follow direction and trust their people do best at it. Often competing in close quarters with other dog-person teams, a dog must pledge full allegiance to his partner and be able to ignore anything else that might be going on.

> ✔ **Sociability:** This sport involves a lot of socializing — with dogs and people, sounds and stimulations, unfamiliar objects, and unpredictable activity. If you go to weekend events, they can last all day. Will your dog be up for it? Will you?

As you're reading over these attributes, remember agility is a team sport. Not only will your dog need these attributes — you will too! Agility requires bending, turning, and running while staying upbeat and focused. The bottom line? While you won't need to scale any walls or leap tall buildings, you will have to exert yourself out there.

Don't overlook agility because you don't think a competitive sport is right for you. When you participate in agility, you're not really competing against someone else — you're competing against yourself. It's just you and your dog against the clock and your own expectations.

Is agility in your future? While only you can decide, let me share one big secret: You can try it just for fun. You don't need to learn every aspect of the sport to have fun with agility. You can think of it as a recreational activity, one that you can explore and enjoy without a major commitment.

Evaluating your dog's body type

Agility evokes a passion that knows no breed or pedigree. Terriers love it; Hounds do too. Companion breeds will happily apply their lap-jumping skills to the cause of completing a course. Sledding dogs, Retrievers, and Working breeds — the sport of agility seems to hold something for each one.

Before getting started, however, consider how practicing agility will affect your dog physically. It may seem like a heavy thought, but it's very important in the broad scheme of things. Injuries, in addition to being painful and life-altering for your dog, can be a huge financial burden to remedy or fix, or force a dog with great potential into an early retirement — all for stresses that can easily be avoided.

One of my most beloved dogs, Whoopsie, thinks like a sporting dog and runs with wild abandon in her dreams as she snoozes on the couch, but there's a glitch in the system . . . she isn't built very well. She's dysplastic in her elbows. She's front-heavy. She's prone to structure tears in her ligaments and joints. After a long hike, she often comes up lame. I still love her to pieces, but I would never dream of taking up agility with her. Sure, she'd be into it, but it would endanger her health and well-being.

Take a minute and imagine your dog's skeleton up on the wall like one of those posters you see when you go to your veterinarian. All dogs are not created equally. Consider how your dog's form will affect his ability to function.

If you observe or take a class, speak to the instructor to ensure he or she will be mindful of your dog's particular needs during practice rounds and mock competitions. A novice Basset Hound can't perform at the same level as an experienced Australian Shepherd. Modify your expectations for the size and breed of your dog. Following are some characteristics that may affect your dog's ability to participate in agility:

✔ **Angular posture:** The perfect agility specimen looks a lot like a Border Collie. Angled hips set to propel forward at top speed, sloped shoulders, which serve as the perfect shock absorbers as the dog leaps, twists, and balances on the obstacles. It's no surprise that this breed excels at the sport of agility, as do Australian Shepherds and Whippets.

✔ **A deep-chest:** As a general rule, deep-chested dogs have a tendency to trot rather than run. They jump by lifting their heavily boned frames up into the air and coming down with a harrumph. Modify jump heights and dissention angles to ease their efforts and the shock to their physique. Keep your enthusiasm high to encourage their speed and participation. Deep-chested breeds include the Giant Mastiff, as well as Sighthounds and Mountain Dogs.

✔ **A straight back:** Dogs with straight backs are flat-lined and not well angled to absorb the shock of repetitive leaps, sharp-angled landings or turns, and jarring stops. When practicing, keep the jumps low and spread the angle of the contact obstacles so the dismount isn't jarring or abrupt. Straight-backed dogs include Corgis, Terriers, Retrievers, and Shetland Sheepdogs.

✔ **A long spine:** While Pretzel-the-Dachshund might get super-charged at the thought of competing, he certainly shouldn't be forced to do repetitive jumps or scale obstacles set at sharp angles. Long dogs have tricky spines and temperamental discs: Be mindful of this — your dog's spine is the only one he's got. Along with Dachshunds, Corgi breeds and Basset Hounds fall into this category.

✔ **A short snout:** Dogs with short snouts have a rougher time oxygenating than other dogs. Don't push them when they're working to catch their breath. These breeds are often barrel-chested and top-heavy as well. Ramps should be set at gradual angles, and jumps should be positioned inches below the elbow. Bulldogs and Pugs fit this characterization.

It's a good idea to check with your veterinarian for recommendations regarding any limitations that may apply specifically to your dog before beginning agility.

Being realistic about sensory limitation

Handicapped dogs are great: They don't complain; they adjust. That said, physical limitations may hinder agility participation. Compromised vision or blindness precludes participation, too. If your dog can't see an obstacle

Okay, no matter what your dog looks like, teaching this balancing trick is both impressive and cute! (See Chapter 10 for balancing tips.)

After your dog learns to hit a target with her paw, you can use the skill to teach many clever-looking tricks like closing the fridge door (see Chapter 7 for specifics) or playing on the computer.

When your dog will fetch your paper, the trick will be to train her not to bring you every paper she sees! (See Chapter 7 for fetching how-tos.)

Certain tricks challenge a dog's patience. Good dog! (See Chapter 10 for the lowdown on the treat-on-the-nose trick.)

Teaching your dog to "Bow" on command — now that's impressive! (Go to Chapter 6 to teach your dog this trick.)

Teaching your dog to "Go to sleep" (see Chapter 10) involves two skills — rolling on his back and the "Stay" command. Teach the skills separately before uniting them.

Some dogs are just happier on two legs than they are on four. Teach this dancing trick to give your dog an outlet! (Turn to Chapter 8 for dance directions.)

From one simple trick like "Paw," you can teach your dog many variations, such as "Wave" and "High five!" (Turn to Chapter 6 for the how-tos.)

Nothing pleases your dog more than working with you. Keep your head back, though — no one wants to get bonked! (See Chapter 8 for the finer points of this trick.)

Leaping through a tiny loop . . . it may look easy, but a dog must gauge his speed, jumping, and balance (find out more about jumping through hoops in Chapter 13). Impressive!

Jumps make up the meat of an agility course. (Get the lowdown on jumping obstacles in Chapter 13.)

Walking the plank (see Chapter 14) is the canine equivalent of walking on a balance beam.

Dogs of every shape and size love the thrill and focused effort of agility training. (Get started in Part IV.)

As soon as a dog learns how to maneuver the see-saw (see Chapter 14), he makes it look effortless!

Weave poles take a high level of concentration. (Go to Chapter 14 for details.)

The A-frame obstacle (see Chapter 14) takes focus and concentration. Often the biggest challenge is teaching a dog a clean dismount.

Many dogs learn to love the tunnel so much that it becomes hard to keep them away from it! (Turn to Chapter 13 to get started.)

Agility tricks don't have to stay on the course — once your dog learns "Over" she'll want to sail over everything! (Check out this command and its variations in Chapter 14.)

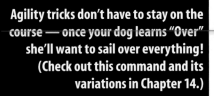

When a dog learns the thrill of catching a Frisbee in mid-air (Chapter 17), she'll go to great lengths to snatch it on the fly!

You can teach Frisbee as a pastime or join a club and compete with your dog in team flying disc games! (Check out Chapter 17.)

clearly, he can't manage it. If you suspect visual problems — or degeneration if your dog is aging — please have the issue checked out before urging him to be active.

Dogs with hearing loss or deafness can do agility just fine. Some organizations have specialty classes; others invite competition at any level. Yours will be a silent theatrical run with plenty of posturing to wow the crowd!

Considering your dog's age

Your dog's age is a big factor when deciding whether he's ready for agility. Off-leash control requires time, training, and maturity — something a young puppy blissfully lacks. Each agility organization has a lower age limit; regardless, most dogs aren't ready for this level of focus until they are one to two years old.

Giving a puppy a head start

The age factor is more than just a maturity issue: There are serious health risks, too. Growing puppies have growth plates, which are areas of soft, immature bone from which bones grow and lengthen. Growth plates don't fully harden with calcium and minerals — a process known as *closing* — until your dog is between 12 and 18 months old. This process takes longer in larger dogs. Strenuous, high-impact, repetitive activities can cause permanent injury to these fragile areas.

But don't shut the book just because you've got a puppy chewing on your shoelace or an adolescent dog making off with your cellphone. There is much you can do to safely prepare your growing puppy or young dog for a future in agility. Here's a checklist:

- ✔ **Socialize your puppy with people and dogs, but control the experience.** Dog parks are fun but can be over-stimulating. Be mindful of who is influencing your puppy and how — don't let him interact with aggressive dogs or rough players of any species.

- ✔ **Expose your dog to a variety of sights, sounds, and experiences.** Walk him through town, in the woods, and near natural bodies of water. Make sure he's comfortable walking on carpet, wood flooring, and AstroTurf.

- ✔ **Bring your puppy to an agility event or class just to watch the older dogs perform.** (Call the organization first to ensure they'll allow non-competing dogs to attend.) Let your dog experience the bang of the teeter-totter, the calls of competitors, the barking, the cheering, and the general happy mayhem associated with agility gatherings.

- ✔ **Encourage your dog's curiosity with exploratory games.** Lay a ladder flat in your yard and lead him over it. Lay a broomstick on the floor and pretend it's a jump. Rest a 12-inch plank on the ground and lure your puppy straight across!

✔ **Get started teaching basic obedience directions like the ones listed in Chapter 4.** Familiarize your maturing puppy with directional cues, such as "Go out" and "Left" or "Right," by repeating these words as you toss a toy or move in each direction.

Don't sit at home, marking the days off on your puppy growth plate calendar. An active, well-socialized puppy will have a real head start in agility.

Advancing during adolescence

Adolescence. Just the word is enough to strike fear into the hearts of many. No matter the species, it can be a challenging time. The good news for dog lovers? Canine adolescence is short — only about eight weeks (typically occurring between the ages of 4–6 months) from beginning to end.

Adolescent dogs are ready to begin more advanced training. They're enthusiastic learners, so use this time to hone your on- and off-leash training skills. Continue to socialize your dog, and direct him in unfamiliar places. Bring him to the train station or a softball game. Enforce his obedience when an off-leash dog is nearby. Take an advanced training class to prepare you for the rigors of working around other dogs and people.

Considering older or veteran dogs

Agility is, for the most part, a younger dog's game. But don't discount the veterans — they can surprise you with their enthusiasm and game.

There's no upper age limit on agility. A few gray hairs on the muzzle won't disqualify your dog — or you — from competing on a recreational or competitive level, but there are a few age-related factors to take into consideration:

✔ Our dogs' bodies age just like ours do. Cartilage weakens, bones become more brittle, and muscle tone and flexibility decrease. Exercise keeps the body fit, but too much vigorous exercise can lead to joint and muscle injuries.

✔ Conditioning is an important part of the training routine for any dog, but for older dogs, it's essential. Keep your senior athlete slim, and make sure all exercise sessions are bracketed by a gradual warm-up and cool-down.

✔ How are your dog's eyes? Cloudy, compromised vision will make it difficult for your dog to gauge his position on the course, and this could present a safety issue. If your dog's vision is poor, it's best to find another activity.

If you're thinking of beginning agility with an older dog, get your veterinarian's approval first. Find an agility instructor who understands your dog's limitations, and adjust jump heights accordingly.

Chapter 12

Laying the Foundations for Agility

I recently took up yoga. Friends promised I would love it. I'd feel more limber, more relaxed. There was even a pose called Downward Facing Dog. How could I resist? I bought a mat and signed myself up. The first few minutes were fine. We closed our eyes and sat cross-legged — the Lotus pose. "Look at me!" I thought. "Doing yoga! Why, this is relaxing." And with that, the instructor gently suggested we do a sequence of moves called the Sun Salutation. Then Warrior. Cobra. And the final straw — the One-Legged King Pigeon.

Is there a Woman Fleeing Yoga pose?

Needless to say, my first few yoga classes were anything but relaxing. Struggling to combine new terminology with unfamiliar techniques left me feeling out of step and lost. But I kept at it. In time, the words and movements started to come together and flow. The same can be said for getting started with agility. Laying a foundation of knowledge and skills can seem daunting, but things begin to flow easily if you stick with it.

In this chapter, I discuss some foundational information and actions you need in order to properly get started with agility. I review how basic training skills are adapted for this sport and list new commands you and your dog will learn together. I discuss how various tools and treats are used to encourage your dog's focus and participation in a sport that will be new to both of you. I provide advice for finding an instructor (for both you and your dog), as well as some pointers for obtaining some of your own agility equipment.

Never fear — soon you'll be talking agility with the best of them!

Modifying Familiar Commands for Agility

Until now, your interactions with your dog have revolved around age-old familiar dog commands and, if you've been learning tricks, some clever cues to prompt her theatrical side. "Sit," "Stay," and "Down" have been your grounding staples. "Follow," "Come," and "Let's go" have prompted movement alongside of you. These commands are used in agility too, but each has its own spin:

- ✔ **"Come"** doesn't finish with a solid, reconnecting hug; instead, it's used to orient and direct your dog as she's moving through a course.

- ✔ **"Down"** isn't an invitation to relax; instead, it directs your dog to drop like a stone on the pause table.

- ✔ **"Stay"** is just a momentary pause in an otherwise adrenaline-pumping race to the finish.

The biggest hitch when working an agility dog is that your dog must be off-leash when practicing and performing. Yes, free — like the wind. Can your dog handle freedom in a social setting? If the thought keeps you up at night, you'll need to review the basics and hone up on your off-lead skills (see Chapter 4). Meanwhile here's a more thorough description of how the basics are modified and used in this sport:

- ✔ **"Come":** The traditional "Come" invites a grounded reconnection. Dogs are taught to either sit in front of their person or stop at their side. Calling a dog on an agility course, however, is used to direct and orient your dog as she's sequencing obstacles. In this case, the command alerts your dog to run in your direction and watch your body cues for more specific direction to the next obstacle. Though some people use the command "Come" on an agility course, many teachers and handlers encourage the use of an alternative cue, such as "Here."

- ✔ **"Sit," "Stand," and "Down":** These commands are staples in every household and a must for trick training, but agility brings each one to a new level. Used on the course, these cues direct a dog to wait her turn or are instructions given on the pause table obstacle. Though agility is generally a fast-moving sport, the *pause table* requires that a dog come to a dead stop, assume a stationary pose for five seconds, and then be off like a rocket when the judge says "Go!"

- ✔ **"Stay" or "Wait":** A stay is a stay is a stay. Truer words were never spoken — accept in the case of agility. In agility, "Stay" does not signal a dog to relax. Instead, "Stay" used on the sporting field means "Hold still for just a few more seconds, and then explode like a rocket."

In timed events, your dog may need to "Stay" at the starting line while you position yourself strategically on the course. "Stay" can be used on the pause table, as well. Many handlers use a different cue to highlight the table maneuver, such as "Wait." In classes or practice runs, this command encourages your dog's self-control when every fiber of her being is urging her to run and jump!

✔ **"Let's go":** This command is more directional than exacting, regardless of your speed. "Let's go" urges your dog to move in your direction, though not straight to your side.

✔ **"Release" (or an equivalent):** Pick a word, any word, to release your dog from a "Stay." Say it with pop-the-cork sounding enthusiasm: "Okay!" "Free!" or "Release!" Pick one and stick to it.

Agility will challenge both you and your dog. Don't be surprised or dismayed if frustrations set in and mistakes happen. When they do, rise above them! Play the role of the all-knowing, benevolent coach. If you're in a situation in which you just don't know what to do next, call your dog back to you and stay upbeat. Remember that anger is not your friend — especially when your dog is off-leash.

Introducing New Agility Commands to Your Dog

You'll be introduced to new commands when you take up agility. Many of them have to do with the new obstacles, while others encourage your dog's direction and speed. As you're out there on the course, envision yourself as the navigator telling your dog which way to go, while she's the executor — bringing your visions to life!

Here's a master list of new commands — some with games you can begin today, and others with skills you'll use on and off the agility course.

✔ **"Go on":** "Go on" sends a dog in front of you to tackle a specified obstacle. Because dogs run faster than people, you'll use it more than you can imagine.

To teach your dog, bait her with a favorite toy. Then hold her collar, tell her to "Stay," and toss the toy out in front of her. Vary the pause time, then release her with "Go on."

Consider this game a two-for-one. You're also teaching your dog to stay while every impulse is riding her to run. It will serve you well when you're teaching your dog to stay at the starting line.

✔ **"Move it":** This is the speed-up cue. Use it or another like it to urge your dog to go faster.

When walking your dog in an open area, command her to "Follow." Say "Move it" as you increase your speed.

✔ **"Through":** This direction commands your dog to move through obstacles like the tunnels and/or jumps.

Find some tunnels in a children's store, lay them out in your living room, and, after reading over the tunnels section in Chapter 13, introduce your dog to this game today!

✔ **"Weave":** This command directs the dog to the weave poles where she will maneuver her body like a wave through poles set 18 to 24 inches apart. Weave poles are one of the most challenging and fun obstacles you'll teach your dog on the agility course. Check out Chapter 14 for the lowdown on weave poles.

✔ **"Up":** This command directs your dog up the A-frame and bridge obstacles.

You can begin to use this command whenever directing your dog up on something — a couch, a rock, or a tree. Always be positive and reward your dog for her efforts.

✔ **"Cross":** This direction tells your dog to cross in front of you as you sequence obstacles on the field.

If your dog has a toy fetish, you can place her in a "Stay" at your side or have a friend hold her; then toss the toy at an angle so she must cross in front of you to retrieve it. Shout your release word and the new cue together: "Okay–Cross."

✔ **"Over," "Hup," "Jump":** These are commands to direct your dog over jumps. Some people like to use one command for every jump, while other people insist on using a different command for each type of jumping obstacle. Flip to Chapter 13 for fun ways to get started on this one!

✔ **"Tire":** This command has an obstacle all its own . . . can you guess? Yup, the tire (or a tire-like hoop).

Flip to Chapter 8 to see how a few fun tricks with a hula hoop can familiarize your dog with this obstacle.

✔ **"Tunnel":** You use this command to direct your dog through tunnels on the agility course. Turn to Chapter 13 for the lowdown on tunnel obstacles.

✔ **"Chute":** This command directs your dog to a closed tunnel. Don't worry — she won't bang her head. Its "closed" end is just an open piece of collapsible fabric that your dog will zip through once she has grown accustomed to it!

✔ **"Plank," "Bridge":** You can use either the "Plank" or "Bridge" command to direct your dog to the teeter or sway bridge.

✔ **"Walk it":** Dogs must be mindful of their footing on the bridge and A-frame obstacles. Use this command to slow your dog down when too much speed could lead to trouble.

Practice "Walk it" with the "Move" command, varying your speed as you walk side by side.

Using Positive Reinforcement with Agility

Imagine this: You're a dog, trying to learn something new. Beside you is your person — the one you trust like no other. It's all good — you're calm and happy, attached to the security of your leash. Suddenly, the leash comes off. Okay . . . still good. You're excited and eager to know what to do next.

Now, one of two things can happen:

✔ Your person guides you, offering clear instructions, rewarding every effort, starting over when things don't feel right, and ignoring your mistakes. This is a little hard, but you're a team! It's going to be great!

✔ Your person grows tense. Instructions are garbled. You're getting confused, so you look to your leader for direction and reassurance but — uh-oh — not a lot of information is there. In fact, it seems like you might be in trouble. This is a little *too* hard and you want to go home!

If you were the dog, which scenario would you pick?

Here's the thing about agility: It's all off-leash. Have I mentioned that? The off-leash part? You're going to ask your dog to concentrate and learn, and then you're going to ask for speed on top of it — all without the assuring guidance of a leash. Establish a bond of trust and an aura of confidence, however, and your dog will be connected to you more securely than with the strongest leash.

Your dog needs to enjoy agility to do agility. If you're a happy, confident, and encouraging leader, it will come together — probably faster than you think. But there's no room for dictators on the field, so check your inner despot at the door and get in the game.

Envisioning cooperation

When you're starting out in agility, it helps to play the Good Movie/Bad Movie game.

Like most people, you'll probably have a few jitters starting out in a new sport. You'll spend a lot of time picturing catastrophes and cataloging what might go wrong. *We'll walk onto the course and my dog won't cooperate! She'll run away! I'll look disjointed and out of sync . . . I might even trip or fall and people will laugh and point and . . .* STOP! This is the bad movie! Rewind! Rewind!

Go back to the part where you and your dog are entering the course. Your dog nails her performance, clearing every obstacle, following your every graceful move and direction. The crowd is hushed — awestruck! While this kind of mastery takes time to perfect, the good movie lets you experience it now.

Remember that your dog can't play the Good Movie/Bad Movie game in her head. She needs to follow your lead and she's happy to, especially if you're kind and encouraging. If *you're* playing the good movie, *she's* playing the good movie. And that's good!

Practicing positive reinforcement

Believe it or not, sometimes the hardest thing to control in agility isn't your dog; it's your temper. The process requires you to learn each obstacle and sequence the course. Your dog needs to focus: simultaneously concentrating and containing herself. And — yes, I'm saying it again — your dog will be off-leash. As in not on the leash.

Sometimes your dog will stay on-course; other times she may fidget or lose focus. Is she being bad? No. She's learning. People learn the same way: One day you're hitting a tennis ball like a pro or conjugating French verbs like a native, then the next day . . . not so great. Everyone — dogs and people — has good learning days and bad ones. Be patient with yourself *and* your dog. Be understanding. Appreciate your dog. Empathize.

Stay positive and upbeat as you explore and learn agility. You'll need to juggle the social aspects of the agility lifestyle, quell your public performance jitters, manage off-leash expectations, and learn to use unfamiliar and challenging equipment — without losing your cool or freaking out your dog.

Okay, so how do you do it? It's easier than you think. The key is positive reinforcement training. Not sure what reinforcement training is all about? The following sections detail three simple ingredients.

Spotlighting what's good

Make a list of things that delight your dog. Treats? A special toy? A game of tug, tag, or fetch? A cheer, a body signal, or a heartfelt hug? Make your list and use all of these, intermittently of course, to praise your dog for even the smallest effort to master an obstacle.

Think about learning from your perspective. Do you want a teacher who rides your every misstep, or one who praises everything you do right?

Framing the mistakes

Think of your dog's mistakes as her confusion — not as stupidity or belligerence. Frame her actions or missteps, determine where she went wrong, and then start over, slowly. Think of different things you can do to help her understand the goal. Review the building-block approach described in Chapter 1, breaking each maneuver into small, easy-to-master steps.

Being a beacon of reassurance

Sometimes a dog needs to be discouraged — if, for example, she interrupts another team, runs off, or gets out of hand. If your dog races off, let her wear a long line. Track the line as she's bolting, then step on it to curtail the burst. Without you saying a word, she'll reach the end of the line and, whap! — correct herself.

As your dog recovers from the unpleasant reaction, be her beacon of reassurance — cheerfully call her to your side. Praise your dog the instant she comes back to you.

While you can't make endless excuses for your dog's behavior, certain issues can be avoided. Did you forget a feeding or potty run? Have you stayed on one obstacle too long? While you may want to repeat a sequence until your dog gets it right, 30 repetitions may do damage to her understanding.

Dogs are a lot like kids: They get overwhelmed when there's too much going on or they're tired, hungry, or need to potty. Then there's that attention span thing. If you push them beyond their focusing capacities, dogs (like kids) start to act up.

The whooped hound doesn't hunt

This adage was passed down through the generations in my family. Translation? If you keep scolding an animal, she'll stay more focused on you than the task at hand. No one likes to be corrected. In agility, there's no place for it. Correcting a dog for missing a contact won't make any sense. Manhandling a dog who's missed an obstacle on a sequence won't help her stay focused and concentrate the next time around. A dog who is jerked, scolded, or corrected will not run a course with joyful abandon — she'll keep looking over her shoulder to study your mood. Remember, dogs are simple, simple, simple creatures. They live in the moment, they delight in your pleasure, and they freeze up whenever they sense anger.

Calling In Reinforcers: The Tools of the Trade

The sport of agility is starting to make some sense to you. You're growing more comfortable with agility terminology. You recognize that there are many organizations that host agility events — each with its own classes, emphasis, and games. You understand the importance of a positive attitude and sense how this time together strengthens the bond between you and your dog. What else could there be? Well, there's one last thing you can't do without: your *reinforcers* — treats and/or toys used to bait and encourage your dog's enthusiasm as she learns how to navigate and complete each obstacle. Though reinforcements aren't allowed during competition, they'll urge your dog's enthusiasm every step of the way, from applying herself on each obstacle to sequencing.

Visit a pet store and you'll find novel little gadgets that store treats inside a toy. These clever items create clever canine mind games and can offer a great incentive to a dog learning agility. Check them out!

Following is a list of more reinforcers you can employ to entice your dog to do your bidding:

- **Treats:** Dogs who love food, love food and will do just about anything to get more of it. You may use food as a lure initially to encourage your dog's interest or guide her into, over, or through an obstacle. While too much food can be distracting, a well-positioned or well-timed reward leaves your dog eager to go around again.

  A lot of people in agility use treat pouches to inspire their dog's drive. Only food-motivated dogs need apply. Filled with delectable goodies, these bags can be tossed in any direction to override hesitation and set your dog on course!

- **Tug toy:** This is the one time I okay a tug-fest. While it's not the right game for a dominant dog, it's a good one to encourage vigor on an agility field. Put the game on cue — "Let's tug!" — and command release after 5–15 seconds.

- **Fetching toy:** Does your dog like to fetch? My last four did — and there was no better way to reward their learning efforts than to toss their ball or Frisbee.

- **Tag:** Dogs playing tag? It's not as outlandish as it sounds. They love to chase and be chased. Put the game on cue, and do a few rounds of loopty-loop to reward their stamina.

- **Clickers:** Though clicker training is described in Chapter 2, its usefulness in the sport of agility cannot be underestimated. The sharp snapping sound, which heralds food or another reward, helps to target a good performance and encourage your dog's drive, enthusiasm, and understanding.

Leashes

Though leashes are considered faux pas once your dog is running sequences or preparing for trials, you can use a leash to hold and guide your dog during the introductory stages of learning the sport. Aside from the trusty hand-held design, two other leashes come in handy:

✔ A short, hand-held or finger loop lead can be used to guide your dog, hold her between practice sessions, and serve as a weighty reminder that someone's paying attention.

✔ A 10- to 20-foot-long line can be used to discourage rampant run-offs (see the earlier section "Being a beacon of reassurance").

A clicker never stands alone! After each click, immediately reward your dog with a tasty tidbit.

✔ **Target discs:** Find out more about target discs in Chapter 2. In the sport of agility, a target disc is a terrific way to teach your dog placement on the field and to help her learn mindfulness on contact obstacles.

Though you can purchase target discs, they're quite easy to make: Use a container lid or cut out a 2- to 4-inch disc. That's it. You can practice these first moves at home:

1. With your clicker in hand, toss the target disc on the ground, and click-reward your dog for any interest. Do this 20 times.

2. Now hold out until your dog paws or noses the disc. Click-reward.

✔ **Target sticks:** These 3- to 4-foot, tent-like poles are used to steady and direct your dog over an obstacle. Initially introduced like point training (see Chapter 2), the stick's length allows you to distance yourself from your dog as you direct her.

You can purchase target sticks or create them out of a ½-inch dowel or tent pole.

Finding A Good Instructor to Help You and Your Dog

The best way to learn any new sport like agility is to find someone who is one part master and the other part great teacher. While someone may have a dazzling competitive record and titles up the wazoo, they also need to take your novice status in stride and adjust the course to suit your dog's beginner needs. An impatient teacher will dampen your enthusiasm and startle your dog. Take time to find the right instructor to introduce you to agility. Meet and interview potential instructors, and watch an ongoing class. Find an instructor who is

Searching for agility on the Web

There are many ways to learn more about the sport of agility. Entire books are devoted to the finer points of learning the techniques and competing with your dog. Web sites abound, as do specialty magazines and periodicals. Scan the Web, check out video reels on YouTube and other sites, and scroll through the following list of Web sites. There are many ways to enjoy learning all there is to know about agility!

✔ **Wikipedia:** Wikipedia provides a great overview of the sport of dog agility. I love the easy cross references. This is a great place to start. `en.wikipedia.org/wiki/Dog_agility`

✔ **YouTube:** I could watch video reels on YouTube for hours. Search "dog agility," kick back, and enjoy yourself. `youtube.com`

✔ **Clean Run:** Perhaps the most thorough site on the Web for all things agility, from rules and regulations to classes and events, this site even has a great presentation of training gear and specialty products. In addition, it publishes its own magazine and catalogs a library of books and videos available for purchase on agility and training. `www.cleanrun.com/`

✔ **United States Dog Agility Association, Inc. (USDAA):** This Web site highlights USDAA news and events and covers the rules and regulations of this group. Because the USDAA is the largest independent author-ity for the sport of dog agility, it's often the sponsor of events throughout the country as well as around the world. `usdaa.com`

✔ **American Kennel Club:** Embedded within the American Kennel Club's site is a great resource for dog agility enthusiasts. Helpful links and articles are offered as well as beginner guides to getting started. In-depth information about their judging standards, class divisions, and breed specifications is well laid out and available for downloading. `www.akc.org/events/agility/`

✔ **Teacup Dog Agility Association:** This Web site lists information about competitive agility for small dogs. In many instances, the specifications and time allotment are modified for size. This site is a good reference for you if your dog is a mini-sized sports enthusiast! `www.k9tdaa.com/`

✔ **North American Dog Agility Council:** The North American Dog Agility Council (NADAC) was formed in 1993 to provide North American dogs and their handlers with a fast, safe, and enjoyable form of the sport of dog agility. NADAC sanctions agility trials sponsored by affiliated clubs. The purpose of a NADAC agility trial is to demonstrate the ability of a dog and her handler to work as a smoothly functioning team. With separate class divisions for Veterans and Junior Handlers and a variety of games, NADAC dog agility offers something for everyone! `www.nadac.com`

✔ **Positive:** Positive reinforcement should be the instructor's claim to fame. Life is too short to get frustrated at a dog. Dogs are like babies — pure innocence and joy. Find an instructor whose positive attitude is infectious. A happy communication style with people will also go a long way in helping you overcome your jitters. A strong emphasis on the most basic skills, like signaling and focusing exercises, will set a strong foundation for what lies ahead.

✔ **Patient with newbies:** A good instructor loves beginners! Everyone who starts out in the sport looks *and feels* befuddled. You and your dog will not be exempt. You'll feel awkward and need plenty of encouragement. Find a teacher who's patient and who takes your newbie questions in stride.

✔ **Safety-conscious:** Safety rules! When you consider a group, look at the equipment too. A good teacher will prioritize safety. Wet or rusted equipment may be slick or loose. A novice dog who slips or falls off unsteady equipment will be emotionally jarred. Safety also includes the other dogs in the class: off-leash, all dogs must be in-control, well-socialized, and nonthreatening to the new students in the group.

✔ **Experienced:** A good instructor should be experienced in competitive agility. Hanging out at weekend trials, he or she will have experience troubleshooting, and be versed in the lingo and the finer points of competing at each level.

✔ **Flexible:** No two dogs are alike! A good teacher adjusts the obstacles according to the size, breed, and experience of each of his or her four-legged pupils. While a dog's height has bearing, it's not the only factor! A dog's experience, personality, and body type must also be taken into consideration. Some dogs have agile, athletic bodies, while others lumber and need more motivation to participate. Finally, different breeds react differently on the course. Some dogs are prone to return to their person's side, while others are perfectly comfortable running ahead. A good instructor should be well-versed in the ways of dogs.

✔ **Creative:** Many techniques are afloat to help troubleshoot a dog's confusion, if, for example, she's prone to leap off a contact obstacle too soon or tunnel when she should weave. Find an instructor who's eager to vary his or her approach to meet your dog's individual challenges.

Choosing between private and group instruction

Everything in life has pros and cons. While private training may seem invaluable — who could argue the perks of working one-on-one with a master? — individual lessons don't simulate a true agility experience. Organized agility events are loud and chaotic. If your dog's used to her private course in your backyard, she won't be able to concentrate. While private lessons can fine-tune your techniques and troubleshoot your dog's moves, you need to find a class or practice group if your hope is to earn titles and challenge yourself on a timed course.

Group classes also come in flavors. A regimented class begins on a specific day and introduces you to agility in a well-organized fashion. These classes are ideal for beginners, but you should still observe a class before you sign up. Because you'll need *some* individual attention, the dog-instructor ratio should be no greater than 6:1.

Drop-in classes and practice groups are also available. These are better choices after you're familiar with the obstacles and can narrow your questions to a specific technique as you use your time to practice your moves.

Perhaps you've discovered a few different instructors in your area. Check them all out. If more than one catches your fancy and you're wondering whether more might be better, here's what I recommend: Start with one instructor. Learn the basics, read some books, and get familiar with the obstacles. Once you get the gist of agility and you're comfortable handling your dog in a group setting, explore other options. As long as everyone is positive and you can filter through instructions to decipher what makes the most sense for you and your dog, you have nothing to lose by taking multiple classes.

Considering specialty camps and agility retreats

For a sport that's relatively new on the scene, agility has sparked a passion that's quite phenomenal. If you feel the obsession rumbling, consider a week-long camp or weekend seminar retreat where you can surround yourself with other enthusiasts and learn from the experts.

Getting Some Agility Equipment of Your Own

While an instructor helps you learn the sport of agility, practice on the obstacles helps you master it! If you live in an urban area, you're likely to find an agility club that has a course to work on during your off days. If you're fortunate enough to have your own yard, you may choose to buy or make some basic equipment.

What's the best equipment to get started with? Jumps, for sure. You can make or rig some very basic jumps from a few rolls of toilet paper and a broomstick. Pause tables can be simulated with a square blanket laid on the ground; and a low version of a crosswalk can be created by placing a 12-inch-wide board on a couple of phone books.

Purchasing agility equipment

Many companies sell agility equipment. Your only concern in purchasing equipment should be for your dog's safety. Decorative taping won't hold its weight if the bearings are loose and threaten your dog's stability. Anyone can pretty up a weave pole, but if it falls over when bumped, it's no good. Here are a few reputable places to find agility equipment:

- ✔ www.carlson-agility.com
- ✔ www.affordableagility.com
- ✔ max200.com

Making some standard pieces

Are you handy? Take a look at CanineCrib.com's Web site at www.canine crib.com/dog/training/agility-course.asp for instructions on how to build your own agility obstacles. Copy the instructions, and head to your local home improvement store. Within an hour, you'll have all you need to start making your own agility course! Of course, only you can assess your carpentry skills. While the jump plans are pretty straightforward, if the poles fall over or the teeter is unstable, your dog may grow wary of the sport. If you're unable to make your own equipment, see the preceding section on purchasing reputable equipment.

Chapter 13

Introducing Your Dog to Jumps, Tunnels, and Tables

In This Chapter

▶ Showing your dog where to jump

▶ Racing through tunnels

▶ Exploring chutes

▶ Mastering the table

*I*magine this: You call out a command, point with an outstretched arm, and your partner races to complete a particular task. ("Wow," you're probably thinking. "Can I teach these skills to the humans in my life?" Perhaps, but that's another book. This is about you and your dog.) The extraordinary levels of communication and enthusiasm that exist between humans and dogs are what make agility such an exhilarating sport.

I've always believed in the innate intelligence of the canine species, and recent studies back me up. According to Professor Stanley Coren, a leading expert on canine intelligence at the University of British Columbia in Vancouver, dogs are capable of understanding up to 250 words and gestures, can count up to five, and can perform simple mathematical calculations.

If your dog has been waiting for a chance to show off his brainpower, agility is the answer! In an introductory agility class, you find out how to direct your dog through a simplified agility course, navigating obstacles with commands and body cues. This chapter gives you an overview of some of the obstacles in an agility course — the jumps, tunnels, and table — and prepares you for the adventures that lie ahead. In Chapter 14, you discover other parts of the course: the contact obstacles and the weave.

Is there a secret to starting with these particular obstacles? Well, simplicity is always the rule, no matter what your species. My advice? Start with the routines that are the easiest to master and least challenging for both of you. You'll get the rush of accomplishment as you inspire your dog's enthusiasm and cooperation!

Planning for a Good Training Session

Once you've decided to take the plunge into agility, you'll be sharing the journey with other participants in various stages of learning. Some will be way ahead of you, making you feel like an eternal freshman. But in time, you'll find yourself lending a hand to a new team, and you'll realize — "Hey! We're getting somewhere!"

In the meantime, keep the following advice in mind as you get started:

- **Make it simple.** Many of the obstacles have adjustable heights, so start at the lowest position. This ensures your dog's safety and success.

- **Find a helper.** Many of the introductory steps require an extra set of hands. Partner up with another newbie, and you'll be doing each other a favor!

- **Use leash control to start.** Keep your dog on-leash in the beginning, and listen to your instructor. Think of holding the leash as holding a child's hand: In the early days of agility, it will make you both feel more secure. Your dog will need to be off-leash eventually to execute the course, but the leash is helpful when directing your dog in the early stages. Wait until your dog really understands the program and your instructor tells you it's okay to go off-lead.

- **Keep your lessons short and sweet.** If you're taking a group class, chunks of time will be spent listening to your instructor and taking turns with the various participants. Your dog won't be "on" for long stretches of time. If you're practicing on your own, a good rule of thumb is to do 3 to 5 repetitions on no more than three obstacles. Use lots of treats and end each practice session with a game. Though every dog is different, and some breeds or personality types might enjoy hours of practice, these dogs are the exception — most dogs burn out (physically and mentally) when pressed to perform!

- **Stay positive.** Throughout the learning phase, you'll have days where you feel confused and awkward. Confusion is a little contagious, and your dog may catch it like a cold. He'll show his confusion by acting up or racing around. If you compound the problem by showing frustration, your dog will misunderstand your displeasure and begin to associate it with the equipment or the activity. He'll want to go home, where everything is predictable and safe.

- **Listen to your dog.** Some days, everything will be going right. Your dog will be eager, your signals will be crystal clear, and the sun will be shining. Other days, your dog will bolt, your knees will hurt, and everything will be just . . . muddy. On those days, lighten your practice load: Simplify the routine, end on a high note, and toss in the towel until another day.

✔ **As you practice, be mindful of your dog's stress signals.** Repetitive motions such as scratching, lip-licking, and barking can be a sign that your dog is losing focus or has overexerted himself. If you've just started your practice session, see whether a walk, ball toss, or some soothing pats will get him on track. If you've been out on the course a while or the weather is extreme, go home and chill. No one — dog or person — likes to be pushed beyond their limits!

✔ **Have fun.** Agility is about having fun and being together. Repeat it like a mantra — "Having fun and being together. Having fun and being together!"

✔ **Keep it slow and simple, and smile!** Remember the three-part cardinal rule when introducing any new obstacle: Keep it *slow* and *simple,* and don't forget to *smile!*

The Jumps: Taking a First Leap into Agility Training

Most dogs love to jump. Teaching them to do it on command can be the easiest step in agility, but there's more to a good jumper than meets the eye! Dogs must not only clear the object but also be able to take a jump at any angle and land squarely.

In this section, I give you advice on setting up the jumps for training. I also explain how to get your dog used to clearing these obstacles — at your direction — in different combinations and from various angles. Finally, I give you some quick tips for tackling the specific kinds of jumps you'll see in an agility trial.

Setting up the jumps for training

Regardless of competition jumping heights, set your jumps very low for training purposes. Make each one easy to clear and fun to do. A jump for a novice jumper should be below the dog's elbow. Got a toy breed? Set the bar on the ground to start. When arranging a set of jumps, leave enough space between them for a proper five-stride approach and a clear landing.

Repetitive stress on your dog's body increases the risk of injury.

As you and your dog get more comfortable with the jumps, you should vary the height to keep your dog ever mindful of the jump set in front of him. Lower the jump during routine practice or on days when the workout is demanding.

Choosing your jump commands

With regards to choosing commands for different jumps, instructors seem divided. Some encourage a one-command-suits-all approach, while other instructors identify each jump separately. I advise you to think of this from your dog's perspective. A whirling dervish who moves before he thinks may do better with one universal command. A dog who can think on his toes may respond better to identifying each jump with a separate command. Here are the most popular commands used in agility circles:

Command	Jump
"Jump," "Over," "Hup"	Single-bar/single-panel jump
"Jump," "Over," "Big Over"	Spread jump
"Jump," "Over," "Big Over"	Broad jump
"Tire," "Hoop"	Tire, hoop

Of course, your dog won't care whether you choose these words or others — just say them consistently and with enthusiasm!

If you're committed to performance agility, wait until your dog is experienced with all the obstacles and fully mature to research competition heights. Each organization listed in Chapter 16 specifies jump heights based on the various classes and your dog's measurement at his withers. Determine which organization you'll register with, and then modify the jump height for competitive practice runs.

Going over: Making the jumps

I remember setting broomsticks on cereal boxes, teaching my dog to jump through my tire swing, and arranging a jumping course out in the side yard when I was a kid. My Husky loved the time we shared together. It wasn't agility then; it was just plain fun!

To teach your dog the agility jumps, you follow a step-by-step process that ends with your ability to direct your dog to any jump from various locations on the field. Can't believe it? Time to get started!

Stage 1: Calling your dog over the jump

Your dog's first introduction to jumping should be easy and fun. Set up a low jump, say "Over," and trot over the jump with your dog. As you move with him, try to get a feel for his movement — ideally give him five full strides to clear the jump and three more when he lands before interrupting his movement. Praise and reward his enthusiasm.

Now you're ready to have him jump on his own:

1. **Have your helper stand and hold your dog in front of the jump as you walk to the far side of the jump.**

   Stand, but don't turn around and face him.

2. **Twist back and make eye contact with your dog; wave a toy or treat cup from the hand on the same side.**

3. **Call, "Over–Come," as your helper releases your dog.**

4. **Click or call out a praise word like "Yes!" as your dog clears the jump.**

   Reward and praise your dog from the side you've twisted from when he reaches you.

Practice twisting, calling, and rewarding your dog from either side. This conditions him to move toward either the right or the left side as you indicate, which will become important as you sequence to other pre-positioned obstacles.

Stage 2: Running alongside

Next, your dog will learn to take jumps as you run alongside him next to the jump. Here's how to accomplish this in jump-training:

1. **Hold your dog in front of the jump and let him watch your helper execute the next step.**

2. **Ask your partner to walk ahead of you, indiscreetly placing a toy, loaded target, and/or treat on the far side of the jump.**

   If your dog hasn't been target-trained, review the technique in Chapter 2.

   Place the reward several strides past the jump to allow your dog to land squarely. Have your helper ready to remove it in case your dog races around the jump.

3. **Release your dog as you say "Over!" and run with him towards the jump. Let him run just ahead of you and take the jump as you navigate to either side of the jump.**

   As you shout "Over," signal, too, with an exaggerated bowling motion directed at the jump. Your signal arm should be closest to the jump.

4. **Click or shout your praise as your dog clears the jump.**

   As he lands, let him enjoy his reward and/or break for a favorite game!

If your dog runs around the jump, have your helper remove the reward quickly. Calmly return your dog to his starting position, and show him the baited target before you release him. If he still dodges the jump, try trotting over the jump with him to let him see the reward, but don't let him have it until he's cleared the jump on his own.

Practice running and signaling from both directions. Your dog should be comfortable jumping with you strategically positioned anywhere on the field.

Stage 3: Encouraging your dog to run ahead

A happy agility dog looks for jumps to clear and obstacles to perform. To condition this level of enthusiasm from the beginning, teach your dog the "Go on" command (see Chapter 12), and use it in this step.

The description *Velcro dog* refers to a dog who clings to his owner and can't think well or enthusiastically on his own. While your dog's affections may reassure you, discourage over-dependence by teaching him to go forward and tackle life . . . one obstacle at a time.

Set the jump very low or lay it on the ground. Then follow these steps:

1. **Have your helper set the lure just beyond the jump or set the target on the other side of the jump yourself.**

2. **Send your dog out with "Go on over" as you let him go.**

   Click or mark the moment he clears the jump. If your dog races around the jump, have your helper remove the reward before he reaches it.

3. **Follow your dog past the obstacle and then turn to play with, praise, and reward him for his efforts.**

Phase out placing the target on the far side of the jump. But don't forget to praise and reward your dog enthusiastically when he clears the jump.

Stage 4: Setting up multiple jumps

Now you're ready for multiple jumps. Lay them out in a direct line, allowing your dog five paces between each one.

Go back to Stage 1, working with your assistant to help your dog understand your new focus. Place the treat at the end of the jump sequence and keep the hurdles low to ensure success and safety!

Stage 5: Adding angles

Enter "dog agility" in the search box on YouTube (www.youtube.com), and watch a competitive run. Notice how each jump's placement sets up the overall performance.

Before you think sequencing, however, practice your jumps one at a time. Teach your dog how to approach and clear each one from any angle, as you encourage him to watch you for direction. Send or run your dog over jumps at different angles, varying your position to the left or the right to simulate a competitive agility experience.

Working on specific types of jumps

A professional course includes many different types of jumps (I describe them in Chapter 11). Here are some tips on approaching specific kinds of jumps:

- **Single jump and panel jump:** These jumps are straightforward: A single bar or flat, wall-like board is positioned for your dog to jump over. Your main goal is to build your dog's success rate and enthusiasm so he doesn't become a "bar knocker." Dogs who clip the jump or dislodge a bar lose points or, worse, are disqualified in competition.

  Keep the jumps low, giving your dog room to clear each one. Positively reward each stage of this learning phase. Your enthusiasm and patience will ensure your dog learns to jump high and clear!

- **Spread jump:** Spread jumps are a spread-out arrangement of several ascending bar jumps that your dog must clear. When practicing, keep the bars low to ensure your dog's success every step of the way!

- **Broad jump:** These low, angled boards are spread out on the ground to simulate a wide environmental obstacle that your dog must jump over (see Figure 13-1). If you're experienced in trial obedience, you'll notice the similarity right away!

  Tip the boards on edge so they're progressively more pronounced and harder to walk over. Once your dog is jumping up and across them, you can lay them down one at a time, from back to front, until the series is laid flat.

  If your dog hits the boards, try laying an uncomfortable surface over them, such as chicken wire.

- **Tire:** A "tire" obstacle is usually an elaborate hoop suspended in a wooden frame. This jump may jar your dog's concentration. When first introducing the tire, make sure it's braced tightly to prevent both motion and sound as your dog acclimates to it. Stay positive, and use plenty of tantalizing food lures and toys. Lower the tire to floor level and kneel down as you bait your dog to come through the circle.

  If your dog's still resistant, use a leash to steady him and lead him through. Toss a toy or treat ahead of him, or let him watch a favorite friend manage the obstacle. Leash him and cheerfully guide him through several times. Once he's coming through when you call him, raise the tire slightly. Good with that? Go back and practice Steps 1–4 in "Going over: Making the jumps."

  Never force your dog through this obstacle. Frustration will ensure one thing, and one thing only: He'll never get near a hoop again. Watch your temper!

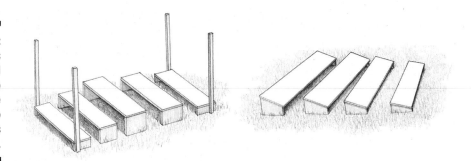

Figure 13-1:
Broad jumps
are laid
out flat to
encourage
a dog to
jump across
them.

Going through Tunnels

Zipping through a tunnel at top speed reminds me of being a kid. The difficulty isn't so much teaching a dog to run through a tunnel as it is teaching him to avoid it to work on other obstacles!

There are two different types of tunnels:

- **Open-ended:** A 15- to 20-foot-long open-ended tunnel that can be positioned straight or curved
- **Closed:** A 12- to15-foot-long closed tunnel or chute with a barrel opening and a collapsible fabric tail that a dog must push through to get out

Make sure each tunnel is secured: Flexible tie-downs are best. You can make one with an overlying strap or tether that's affixed to sand-filled water jugs on either side.

Does your dog get jazzed up when he sees the tunnel? If your dog is obsessed, he's not alone: Dogs who prioritize the tunnels are called *tunnel suckers*. I love that! If I were a dog, I'm sure I'd be a tunnel sucker too.

Introducing your dog to open-ended tunnels

Begin training on the straight, open-ended tunnel. Let your dog explore the tunnel as you walk along the outside of it together. Look down the hollow as though you were exploring a cave. If your dog grows wary, avoid looking at or reassuring him — your attention will reinforce his concern. Instead, crawl into the opening in sheer amazement, rewarding any sign of confidence.

Two unusual-looking tunnels are used to compete for UKC titles. The hoop tunnel and crawl tunnel are open frames that your dog must learn to navigate in the same way he learns to move through the tunnels I discuss in the following sections.

When practicing your tunnel runs, direct your dog from both the right and left side. Later, your position will help orient him toward the next obstacle.

Stage 1: Calling your dog through

Ask a helper to assist you. If possible, scrunch up the tunnel to shorten its length. Then proceed as follows:

1. **Ask your helper to hold your dog at the mouth of the tunnel.**

2. **Walk around to the opposite end, kneel down, and wave toys or treats as you call out to your dog.**

3. **Have your helper release your dog when you shout, "Tunnel!"**

   If your dog shoots through, reward and praise him enthusiastically.

   If he balks, stay calm and do whatever it takes to fan his enthusiasm . . . find more tasty treats, use a host of favorite toys, or position his favorite dog friend at the far end of the tunnel.

Super-sized tall breeds will need to scrunch to get into the large tunnel. They can do it — I've witnessed it with my own eyes! To encourage your large breed into the tunnel, make it as short as possible. Lure him in with a tantalizing treat or favorite toy.

Stage 2: Running alongside

The next step is to teach your dog to run through the tunnel as you run alongside it.

1. **Set up and secure the tunnel in a straight line.**

2. **Hold your dog at the mouth of the tunnel while your helper maneuvers to the far end with a baited target.**

   Once your helper has your dog's attention, ask him or her to set the target on the ground.

3. **Release your dog, saying "Tunnel!" with enthusiasm. Thrust the arm closest to your dog forward in a bowling motion.**

   If your dog ducks in, run alongside him, cheering him on as you do, so he can better orient himself to your position as he exits. Reward him enthusiastically!

   If your dog runs around the tunnel or is otherwise confused, ask your helper to remove the reward, ignore him, and start over again.

Practice running along both sides of the tunnel. As you learn sequencing, the side you'll stand on will depend on the location of the other obstacles.

This obstacle is very, very exciting. Some dogs get wound up and forget their manners. To help ground your dog, let him drag a light leash. Should he start to zoom off, you'll have an easy way to stop him. Laugh it off; then up the quality of your food rewards or practice just before mealtime, and stay positive!

Stage 3: Sending your dog out

Next, you teach your dog to race ahead of you to take the tunnel:

1. **Keep the tunnel straight and shortened.**

2. **Stand way back, and run toward the tunnel saying "Go on–Tunnel!"**

3. **Slow your pace so that your dog gets ahead of you.**

4. **Ask a friend to toss a treat pouch or a toy to your dog as he emerges from the tunnel (or, if you're fast enough, greet him yourself!).**

The chute: Introducing your dog to closed tunnels

The closed tunnel is slightly more complicated than the open version. Here your dog must run into an open barrel without being able to see his way out. What's blocking his view? A collapsed fabric tail, known as the chute. Hmmm . . . this obstacle requires trust!

Make sure your dog doesn't get tangled in the chute. Fluff it before and after each use.

The steps to getting your dog to navigate a closed tunnel are similar to those in the preceding section on open-ended tunnels, but with the following variations.

Stage 1: Variations on the call-through

If possible, get your dog used to going through the tunnel without the cloth section attached. Remove the cloth section and call your dog through the barrel. Repeat Steps 1–3 as outlined in the preceding section on open tunnels. When your dog's familiar with the equipment, place the collapsible section on the barrel and proceed:

1. **Fold the fabric section back like a pant cuff, making it as short as possible.**

2. **Hold the fabric open so that your dog is able to see through the tunnel.**

3. **Have your helper hold your dog back, then call your dog through as described in the earlier section, "Stage 1: Calling your dog through."**

   Praise and reward him enthusiastically as soon as he enters the chute.

4. **Once your dog is confidently racing through the tunnel, drop the fabric on his back gently as he exits the chute.**

5. **Gradually drop it earlier and earlier — using your cheerful enthusiasm to reassure him that everything is okay.**

Some dogs freak out when the chute covers their head. Delay this as long as possible — when you're first dropping the fabric, make sure it doesn't cover his eyes.

You can practice a game of peekaboo with a lightweight towel and some favorite treats. Toss the towel over your dog's head and say, "Peekaboo," as you whisk it off and reward him!

Stage 2: Variations on running alongside

Here you repeat Stage 1, but you enlist the help of a friend, freeing you to run alongside your dog.

1. **Ask your friend to fold back the chute and hold it open.**

2. **Have him or her wave the baited target so your dog sees it, and then drop it on the ground at the end of the opening.**

3. **Shout "Chute" and signal with your full-arm swing (the bowling motion) as you release your dog and let him race through.**

4. **Run out to meet and congratulate your dog with praise and play.**

5. **Have your friend lengthen and drop the fabric as you did in the preceding section.**

Run on either side of the chute to condition your dog to locate you as he moves through.

Stage 3: Variations on sending your dog out

Once your dog is comfortable moving through the chute, you're ready for the last stage. Ask your friend to hold the tunnel open for the first couple of send-outs.

1. **Stand back and run toward the tunnel, shouting "Go on–Chute" as you signal and release your dog from your grasp.**

2. **Slow your pace to let him race on ahead of you.**

3. **Ask your helper to toss a toy or treat bag down, so that your dog is rewarded the moment he emerges.**

    Alternatively, run alongside the chute and do this yourself. When you reach your dog, play with and reward him some more!

Modifying tunnel positions

In competition, your dog will have to navigate the tunnel on course. At higher levels, the open tunnel may be curved so that your dog will have to run to an opening that's out of sight. Here are some exercises to challenge your dog's tunnel comprehension:

- **Curved open tunnel:** Curve the tunnel, both to the left and right. Send your dog from either side, conditioning him to take your direction from anywhere on the field.

- **Hidden opening:** From the same curved layout, gradually angle back away from the curve so you're sending your dog around the tunnel to enter it. Use dramatic bowling signals to urge your dog to navigate around to the opening. Toss a toy/treat out as he races through. Bend the tunnel the other way and work the same exercise from the opposite side.

Waiting on Tables

The table obstacle tests your dog's ability to put on the brakes. While the rest of the agility course is pure form, function, and speed, the table is the one obstacle where your dog must come to a complete stop and hold a specific position for a full five seconds.

If you're planning on getting some equipment to practice at home, put "table" near the top of your list. Why? The skills you teach here have side benefits in everyday life: For instance, when the doorbell rings or your dog sees a squirrel, the table can help ground your overstimulated dog.

A dog who has mastered the table has been taught the obstacle with a fine balance of patience and enthusiasm. You can spot this dog a mile away! He will

- Run directly to the table without hesitation.

- Quickly respond to "Sit" or "Down" as directed.

- Stay steady as a rock, yet be poised to spring when he hears his release cue.

- Fly off tilt and onto the next obstacle, when given the cue.

But aren't you supposed to be teaching your dog to stay *off* the table? Well, yes, when it comes to your furniture, but the agility table is a different type of table. It's low and square with a roughened surface area to prevent slipping (you can even jury-rig a table out of a low, sturdy, resurfaced coffee table — sanded and coated with sand-textured paint or non-slip vinyl strips). The height of the table is fully adjustable, and you can modify it depending on your dog's height.

This section covers four stages to teaching the table. Practice each stage separately before chaining them together.

Stage 1: Encouraging quick positioning

The first stage is done off the table: You need to speed up your dog's reaction time to the "Sit" and "Down" commands. If he's a little rusty, flip to Chapter 4 and perfect the basics.

Use your dog's favorite lures and a clicker or word cue to highlight his speediest renditions. Begin with the speedy "Sit." When your dog gets the knack of that, move on to the speedy "Down." Follow these steps:

1. **Give the "Sit" or "Down" command as you lure your dog into position.**

2. **Reward your dog's initial cooperation — no matter what his speed.**

3. **Then, withhold the treat for faster positioning, urging him with faster luring motions and more urgent tones.**

4. **When he nails his first speedy posture, give him a jackpot reward — a fistful of treats!**

Stage 2: Going to the table!

After your dog has mastered the speedy "Sit" and "Down," teach him to run to the table and get on it with eager enthusiasm.

Make table time special by pulling the table out when practicing, but storing it away when not in use.

When you first approach the table, let your dog explore it . . . allow him to sniff it, put his paws on it, jump on it, and so forth. If your dog gives you a double-take, do your best to erase his skepticism by staying enthusiastic and encouraging your dog to climb up. You're ready for the send-off!

1. **Ask a friend to stand behind the table with a loaded target disc — a target disc laced with a treat.**

   Have your friend wave the disc to get your dog's attention.

2. **Stand back 5 to 10 feet. Shout "Table" as you let your dog go.**

3. **Mark the moment he lands on the table with a clicker or a praise cue such as "Yes," or "Good!"**

   Let him have the target reward by approaching behind him and praising galore.

Always use your release word, for example, "Okay," to end the praise fest. You're conditioning your dog to get off when he hears the word cue.

Increase your dog's understanding by practicing from different angles and increasing the send-off distance.

Once you've accomplished all this, try practicing solo:

1. **Show your dog the target and place it back and slightly off the table's center.**

2. **Bring your dog back, and then release him with the command, "Table!"**

3. **Run with him to the table. If he leaps on, mark it with your word cue and/or clicker, and stop in front of the table and praise him.**

   If he's hesitant or runs by, move to the opposite side and encourage him to get on from the front.

   If he ducks behind and tries getting up on the far side, put him on a short tab leash and calmly maneuver him back to the front side.

4. **Once he has mastered jumping on the table, send him from different angles and distances.**

   Always release your dog from the table with "Okay."

Some dogs approach the table with such force and excitement they slip off. If this happens to your dog, shout his name as he nears the table.

Now phase out your use of the target:

1. **Put the target up on the table without lures.**

   Mark the moment he hits the target, and then run up and reward him by hand.

2. **Remove the target altogether.**

   Reward your dog instead with a marker cue (click or word) and treats.

Stage 3: Practicing table positions

Once your dog is super-happy about the table, you're ready to introduce your stationary commands, combining quick positioning (Stage 1) with going to the table (Stage 2):

1. **Bring out the table. Practice a few familiar runs (see the preceding section) to stoke your dog's enthusiasm.**

2. **Send your dog to the table by commanding "Table!" When all four paws hit the table, direct "Sit."**

   Verbalize clearly and with urgency.

   Command from an upright posture — your dog may misconstrue any bending forward as threatening.

3. **Cue or click and reward your dog the instant he nails the posture.**

   At this stage, get close enough to your dog to treat him while he's in position. Otherwise, you'll be conditioning a position-pop-up — a big no-no in this sport!

4. **Work on the quick "Down" the same way you approach the "Sit" cue in Stages 1–3.**

Your only focus at this point is to teach quick positioning.

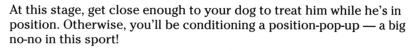

Stage 4: Holding — 1-2-3-4-5 GO!

Once your dog will assume whatever posture you direct on the table, you're ready for the final move: holding still! In trial, the judge will stand near you and count to five: Initially, vary the holding time from 5 to 10 seconds.

You can practice this move at home with or without a table. Do your quick "Sit" or "Down," count out loud, and then release with "Okay!" Use a more urgent tone than that of your everyday command voice so your dog will know these short counts to five are different than your other, lengthier, expectations. Follow these steps:

1. **On every third "Table" run, add the command "Stay" after your "Sit" or "Down" positioning cue.**

   Vary the stay time from 5 to 10 seconds.

2. **Hold the treat in your hand while your dog holds the position, giving him the food just before you release with "Okay!"**

3. **Is your dog holding his "Stay"? Ask someone to volunteer as the judge — standing next to the table and counting "1-2-3-4-5 GO!"**

The bottom line? You don't want this obstacle to dampen your dog's enthusiasm for agility. Make it a fun and exciting challenge, and your dog will look forward to it as much as the other obstacles on the field!

Chapter 14

Teaching the A-Frame, Dog Walk, Teeter, and Weave Poles

In This Chapter

▶ Getting your dog to nail the contacts every time

▶ Navigating the A-frame, dog walk, and teeter

▶ Perfecting the weave poles

The obstacles I discuss in Chapter 13 (the jumps, table, and tunnels) are just to whet your appetite for the sport. Now it's time to test your teaching abilities and your dog's concentration with the contact obstacles and the weave poles. Still fun, each one poses its own unique challenges.

The *contact obstacles* — the A-frame, dog walk, and teeter — are so named because each requires your dog to touch a marked zone as she gets on and off the obstacle. In agility, these zones are referred to as *contacts,* and they're differentiated by a distinct, two-toned color scheme — the contact zones are a different color than the rest of the obstacle. They're designed to not only ensure safe navigation on these raised platforms, but also to provide competition judges a means to confirm that your dog touches down as she performs the obstacle. Of course, your dog doesn't get the safety bit — sometimes rushing the obstacle and flying off early seem more exciting. It's your job to enforce the safety card, reining in her enthusiasm and teaching her to nail her contacts every time.

A master agility dog can make blowing through 12 weave poles in under five seconds look quite easy. Many professionals, however, contend that teaching your dog to weave — properly — is one of the greatest challenges in agility. Weaving certainly isn't a natural motion, but most dogs rise to the challenge, and once they "get it," shimmy through as if it was their idea!

In this chapter, I tell you how to introduce your dog to these challenging obstacles. You find out ways to keep your dog safe — and avoid penalties — by getting your dog used to touching the contact zones. I also give you some techniques for introducing the contact obstacles and helping your dog master the weave.

Using Inventive Ways to Teach Contacts

Contact obstacles look pretty straightforward. You teach your dog to run up and then down. What's so challenging about that? The test in the training is to teach your dog to hit the contact zones on the way up *and* on the way down. Much easier said than done.

Why do dogs miss their contacts? It's known as the *leap factor* — if the dog could speak, she'd ask "Why slow down cautiously when I can just leap on and off?" The enthusiasm is good, but the carelessness is dangerous. No one should get injured in agility.

Contact zones weren't created to rattle anyone's concentration; the zones are there to ensure your dog's physical safety. In competition, dogs lose points or are disqualified if they don't touch at least one paw in both zones.

So how can you ensure your dog learns this all-important concept from the start? Well, the most deeply ingrained habit is the one that's learned first — so teach it once and teach it right. You'll be off to a very good start. This section gives you some techniques for getting your dog to touch the contacts. Later, in "Cruising the Contact Obstacles," I tell you how to apply these tips when introducing your dog to the A-frame, dog walk, and teeter.

Following the cardinal rules

There are many different techniques to teach a dog to *stick* (touch) the contact zones. In the following sections, you explore some new, novel, and upbeat methods. But first, remember these cardinal rules:

- **Think safety first:** Each obstacle raises your dog off the ground. What's up can fall down. Work with a helper initially to ensure your dog doesn't fall over the edge of the obstacle or jump off in fear or excitement during the early learning phases. Like kids, dogs are delightfully unaware of their mortality.

   If your dog falls off any apparatus, check to ensure that she hasn't sustained any injuries. If your dog is lame or can't move her neck, stop immediately and find an animal hospital. Pushing an injured dog can lead to permanent handicaps — at best, this means the end of her agility career; the worst-case scenario could leave your dog permanently disabled.

- **Stay positive:** Some days agility will get the better of you. You'll feel aggravated with your progress and wish it could be faster. Promise me you won't take your frustrations out on your dog. One angry jerk can taint your dog's enthusiasm for good. A cheerful attitude, tempered by the knowledge that things always improve, ensures your dog's enthusiasm to try, try again.

✔ **Remember to take it slow and steady:** Contact obstacles can take months, even years, to perfect. If your personality demands more immediate gratification, you won't find it on an agility course. These moves are sculpted step by step over time.

✔ **Vary your approach:** As you practice the methods, check in with your partner — your dog. If she's not getting something, don't press the issue. There are many ways to teach these contact obstacles; find one that works for both of you.

As you approach each obstacle, try to create a habitual rhythm: a way of guiding your dog on and off that has body flow so your dog's muscles won't forget, otherwise known as *muscle memory*. Think of it like riding a bike . . . once taught, never forgotten.

Promoting pausing: Two on–two off

Imagine your dog racing up one of the elevated contacts, crossing over or angling down, and then stopping on a dime with her front paws off the obstacle and her two hind ones firmly planted in the contact zone. After a millisecond pause, she's up and racing off. This *two on–two off* approach guarantees a creditable performance as well as a generally safe one.

If you begin training the obstacles by *back-chaining* — working on the last step first — your dog will better understand the two on–two off dismount. While it may seem peculiar to introduce an obstacle by teaching the last step first, remember the agility motto: taught right, never forgotten.

In this section, I tell you how to get your dog ready for this method. I also explain how to put it to use when you introduce your dog to the obstacles.

The two on–two off requires your dog to put on the brakes — quickly. Check with your trainer and your veterinarian to ensure this approach won't put undue strain on your dog's shoulders and back.

Off-course

To teach two on–two off at home, you'll use a target disc from the start — go to Chapter 2 to get up to speed if your dog doesn't know about targeting. Then start doing the following exercise at home:

1. **Find a wide, low landing (such as a hearth or step), or rig a low rise by laying a wide, flat board on bricks at either end.**

2. **Encourage your dog onto the landing; then lure her front end off the step. Face her and command "Wait."**

   Reward her as you click and treat or mark the moment with a positive "Yes," followed by food rewards and/or toys.

3. **Release her from the step with "Okay."**

4. **Once your dog maneuvers into this position eagerly, place a target down in front of her so she can reach it comfortably without moving out of position. Say "Contact–Target."**

   Reward her as she paws or noses the target.

5. **Command your dog to "Stay" as you gradually add distractions to test her focus.**

   Toss toys, and have people or other pets present to test your dog's ability to hold her position no matter what.

On-course

Reinforce the two on–two off technique when you first introduce your dog to the obstacle. Proceed as follows:

1. **On-leash, lift your dog onto the high end of the declining side of the obstacle, or guide her up the backside of the A-frame and then turn her around so she's facing the ground.**

   Ask your helper to block her from falling off the opposite side.

   Avoid maneuvering a frightened or oversized dog. Instead, lure the dog up the incline slowly (and down the same way in Step 3).

2. **Have your helper place a target laced with toys or treats on the ground just beyond the contact zone.**

3. **Walk her down the obstacle using familiar commands: "Contact–Target." Reward your dog enthusiastically as you release her with "Okay."**

   The moment your dog gets it, offer a jackpot of rewards and play a happy game.

4. **Gradually increase your dog's steadiness through practice, switching sides and varying distractions so she's able to concentrate no matter where you are or what's going on around her.**

5. **Over time, remove the target — intermittently at first and then altogether.**

   Your dog will often do the "ghost target" move, where she noses or paws the ground as though the target was still there.

Discouraging leaps: Duck under

Many dogs can be taught muscle memory with a handy little trick I like to call the *duck under*. To get off the contact obstacle, the dog initially has to go under an arc you've made of PVC tubing or a hula hoop you've cut in half. Of course, the dog shouldn't really have to duck, but teaching her this trick ensures she doesn't leap on or off the obstacle. Here's how to use this trick both off- and on-course.

Off-course

To start teaching your dog to duck under away from the agility course, do the following:

1. **Steady the arc in the middle of an open floor or field.**

2. **Teach your dog to run under the arc by tossing a toy or treat bag through it as you trot towards it. Call out "Contact!" and try directing her using your bowling signal as she passes through.**

   If your dog doesn't follow the toy through at first, guide her through on a short leash.

3. **Reward her passage!**

On-course

Once you've got the rhythm on the ground, you're ready to use your prop on the actual obstacle. Proceed as follows:

1. **Place the arc at the base of the decline.**

2. **Position your dog at the high end of the decline.**

3. **Have a helper position the target and block your dog once she's on the obstacle.**

4. **Lead your dog down the decline as you say "Contact!" in an enthusiastic tone.**

   Muscle memory — it's a beautiful thing.

5. **Gradually phase off your dependency on the arc itself.**

   If your dog's memory ever lapses, bring it out and start over from the top!

If you're breaking a bad habit, relearning the right way will take longer, but it's a cheerful, fun way to go about the task. Hula, anyone?

This technique also works wonders for dogs who are prone to jump *on* to the contact obstacles. Place the arc just before the incline, and command "Contact" as you send your dog up.

Luring your dog into the zone: Jump over

Jump over has the same general flavor as duck under (see the preceding section), but with this strategy, you use a low jump positioned three strides from the base of the contact obstacle to encourage your dog to run through the contact zone so she can make the jump. A low 4- to 6-inch jump will do — the point is to get your dog to run through the contact zone, not to work on her jumping skills. Once your dog has discovered the joy of leaping, she won't be able to resist. Gradually phase off your jump dependency by removing the jump periodically, and then altogether. You can always resurrect the jump if your dog lapses.

Directing your dog: Follow the target stick

In Chapter 2, I discuss the target stick — a long, tent-like pole that a dog learns to trace and follow with her nose. It's a handy way to teach many tricks and can be used to direct dogs in agility, too. With regards to teaching your dog to pass through her contact zone, use the target stick like an arrow to habitually move your dog over the zones as you say "Contact!" The goal is muscle memory, creating a good habit that sticks.

Use your helper to spot your dog in the early stages. Sometimes the dog's focus on the target stick is so intense that she loses focus on her footing.

Cruising the Contact Obstacles

Getting your dog to touch the contacts on the obstacles is a matter of staying safe and racking up points. After you've decided how to encourage this safety measure (see the preceding section), you're ready to introduce your dog to the contact obstacles. In this section, I give you specific advice on introducing your dog to the A-frame, dog walk, and teeter.

The most common directions given for contact obstacles include "Frame it," "Teeter," "Walk it," and "Bridge." To remind your dog to stick her contacts or gauge her speed, include "Easy," "Touch," "Contact," or "Wait." Release your dog with the command "Okay!"

Acing the A-frame

Envision this: A dog sails through an agility field, racing toward the A-frame at good speed. She heads straight for this visual obstruction. At the last moment, she angles up into the contact zone, then actually catches air as she skywrites the letter "A." On the way down, she checks her speed slightly so she undoubtedly lands her downward contact, and off she goes, on to the next obstacle.

The A-frame is a truly beautiful thing. To condition your dog's movement, practice the dismount first (known as *back-chaining*) to help your dog learn to run through the contact zones. Once this is accomplished you can work on your approach to and motions over the frame as you chain together the rest of the steps, as follows:

1. **Find a helper for the initial learning stages.**

2. **Lower the frame to its lowest point.**

3. **Put your dog on-leash, and surprise her with food or toys.**

   When practicing on-leash, do your best to keep the leash loose. A tightened collar can throw your dog off balance and slows your dog on the very obstacles for which she needs momentum the most.

4. **Lure her up the frame saying a chosen command, such as "Frame!" or "Climb!"**

   If your dog balks, ease off. Let her watch other dogs manage the frame. Climb it yourself. Do whatever it takes to help her overcome that initial trepidation.

5. **Don't allow your dog to stop on the obstacle, even as you're rounding the top of it.**

   Encourage her to move quickly as you lure her forward.

6. **Once your dog is cooperating on-leash, raise the frame to its normal position (5 to 6 feet).**

Perfected that? Is your dog excited to scale the A-frame? You're in good shape. Now you're ready to practice off-leash. Your helper should continue to spot your dog. Move toward the frame using your familiar command and a bowling signal with the arm closest to the obstacle.

If at any point your dog reverts back or tests the crazy jump-off maneuver, back-chain it, and start over. Stay happy — you need your dog's pumped enthusiasm to complete all the obstacles on an agility course.

Staying balanced on the dog walk

The dog walk is a bit precarious. A raised, 12-foot-long, 4-foot-high, 12-inch-wide bridge extends between two planks — think balance beam for dogs. Mindful of their footing, few dogs will fall off if they walk it, but you will eventually be asking for speed. A slow and steady training regime ensures that your dog will be more mindful of her footing when you speed things up. Here's how to get your dog ready for the dog walk, both on and off the agility course.

Off-course

Introduce this fun game in a familiar, non-distracting setting. Here's what to do:

1. **Lay a wooden plank along the floor.**

   Ideally, set the plank against a wall to discourage darting.

2. **Use treats to lure your dog (or puppy) onto the plank on-leash.**

3. **Guide her down the entire length of the board, praising and treating your dog as you go.**

4. **Lead her straight off the end — straight off, every time.**

5. **Once she's comfortable with this exercise, begin to use your agility command word: "Plank!" or "Walk it!"**

6. **Direct your dog to run the plank in both directions, pairing the command with a bowling arm signal whenever possible.**

7. **Remove the leash, but keep enforcing the entire run — straight off, every time.**

8. **Elevate one end of the dog walk a few inches (use a big book or a brick). It will seem awkward. Go back to Step 2. Lure your dog on-leash as you command and reward her. Proceed through Step 7 using this configuration.**

9. **Now elevate both ends and repeat Steps 2–7.**

Got that? You're ready for the real deal!

On-course

When possible, introduce your dog using the *baby dog walk* — it's lower and safer than the raised version, and it seems less scary to your dog. Here's how it works:

1. **Find a helper to spot your dog on the opposite side of the plank.**

2. **Lure your dog on-leash, as you did for the A-frame (see the earlier section, "Acing the A-frame").**

If your dog is hesitant, create a Hansel-and-Gretel pathway with favorite treats. Use this grazing method a few times (and only if necessary) to encourage your dog's enthusiasm on this obstacle.

Stay even with your dog's head, and avoid quick motions, which may excite a departing leap. Praise your dog and urge her to pick up speed.

Hold the leash loosely to prevent unconsciously slowing your dog's progression.

When your dog can manage this obstacle with comfort, you're ready to try the official dog walk! For the raised dog walk, repeat the preceding steps, asking your helper to channel your dog's movements to prevent early slipping. If your dog does fall, stay as calm and cheerful as possible. As they say in horseback and bike riding: If you fall off, get up, get back on, and try, try again!

Teaching the teeter-totter

Okay — here's a twist. This obstacle moves. Like a seesaw. As your dog maneuvers it solo. Seriously! Your dog will shimmy up the board (with unbelievable enthusiasm), hold still until the teeter lowers, and then race off and onto the next apparatus. Cool beans.

To talk your dog into this one, teach it slow and steadily. If you rush into it, your dog may get truly spooked — making it much harder to tune into her inner teeter joy.

Getting your dog used to the motion at home

The following exercise piggybacks on the one I describe in the preceding section on teaching your dog the dog walk, so if you haven't mastered that one already, start there. Once your dog is comfortable walking on a stationary board, proceed as follows:

1. **Place a round object (like a dowel or PVC section) under the center of the board.**

2. **Place your dog on-leash, and guide her over the plank and straight off the end. Straight off, every time.**

3. **As your dog's confidence grows, work this homespun teeter off-leash, commanding your course cue, such as "Teeter!" and emphasizing the direction with a dramatic bowling signal directing your dog to the obstacle.**

Dogs can be startled by the bang of the teeter as it hits the ground. Condition your dog to the sound of the big bang. Ask a friend to drop a large book on a hard floor as you play on your homespun teeter. In addition, go to some agility competitions: Your dog will grow accustomed to the noise.

Practicing on the baby teeter

If possible, find a baby teeter to practice on initially. If your dog is sensitive to sounds, ask your agility instructor to wrap a pillow around the end of it to muffle the sound and lessen the startle factor.

Having a helper is a must. He or she will

✔ Channel your dog as you work her across the teeter

✔ Be there to lower the high end gradually as your dog crosses the apex of the teeter

Initially your helper should lower the teeter gradually so that the shift doesn't frighten your dog. As your dog's confidence builds, have the helper drop it partway, then further and further until your dog is conditioned to the movement.

Over 20 repetitions, your helper can incrementally let the board drop until your dog is maneuvering it on her own.

Practice this obstacle on both sides to simulate a true agility experience. Depending on where your next obstacle is located, you'll need to position yourself closest to it.

Making sure your dog hits the contact zones

Like the other obstacles, the teeter has two contact zones. The following three methods help you ensure that your dog hits her contacts every time:

✔ **Pause and drop:** This is a common and safe method, but if you're a speed freak — or your dog is — it takes the most time to complete. Here, you teach your dog to stop at the apex of the teeter and pause until it securely hits the ground (see Figure 14-1). If this method appeals to you, say "Wait" as your dog nears the center, and then say "Go!" when it's safe to proceed.

Figure 14-1:
Pause and drop on the teeter.

✔ **Run through and crouch:** With this method, your dog races right to the end of the teeter and crouches as it lowers to the ground, as shown in Figure 14-2. It's a speedy technique, but needs to be taught mindfully to prevent your dog from leaping off before the plank hits the ground.

• To lessen the initial intensity, ask a helper to guide the plank down as your dog races off the end of it. Gradually have your helper phase off his or her protective hold. Done incrementally, your dog will grow accustomed to the teeter's motion.

• Lure and/or guide your dog to the end of the plank on-leash. Command a quick "Down" or "Crouch!" at the end, and then say "Okay!" or "Go!" when the teeter is secure.

Always insist that your dog wait until you release her to race off the teeter. A free racer is likely to hurt herself by leaping off too soon.

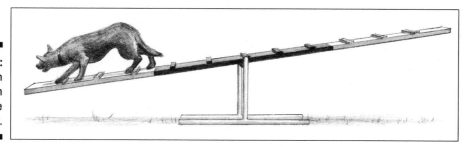

Figure 14-2:
Run through
and crouch
on the
teeter.

TIP

✔ **Two on–two off:** Employ the use of a target disc, strategically placed just beyond the dog's reach at the end of the teeter before you approach the front end of the obstacle, as I explain in the earlier section "Promoting pausing: Two on–two off."

Initially, back-chain this move to help your dog recognize your expectation.

Working up to the official teeter

Once your dog is eagerly moving across the baby teeter, you're ready for the true experience. Follow these essential steps (see the previous sections for more details):

1. **Lower the official full-size teeter to its lowest point.**

2. **Work with a helper, to both channel your dog and lower the high end of the teeter gradually.**

3. **Guide your dog on-leash until she's steady and confident with the obstacle's height.**

4. **Enforce a method of shifting the obstacle's weight.**

5. **Release your dog to dismount once the obstacle is safely on the ground.**

Raise the teeter gradually to its competition height, and remember — if your dog falls off or is suddenly spooked, stay calm. After checking for injuries, return to your early baby steps and ask your helper to spot your dog until she regains her confidence.

Weave Poles: Teaching the Ol' Bob-and-Weave

To be a spectator seeing a dog weaving in action is to witness a motion that blends excitement and beauty. You watch . . . holding your breath . . . letting out a scream of elated joy or crushed disappointment. With the weave poles, there's one way in and one way out — scripted and ordered, but subtle in execution. Can your dog do this? The trick is in the training.

Envision it before you begin. Your dog will enter the series of poles from the right — always from the right — no matter her angle or position on the field. Once into the poles, her concentration will lock, and her head will be down, focused on the task. Weaving through the poles, she'll exit from either side, depending on the number of poles standing. Then your dog will look to you for a directional signal and be off to the next obstacle!

It's exhilarating, this vision of you and your dog held together in the moment, but it won't happen overnight. If your dog is new to the sport, teaching her to navigate the weave poles may take months to shape. In fact, to many newbie agility dogs, the poles themselves are pretty unimpressive. Erect, motionless — good for peeing on perhaps, but they don't even carry much scent. It's your effort that transforms the poles into an obstacle that challenges your dog's competitive spirit. Your eagerness to train your dog to twist pole-to-pole inspires your dog's enthusiasm as she grasps your expectations.

In this section I offer a few different techniques that trainers use to introduce dogs to the weave poles. Read through and envision them before you begin.

If you're using the push–pull or collar weave techniques (I explain these in upcoming sections), practice with shortened poles. The idea of the poles looming overhead or the notion of getting impaled on a pole can seem threatening to a dog, who may grow wary of the poles! Always start with poles 24 inches apart. Although regulation distance may be tighter — 18 inches — you can narrow the spacing once your dog has mastered this technique.

Channeling: Letting the poles be your guides

Evolution can be a beautiful thing. Running water. Sanitation. For agility dogs learning to weave, the channeling method is heaven-sent.

This training involves a series of steps and some additional props, which can be bought or made. While it may seem more labor-intensive than pulling your dog back and forth through the obstacle, it guarantees a much more positive association to the poles and a far higher success rate. All that — and it's fun too!

Calling through

Arrange two sets of poles called *channel weaves* parallel to one another to create a channel. Your mission is to teach your dog to run down the middle at top speed. Here's how:

1. **Ask your helper to hold your dog at one end while you center yourself at the opposite end.**

2. **Place a target laced with treats at the end of the channel.**

3. **Call your dog, and reward her enthusiastically when she succeeds.**

   If she ducks out of the poles, have your helper run her through the channel to show her the goodies/toys — but don't give them to her until she has run the channel.

4. **Start shouting "Weave!" as your dog races through the channel, as shown in Figure 14-3.**

5. **Move the poles closer together until the channel is nearly brushing your dog's shoulders.**

   If, as you move the poles together, your dog consistently breaks out, you're proceeding too fast. Teaching poles can takes months, so pull the poles apart, and work with baited targets and a helper until your dog is ultra-clear that she's to run straight through the poles, not around them!

Figure 14-3:
Calling your dog through the channel.

You can purchase channel weaves that have various adaptations to enable accurate positioning as your dog learns to move through the poles. See Chapter 12 for locations to buy agility equipment.

Running alongside

After your dog has mastered running through the channel (see the preceding section), practice running alongside your dog as she runs the channel.

Shout "Weave!" as you run towards the poles. When your dog enters, continue to run alongside her — if possible, next to her head to encourage her to stay focused as she blasts through.

Run on both sides of your dog. Test your encouragements — does your dog do better if you praise her as she weaves, or does that over-excite her? If your dog runs out, send her back in and wait to praise her until she finishes the sequence.

Move the poles together until they are lightly brushing your dog's shoulders as she races through.

If your dog curves off-course, use a baited target at the end of the channel. Walk straight down the channel to place the lure, either leaving your dog in a "Stay" or holding her on-leash.

Now you're ready to teach your dog to weave. Follow these steps:

1. **Arrange the poles in a slightly staggered way, so that your dog won't actually have to twist to get through them.**

2. **Place guides on your poles, as shown in Figure 14-4.**

   Guides are low-set, curved tubing or wires positioned pole-to-pole to condition your dog to stay in the obstacle and to navigate it properly. Guides can be purchased or homemade: See Chapter 12.

3. **Let your dog sniff the guides before sending her through the obstacle.**

4. **Lead your dog to the poles. When she's eager to run, release your hold and shout "Weave!"**

   If your dog is leery of the guides, ask a helper to either bait her or hold her while you bait her through the first few times. If she jumps out of the obstacle, lead her back calmly. You can also guide her through the new arrangement on-leash — always rewarding the exit — until she's more comfortable with the setup.

5. **Run near your dog as you encourage her through the poles. Stay alongside her head, and reward her with a tossed treat bag or toy as she exits.**

6. **Once she's consistently making it through the obstacle, approach the poles off-leash from varying positions and distances.**

7. **Next, move the poles together in a straight line, eliminating the staggered arrangement. Space the poles 24 inches apart to start. Leave your guides in place, and practice with this new configuration (see Figure 14-5).**

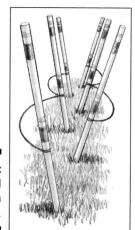

Figure 14-4:
Staggered
poles with
guides.

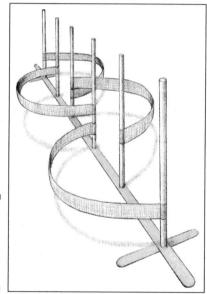

Figure 14-5:
Poles in a
straight line
with guides
in place.

It may seem odd to your dog at first: Lined-up poles are harder to differentiate.

In competition, the space between the poles can range from 18 to 24 inches. Set the poles at 24 inches during the initial stages of training, but gradually shorten the distance; then vary it so your dog will reliably perform the weave regardless of the spacing.

Always enter the poles from the right side. If your dog is confused, guide her through the opening with her collar or a leash. As she gets familiar with the setup and reliably enters the poles from the right side, vary your entry run from different angles or positions around the pole. The goal is to teach your dog how to properly enter the poles *from the right side*, no matter how she is approaching them.

Use a baited target positioned 3 to 5 feet from the last pole to encourage your dog's forward focus and/or toss a treat bag or toy forward as your dog emerges from the poles. If she looks to you for direction, keep your head down and don't look back or direct her. Dogs who look to their handler while weaving often miss a pole and are slowed from the task.

Is your dog performing her weaves with the guides in place? You're almost there!

8. **To phase off the guides, practice a random disappearing act. Begin eliminating one center guide at a time.**

    Did your dog blow through unhindered? Good, put that guide back on and remove another mid-section guide. Now put that one on and take another off.

9. **Now start removing two non-sequential guides (for example, the guides between the third and fourth poles and the eighth and ninth poles.)**

10. **The last guides to remove are those that help your dog navigate into and out of the weaves, the guides between the first and second and the eleventh and twelfth poles.**

The rule of thumb when removing guides is to be verrrryyyy flexible. If your dog dashes out — don't be afraid to put them right back on! Muscle memory strikes again. It's your goal to shape positive, successful muscle memory — but it can work against you if you allow your dog to make routine mistakes.

Traditional techniques

Before the enlightened technique of channeling, people used to just work their dogs through the poles holding their leashes or collars. Here's a quick summary of these techniques, which many trainers and handlers still use to teach their dogs the poles.

The collar weave: Grasping the collar

Grasp your dog's collar firmly, move her back and forth through the poles, and voilà — canine comprehension! When I first saw the collar weave method in practice, I thought "Huh?" It looked a little like rough manhandling, but the word is that for the right dog — one who can learn when shown a routine — and the right handler — one who's fit and coordinated — this method can be extremely effective.

Troubleshooting the weave poles

Here are some key mistakes people make when teaching the weave poles and how you can avoid them.

Many people are so enthusiastic when they're running a course that they make mistakes as they head into the poles. If directions come too late, the dog may have a hard time orienting to the poles; if the handler runs at the poles, the dog will have a hard time gauging herself to enter in.

To avoid this, dramatically signal and call out your verbal cue, for example, "Weave!" as your dog dismounts the preceding obstacle. Then slow down as you approach the poles to make a successful entry. As your dog performs the weaving motions, steadily move alongside her head: If you slow down, your dog may turn to eye you, and if you run ahead, she may break out to keep up with your pace.

Finally, be mindful of your motions during your dog's maneuvering. Something as absent-minded as a head scratch can break her concentration, resulting in a disqualifying run.

Initially, the poles should be shortened to allow the handler to reach over and guide his or her dog. Here's what this method looks like:

1. **The newbie dog sniffs the poles.**

2. **At the first pole, the handler grasps the dog's collar and steers the dog through the poles.**

3. **As the dog catches on, the command "Weave" is used and the pace increased to as fast as the dog and the person can move as one.**

4. **The handler gradually lets go of the dog.**

This method, when effective, may take a while to solidify. Many of the dogs get über-dependent on their handlers' interactions, and it can take many months to fade off the physical direction.

The push–pull: Using the leash

The push–pull method involves guiding your dog through the poles on-leash until she learns to weave on her own. When agility first began, this was the way it was done — a kind of show and tell. However, agility trainers have grown more enlightened since the sport's inception, and this method is rarely put into practice today. Nevertheless, it does work for some dogs.

Here's how the push–pull method works:

1. **Using the leash, the dog is maneuvered through the poles.**

   Fewer poles are used to encourage a dog's success rate.

2. **Rewards and treats are offered after a run-through.**

3. **The command "Weave" is added after the dog understands the expectation.**

4. **The leash is eventually removed as the dog's confidence increases.**

   A short leash may be left on to help redirect a missed turn.

5. **Eventually, the dog is encouraged to move in front and work solo as the handler shifts sides and directs from various angles.**

The issue with the push–pull is that it requires a lot of physical involvement and restrictive leash maneuvering. The constant handling slows a dog's natural pace . . . and we're back to that muscle memory concept again! Your dog's first association with the poles should be free-flowing and fast!

Chapter 15

Sequencing and Troubleshooting Your Agility Moves

*H*ave you ever longed to be the captain of a team? A movie director? A conductor? Here's your opportunity. Of course it would be fabulous if you could take a shrinking pill that would allow you to ride your dog like a pony — steering him to each obstacle as you directed and cheered him along. But alas, that would make it too easy. The challenge of agility is learning to steer your dog with words and signals alone. How can this be done? By following a formula of well-established moves that are easy to learn.

In this chapter you find out about these moves and how to teach your dog to sequence up to 20 obstacles in a row. No joke! Working piece-by-piece, slowly and steadily, you'll be out there directing your superstar athlete who'll look to you with eagerness and respect . . . and before you know it, people will look to you with awe and envy, thinking "What a harmonious pair!"

Before we finish, we troubleshoot problems that befall many newbie handlers. The good news/bad news here is that most problems result from human misjudgment and handling errors. But human errors are way easier to correct than dog-related issues, so don't fear your missteps!

Mixing Obstacles

Envision a competitive agility course — 16 to 20 obstacles laid out and pre-arranged in various positions and angles on the field. There's one starting point and one finish line. You and your dog come out together, focused on finishing the course in record time. If it's a true competition, you're scored; if it's just a test run, you're your own judge, using the results to gauge your readiness and skills.

Eventually, your dog — yes, your dog — will move seamlessly through a course of up to 20 obstacles. But don't get overwhelmed; it's a building process, and what seems far-fetched now will come together over time. Eventually, you'll move from the starting gate to the finish line in under three minutes.

Initially, you combine two or three obstacles your dog has mastered. Begin with two or three jumps in a straight line. As your dog masters the straight sequence, angle them in a slight curve. Then add a tunnel. Then a well-honed contact obstacle. Slowly chain more and more obstacles together and vary the positioning as you learn different directing moves. For instance, you may start with two jumps, and then toss in a third — or maybe a tunnel or contact obstacle — increasing the number of obstacles in your sequence.

At some point, you can set up your own mini-course. Please don't wing this, especially if your aim is competition. Figure out sequencing with the help of your agility teacher before you try it at home. Bad habits are hard to break — no matter how many legs you stand on!

You can visit the Agility Course Maps Web site (`agilitycoursemaps.com/CourseMap.aspx`) to see a few official sample courses that you can try after you know how to signal and direct your dog from one obstacle to the next. Look for a Novice or Starters level course — it may not be on the first page.

To figure out the spacing of the obstacles, speak to a professional. The distances between obstacles and the heights and measurements of the equipment are determined in large part by the size and breed of your dog.

Obstacle spacing is crucial when sequencing a course. If obstacles are bunched, there will be little flow because much of the dog's concentration will be wrapped around gauging his speed and approach. Spread them out and time will be lost racing back and forth, not to mention the dogs who can quickly outrun their handlers!

When setting up a practice course, there are a few general rules of thumb. The obstacles should be placed so that the dog has 18 to 21 inches of straight runway to approach all jumping, tire, or spread jumps; when a contact obstacle is presented, the dog should be directed to approach the plank straight on. When angles are added to the course layout, there needs to be a greater distance allotment to allow the dog to direct himself to the next obstacle. There are programs available online that allow you to design a course tailored for the coordinates of your location and the measurements of your dog. My favorite is Clean Run Course Designer 3, which you can explore at `www.coursedesigner.com/newcd3;jsessionid=2B356C4442826D69A48A4093E100873F`.

Directing Your Dog to Do a Sequence of Obstacles

When your dog is eager to practice, reliably consistent in completing an obstacle, and responsive to your directions, you're ready to begin *sequencing*, arranging more than one obstacle and directing your dog in a pre-determined order. There are two parts to this process:

- ✔ Teaching your dog to perform a series of obstacles, arranged in various fashions

- ✔ Learning how to direct your dog and choreograph your motions to minimize your footwork and maximize your dog's speed

When you begin sequencing obstacles together, include only those that your dog loves on a standalone basis. If he's having trouble with one, for example, the dog walk, you may begin some sequencing moves that exclude the dog walk as you continue to practice this obstacle individually. Remember, your dog's success is based on two things: his understanding of each obstacle and your proficiency in giving him clear, understandable directions.

Giving commands and hand signals

If you've trained your dog in obedience, check your inner drill sergeant at the door. Many of the tried-and-true obedience rules — use commands only once, keep your praise calm or you'll excite your dog, always work your dog on your left side — simply don't apply to this sport. On the agility field, you'll likely find yourself shouting. Excitedly, eagerly! You'll often repeat commands as you urge your dog through the course. Don't worry, you're not making mistakes! You're simply reflecting the nature of the game — and your verbal encouragement should bring on a canine-adrenaline rush.

When I trained in agility, I liked to think of myself as an ocean current — urging my dog's enthusiasm with words and motions to help her navigate the way. I knew she was excitable and athletic, and her focus was drawn in 15 directions all at once. It was up to me to keep her attention, to be the powerful current, so she would stay focused and ride the wave!

When you're out there, you have two tools at your disposal to steady your dog and direct his way: commands and body signals. Use both simultaneously, focus on your timing, and watch your dog looking to you to light his way. Here's how to use these tools:

- ✔ **Loud, excited, urgent commands:** As you navigate your dog around an agility course, give your directional commands with urgency and joy! Work on clear comprehension and directing body signals so your dog gets the visual on first command — think of your directions as a steering wheel that will . . . *eventually* . . . guide your dog across an ever-changing course configuration.

Always remember that you won't be penalized for repeating your command should you need to do so. Agility is *very* different from everyday life, so say your directions loudly, repeat yourself if necessary, and urge your dog with an excited tone!

✔ **Big body signals:** When you want to send your dog off in one direction or another, don't use a subtle hand gesture — use your whole arm as though it has the power to push your dog in the right direction. *Bowling signals* — large, theatrical, bowling-like arm sweeps — should be used to direct your dog every path of the way. When you want your dog to race to an obstacle, don't walk toward it; run fast and keep your eyes fixed on where he should go as you lean toward the obstacle with your whole torso and wave your arms to urge his excitement!

When signaling, use the arm or hand closest to the obstacles.

Commands and signals work in tandem. Your dog listens for your directions — and is powerfully swayed by your encouragement — but he depends on your signals to help him make split-second directional decisions. Think electricity here — the more animation you put out, the higher the voltage. Your dog responds to whatever you send out, so ramp it up!

Getting a handle on handling

While your dog may be eager to learn sequencing, it's up to you to simplify it. No matter how well he knows each individual obstacle, the new, multi-obstacle configurations will be something completely new — and your dog will be clueless.

Did you think you'd just wing it, running around the course telling your dog which way to go? The problem is that your dog can outpace you in a nanosecond, and if he loses sight of you, he'll stop in his tracks, utterly bewildered yet still pulsing with adrenaline — a tough combination. That's why learning to direct him with verbal and body cues is important.

Before you teach your dog how to move about an agility course, study and learn the human moves. Study the commands. See how they differ between the way you use them with your dog in your routine life and the way they're used to direct your dog's placement on the course. Once you see the science that belies the chaos, you'll feel more confident directing your dog.

Fortunately, there are fine-tuned "human" techniques for sequencing agility obstacles, and I cover them here. Take time to envision, learn, and practice them (when possible without your dog and in front of an experienced handler) before you begin! Once you embrace the integral role you'll play on the field and feel comfortable with the commands and body cues, you're ready to work with, teach, and direct your dog.

Teaching "Here"

"Here" is similar to the "Come" command — it tells your dog to run toward you. The difference? "Come" invites a reconnection — a stop-and-share-the-moment. Agility requires top speed — so "Come" isn't the ideal choice.

On the course, "Here" directs your dog toward you — then you need to quickly send him to the next obstacle, for example, "Tire" or "Frame." Practice your timing — shouting and signaling to the next obstacle before your dog reaches you. Invigorating!

"Here" should alert your dog to turn quickly in your direction. Wave a toy or a cup of treats, and shout "Here" as you step back away from your dog or call to him from a distance. As he runs in your direction, toss the object in one direction or the other shouting "Go left" or "Go right" as you do.

Getting your dog to lead out

Okay, I'm going to state the obvious. You have two legs; your dog has four. No matter his size, he'll outpace you. Rather than slowing his progression, teach him to *lead out* — to race ahead of you and take whatever obstacle you point him toward.

Most people tell their dogs to "Get out" or "Go on." Use one command consistently, and practice the playful exercises found in Chapter 12. Taught properly, your dog will grow confident racing ahead of you.

The "Get out" command rarely stands alone. Once you teach your dog to race ahead of you, you need to incorporate directions that send him toward the next obstacle. Use your dramatic bowling body signals to point to the chosen obstacle and a verbal cue to further specify it, for example, "Get out–Tire!"

The command "Get out" has a lot of uses on the agility field. Once your dog has mastered his obstacles and is eager to perform them, you may notice that you're holding him back . . . it's the two-leg to four-leg ratio. If your dog is outpacing you on the way to an obstacle, you can use "Get out" to support his initiative and vision. In competitions, you'll likely use this move at the very end of the course, sending your dog out to take the last series of obstacles and cross the finish line solo.

Using call-offs

Call-offs are used on-course to call a dog away from an incorrect obstacle. You may call out the name of the proper obstacle, "Go left or "Go right," or "Here" if you're well positioned to bring the dog toward the right one. Envision your dog running a course of preset obstacles. As he finishes one obstacle, he has two choices: run straight and take the obstacle that faces him, or turn and take one that is out of his line of vision. Left to his own devices, he'd probably choose the obstacle facing him, but agility is a team sport . . . and that's cool. Call-offs teach your dog to inhibit his impulses, turning away from one obstacle and prioritizing your directional cues. The excitement of trial agility is that each course is a maze that you navigate together.

While these maneuvers are generally used in higher-level competition, they sharpen even a novice dog's concentration.

"Go left," "Go right"

While this may sound like an exercise for the trick chapters, your dog can learn his left from his right — and you can use these commands to direct him on the field.

In Chapter 13, I introduce you to a fun game, tossing rewards to either side and routinely shouting out the appropriate cue. The following exercise challenges your dog's comprehension:

1. **Set up two low jumps side by side.**
2. **Walk out beyond the jumps 15–20 feet, while leaving your dog in a "Sit–Stay" facing the jumps.**
3. **Stand in the center of the two jumps.**
4. **Command "Here–Left," as you dramatically signal with your left arm and run across to the middle of the left jump.**

   If necessary, use a helper to guide your dog.

5. **Now practice "Here–right," reversing your directional cues.**

When you're working a course, use the commands "Go left" and "Go right" to help your dog navigate the obstacles, especially when the layout is tight and confusing.

Traps are never a good thing. An agility trap is set by positioning the exit of one obstacle in line with the entry of another but requiring the dog to completely avoid it. It's the handler's job to call his or her dog off-course and direct the dog to another, often less-obvious obstacle. A common trap involves the tunnel placed directly under the A-frame: Because the tunnel is a hard obstacle to avoid anyway, the temptation is compounded! Traps are usually found in higher-level competitions — but practice them early, just in case one crops up sooner than you expect.

Footwork on the field

When working a sequenced course, your dog's success or failure often depends on your footwork, steadiness, and clarity. If you mix up your signals or blurt out the wrong direction, you dog won't know what to do — he'll simply respond. This blind devotion can result in a missed obstacle or a dog who's off-course and/or out of sync. Before you get nervous, a quick review is in order — knowledge is power, no matter what your activity!

Deciding where to position yourself

As you direct your dog, you want to position yourself to minimize your mobility (too much activity disorients your dog) while staying visible to your dog as he maneuvers each obstacle.

Check out Figure 15-1. Identify the *inside line* or center footprint of the course versus the *outside line,* the course path that encircles all the equipment. The inside line keeps you on the inside path of the obstacles so you can direct your dog like the arms of a clock. The outside line puts you outside of the center, or on the periphery of the course. In trials, you'll have time to walk the course ahead of time to determine the best path for directing your dog during a competitive run.

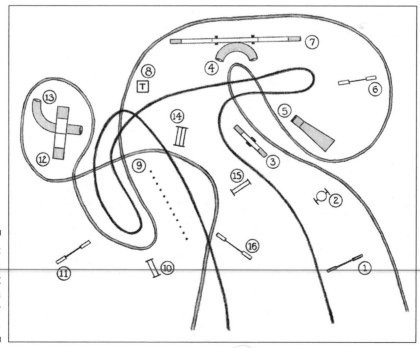

Figure 15-1:
Choose a
path that
minimizes
your
movement.

If your dog will "Stay" at the starting line, you can walk out and stand right next to the first set of obstacles. In this instance, you can call your dog right to you using the "Here" command.

As your dog is running forward, position yourself to direct him to the next obstacle. If you're able to stand next to a jump, for example, you can shout "Here–Over" to signal the jump. If the tunnel is next, you can just shout "Tunnel" as your dog clears the obstacle. With agility, you never know what configuration you'll get, but you'll have fun piecing it all together.

Practice your timing: As your dog is taking the preceding obstacle, move toward the next obstacle and command the next move. No time for a hug!

Working on both sides

At home, my dog Shayna always followed on my left side. When she approached me on the couch it was always to my left. When practicing tricks, she skewed her posture to the . . . you guessed it . . . left. But on an agility field, she would work on either side of me. As we moved quickly around the course, I would sometimes be in front of or behind her, often maneuvering my position to the left or right depending on the path of the prearranged course. As both of us moved through the obstacles, my positioning helped her orient her next move. From her perspective, my positioning was unpredictable, but watching me would help her orient herself on the course.

Throughout the learning phase, mix it up: Stand both to the right and left side of an obstacle. Use your vocal cues and body signals to guide your dog from one obstacle to the next.

Crossing your dog's path

As you learn to handle more obstacles, you may see a course configuration that shifts the inside line. To make the most of your footwork, you may need to cross your dog's path in order to direct him to the next move. Here's how crosses work:

- ✔ **Crossover (cross-in-front):** If you need to cross in front of your dog, the only thing to practice is timing. If you're too late, you may ram into your dog or pull his attention away from the next obstacle in the progression.

  Study each course before running it with your dog. When you determine a crossover is the best move — perhaps the tunnel is curved away from the center and upon exiting your dog will need to change direction, or the jump/contact obstacles are lined up so that your dog will have to turn off the center line to take it — envision making the cross the moment your dog has committed to the preceding obstacle, but long before he's completed it. Of course we're talking about milliseconds; nevertheless, cross early and cross quickly. Call out the next direction as your dog completes each obstacle — he won't skip a beat!

✔ **Cross behind:** Some courses change their inside lines in other directions that necessitate a cross behind. Here you would cross behind your dog as he took an obstacle in order to position yourself to direct his next movement. This would be a good move when your dog must turn 180 degrees to move to the next obstacle. The tunnel is the ideal obstacle with which to make this shift because it gives you that extra millisecond to make your shift, though you may need to make this move elsewhere as well. Similar to crossovers, steady your timing. Once your dog has committed to the obstacle in front of him, make your cross. Shout your next direction as your dog completes the obstacle and make sure he can find you the instant he reorients himself on the field.

Troubleshooting

Believe it or not, the hardest thing to manage on an agility field isn't your dog . . . it's yourself: your handling techniques, your footwork, and your temper. You'll have good days and not-so-good days. Like you, your dog will also have on days and off days — days he'll be steaming up the car windows and days he'd probably rather hang out at home. But the difference between you and your dog is that you can articulate your feelings. You can pop a couple of aspirin and call off the show when you're feeling under the weather. Your dog can't tell anyone anything — it's up to you to know your dog, to "listen" to him, to dissect his behavior, and to trace any inconsistencies to their root causes.

In this section, you discover how to read your dog's physical discomfort signs as well as how to troubleshoot problems like missed contacts and incomplete jumps. You also learn to take an up-close look at yourself to discover if, by chance, your handling is creating confusion. Many times it's important to ask what you're doing wrong!

Respecting your dog's physical inhibitions

If your dog is having trouble on the agility course, physical limitations are some of the first things to watch for. In this section, I discuss illness and injury as well as breed limitations, whether they're related to your dog's body shape or demeanor.

Watching out for illness and injury

Think of the last time you had an ache or a pain . . . perhaps it was that awkward misstep that tweaked your ankle, something you ate, or a sporty excursion that left you zapped of your normal get-up-and-go. You can't control everything; like everyone else, you learn to roll with the punches. Well, your dog is no different: He's not a machine. Trapped in his mammalian frame, his body can and often does suffer similar shutdowns.

Learn to read your dog — watch his movements, expressions, and behavior. If he's having an off day, consider why.

Take some time to know your dog. Watch him on his best day. Look at how he moves; count his strides as he approaches the single-bar jump; note the happy gleam in his eye as he watches you for his next cue. Record these moments in your head for comparison purposes. Also take his resting temperature, and pass your hands along his legs, hips, and joints. Notice how he reacts to your touch.

If you suspect injury or illness, caress your dog, speak to him calmly, and slow down. If you push him through or force him to practice, you may damage his enthusiasm for the sport, and thus your agility career. In my mind, it just isn't worth it. Treat your dog as you'd like to be treated.

Many injuries and illnesses require a veterinarian's attention. Reference Chapter 21 for physical conditions, and note those that do.

Recognizing breed limits

More dogs can think like a Border Collie than move like one. No matter how eager your dog is to do agility, respect his breed restrictions (see Chapter 11). Place obstacles at heights and angles that limit joint stress and maximize your dog's success rate.

If your dog is refusing ramps, balking at jump heights, or refusing to follow your lead, consider the obstacle's position: Has it changed or been raised? Your dog's physical stature dictates how obstacles are set for repetitive practice.

Next consider your training approach. Some dog breeds, such as the Border Collie, the Australian Shepherd, and the Golden Retriever, thrive on repetition. These breeds have their own inner dictator pushing them to strive for perfection. Repetitive practice helps them to nail a performance strategy.

Other breeds are not bred for repetitive work, including many instinctively driven breeds like Terriers, Nordic breeds, and Hounds. These dogs snub routine practice. When working them, the best reward for a breakthrough performance is a few days practice-free. They seem to encode success better when they're allowed to sleep on it!

Handling the dog who acts up

My daughter's a ham. She's delightful, funny, and loves a big audience. Why talk when you can shout? Why stand when you can dance? Why sit still when you can make a funny face and scratch your dog's head with your big toe?

Dogs have personalities, too. Many of the dogs who act up are comics: smart, energetic dogs that dance on the edge of good behavior. These dogs hear laughter like praise — a chuckle guarantees a repeat performance. Personally, I find it hard not to be jealous — what a wonderful way to deal with life's stress.

So how can you manage your comedian? Try the French-fry cure. Find an über-treat that your little jokester will do back flips for: a mind-bending reward that he only gets on special days. Use your chosen tidbit to keep his attention: He'll soon learn to focus on you no matter what the distractions.

Treat rewards are allowed during practice runs and match competitions. Though you can't reward your dog in the midst of a trial run, you can certainly give him a jackpot at the end!

If your dog acts up and you're left empty-handed, remember that a dog who acts up is still a little stressed. While having all eyes on you is a bit of a thrill, it can be jarring! Though he looks like the life of the party, he's jumbled up inside. Stay calm and remember these cardinal rules:

✔ Don't look at him. Any attention — negative or positive — will egg him on. Let him freak out and keep a watch out of the corner of your eye, but don't shout or track his movements.

✔ When your dog calms down, sit down and tie your shoe (or pretend to). If he's still wary of you, try the "Ouch — I'm really injured" move. Shriek like you've been shot. When he looks to see what happened, fall on the ground and clutch your leg in pain. When he runs over, calmly reach up and grasp his collar; then put his leash on and walk off the course. Keep your cool, lower your head, and look at the ground. Don't reconnect or let him have anyone's attention for at least five minutes: No attention or treats for that performance.

Of all the things that can happen during a trial, having your dog go wild is perhaps the most embarrassing. While controlling one's temper is a tall order, lashing out at a dog only guarantees more stress and an inhibited agility performance.

Fixing obstacle errors

Your dog may be having trouble with the obstacles — flying past the contact zones, refusing to do an obstacle, knocking down bars on the jumps, or choosing to do an obstacle out of order. In this section, you find out how to get your dog back on track.

Missing contacts

Some dogs dream of flying. Fast-paced and excitable, these dogs love a sequenced course and race to beat the clock. Contact zones — on the A-frame, dog walk, and teeter obstacles — slow them down. While the mindfulness exercises found in Chapter 14 can help a dog to gain more awareness of your expectations and condition muscle memory, touching the contacts can still be a struggle in the heat of the moment.

If you're having trouble, try teaching your dog a cue word during your practice runs: a word you can repeat during trials, such as "Easy." This word can help remind your dog to slow down just enough to nail his targets!

Refusing an obstacle

Dogs always have a perfectly good reason for refusing an obstacle. If only they could speak! The most common refusals happen when

- A dog is sick or injured.
- He doesn't have enough runway space.
- The obstacle is raised too high.
- The signals or directions are unclear.
- He makes an unsteady entry onto a ramp or tunnel.
- He's momentarily confused as to which obstacle to take.

Many of these faux pas are handler's errors, and this is good news. If you're having these issues, look at how you can change. No one can learn these steps overnight — it took me a long while! Find a master to watch and critique you. Listen and learn — your dog will be so glad you did!

Double check to ensure your dog is in good physical condition and the obstacles are set to ensure his success: Nothing is more frustrating for dogs than being pushed beyond their limits. They want a clear run too!

Knocking down bars

Dogs can get in a bad habit of knocking down bars as they clear jumps. Some nick the bar with their hind legs, often not even realizing what they've done. Other dogs push off with their hind legs or bump the bar on the way up. What to do?

First, stay calm when it happens. If you rush in and give your dog attention — negative or positive — he'll often do it again just to get you to come near him. Retrieve your dog, review the jumping section in Chapter 13, and follow these tips:

- Consider your practice jumping height. While you don't want to work at competitive heights full time, it's important that your dog be able to clear this height reliably. Set the jump to this height every fifth run to ensure your dog can clear it.

✔ If your dog is oblivious to the fact that the bar is coming down, check the bar itself. Is it made of lightweight plastic? Fill the bar with sand, and plug the ends of it. If it's already weighty, toss some screws in a soda can and tie it to the end of the bar. When your dog hits it, he'll know.

✔ Each time your dog knocks down a bar, ignore the mistake and set your sights on teaching him a better approach. Set the bar low to encourage full clearance, and reward him like a newbie. The contrast will make it clear. Slowly raise the bar to its appropriate height.

Going off-course

A dog is off-course when he takes an obstacle out of sequence or takes one that's not included in the course. When this happens, always stay calm. Consider whether your dog is mature enough to run a sequence.

Another mistake that can lead to an off-course reaction is a habit that's created during practice runs — when a handler either calls or sends his or her dog back over a missed obstacle. Always approach obstacles from a predetermined direction. If your dog misses an obstacle, step away and call him to your side. Take him back and start from the top.

Reining yourself in

Sometimes, you just have to let your dog go — to run the course, that is. Playing the role of an overbearing parent causes your dog to become too dependent on you, and it can get you and your dog disqualified in competition. In this section, I discuss problems with guiding your dog too closely.

Overhandling

Overhandling is a term used in competition where the handler uses his or her body or voice to over-direct a dog or to prevent the dog from making a directional mistake. Often when dogs are first learning how to sequence a series of obstacles, a leash is needed to guide them through the equipment. Initial off-leash maneuvers often involve physical direction too. Hands are used to manipulate motions, spot efforts, and reassure insecure dogs. Praise and rewards are doled out on a regular basis.

This newbie involvement can lead to interactive dependency and insecurities if overused. When dogs aren't weaned from this constant reassurance, solo performances can be hard for them to manage.

In competitions, overhandling may lead to disqualification. Constant interference or a dog's overdependence on your guidance conveys to all spectators that you aren't quite ready for this challenge. Don't push yourself; don't pressure your dog. Review the weaning steps in Chapters 13 and 14 to ready yourself for a complete course run-through.

Blocking

To envision a blocking move, imagine a dog racing out of the tunnel and having two equally distant obstacle choices. Instead of guiding him with a command or signal, the handler simply stands in front of the off-obstacle's entry path. That's *blocking* — it's fudging with a capital "F."

Blocking is another form of overinteraction. Though slightly more subtle than overhandling, no one can fool a judge. If practiced too often, a dog will grow mindfully aware of the body position of his handler and use it to determine his course.

Chapter 16

Competing in Agility: Ready, Set, Go!

While no one has to enter trials or earn titles to enjoy the sport of agility, if you stick with it and get pretty good at it, you just might find yourself daydreaming about a timed run and ribbons adorning your walls. I've been to many agility events. They're a blast, whether you're a spectator or a participant. Search for one in your area and spend a day there. If you're anything like me, you'll be shouting, cheering, and whooping in no time. Wear your best jumping-up-and-down shoes, and expect to go home hoarse.

Competition is 10 percent hype and 90 percent concentration. Most people get a few butterflies on judgment day, but your dog will be oblivious to what's going on. Think of competitions as social gatherings where you meet people who share similar interests. Cop a breezy attitude as you wait your turn, then focus on the task at hand as though you were running the sequence in your backyard or on a practice field. Confidence is catching — the less you worry, the more comfortable and eager your dog will be on-course.

Remember that the only difference between you and your competitors is experience: Once you learn the ropes, it will be your turn to reach back and guide a newbie. For now, gratefully look to others for help.

In this chapter you find what you need to know about agility events, from the difference between match and trial competitions to how to register and prepare yourself. Though no one will say you must participate, don't be surprised if you get drawn in!

You can't fool your dog! If your nerves get the better of you as you prepare for competition, your dog will attribute it to the circumstances at hand. She may grow so concerned about you that she wouldn't dream of leaving your side to concentrate on her performance.

Entering Agility Events

Once you feel confident sequencing and completing an agility course, you may feel drawn to competition, earning titles, and going to weekend events. Let me forewarn you: The first steps can seem a little confusing. There are match trials — kind of like practice runs where you're judged as though you're at an official competition, but it's unofficial in the sense that you can't earn points towards an agility title. True title-earning competitions are run by agility organizations, five of which are listed in Table 16-1. Each organization has its own standards for competition as well as levels, classes, and titles, which can best be understood by studying their "Rules and Regulations" guidelines or visiting their Web site. In this section, I outline differences between matches and trials, give you an overview of several national agility organizations, provide definitions for class competitions and titles, and tell you how to sign up to compete.

Choosing between matches and competitive trials

It's helpful to understand the difference between matches and competitive trials. *Matches* are organized and run by regional agility clubs that set up pseudo-competitions to prepare teams to work toward earning titles. While the structure is similar to that of a competitive trial, these weekend get-togethers are held to give dogs the opportunity to practice sequenced runs and to help newbies prepare for the rigors of competition in a fun, friendly environment.

Matches are a great place to work out any kinks in your routine. These events are publicized, but far less official — there's often no premium list (see the section "Signing up" for more details) or advance registration. They may draw big crowds, but a good run — although earning applause and congratulations — doesn't earn you points toward any titles. Matches are an excellent way to practice your routines: Once you feel confident on the course, you'll be ready to move into more competitive venues.

On the other hand, *competitive trials* are very formal. You must register early, and you'll receive a premium list. It's important to sign up early because only a certain number of trials are run on any given day. Seasoned agility dogs can earn a great many titles from many different organizations. In the next section, I list five different sanctioned agility clubs. There are other organizations, too: Look for ones that have a strong hold in your part of the country. Once you go to a trial, your name will be put on a list and you'll get routine mailings of competitive events held in your area.

Agility titling lingo

The rule of thumb in listing titles is that championship titles, as well as all UKC titles, are placed in front of a dog's name, while all other titles are placed behind it. Lolly's Bit-by-Bit NF, a Golden Retriever who gained her Novice Fast title, is the daughter of U-ACH ADCH Lolly's Special Girl OA, OAJ, OAC, AXJ, who has many titles to her credit. (*Note:* U-ACH = UKC Agility Champion; ADCH = USDAA Agility Dog Champion; OA = AKC Open Agility; OAJ = AKC Open Agility Jumpers with Weaves; OAC = NADAC Open Agility Certificate; AJX = Excellent Jumpers with Weaves.)

Finding events through agility organizations

Agility matches and competitive trials are put on by various agility clubs and organizations. By the time you're ready to enter a match or trial, you'll likely be involved with an agility group that can point your way to an event. But if you're going solo, you can find information about agility events in your area by contacting national agility clubs, as listed in Table 16-1.

If you can, find an organization that reflects your ideals and enter the competitions it sponsors. All agility organizations are not equal. Each one stresses different parts of the game. Some organizations emphasize speed, while others stress safety. One organization has longer completion times, thus enabling slower dogs to succeed, while another takes breed limitations to heart — varying jump heights to accommodate your dog's size and body type. See Table 16-1 for a list of the top five agility organizations in the United States and what they focus on.

Table 16-1 National Agility Organizations and What They Emphasize

Organization	Emphasis
The United States Dog Agility Association (USDAA) www.usdaa.com	This club promotes agility worldwide, sponsoring a yearly event in America that attracts competitors from around the world. The USDAA also sponsors a team to compete internationally. The courses are competitive, and events are divided into two categories: Championship Level, which consists of top-level courses that challenge a dog's vitality and the team's choreography; and Performance Level, which is more recreational.

(continued)

Table 16-1 *(continued)*

Organization	Emphasis
American Kennel Club (AKC) www.akc.org	The AKC offers a challenging course while allowing course times that accommodate a variety of breeds and sizes. The AKC also offers a Preferred class that lowers jump heights and lengthens the course completion time to benefit veteran (senior) or special needs teams.
United Kennel Club (UKC) www.ukcdogs.com	The UKC allows more time than the other organizations for each team to complete the course. The jump heights are lower as well.
North American Dog Agility Council (NADAC) www.nadac.com	This group stresses speed, with course times that challenge even the best teams. Specialty classes allow for dogs and human handlers of all ages and abilities.
Canine Performance Events (CPE) www.k9cpe.com	CPE is the newest organized club on the scene. It emphasizes the fun and recreational side of agility. The courses are challenging without being too rigorous. CPE offers a host of games that spotlight passions for various obstacles.

Checking out the classes of competition

In the United States, many organizations hold weekend matches and gatherings to judge and time the performances of individual teams, consisting of one dog and her handler. Each organization has standard classes and nonstandard classes. *Standard classes* include obstacles with varying degrees of difficulty. *Non-standard classes* are games that emphasize different aspects of the sport.

Standard classes

A team who has mastered each of the obstacles in agility and can sequence them in varying order may choose to register and compete with a recognized organization. Each organization awards titles to dogs who successfully run a set number of courses. Additionally, these groups divide registrants into three competition levels: beginner or novice, advanced, and expert or masters. (*Note:* The names of the levels may vary, depending on the sponsoring organization.)

A beginner or novice level course consists of 13 to 15 obstacles, widely spaced for ease of communication and completion. Once a dog masters the beginner's course and has three qualifying runs, she gets a title that represents this accomplishment. Good dog!

The next challenge is the advanced course, and then comes the master course. These courses contain 18 to 20 obstacles, arranged closer together. Faster, more difficult maneuvers are required, testing a team's ability to discern and direct. Fewer dogs can master the advanced course, and only when a title has been achieved at that level can they test their skills at the master (or expert) level competition.

Non-standard classes

When competing for titles, standard classes are the bread and butter of the weekend trials; non-standard classes are the fancy jam spread on top. Talk to anyone involved in agility and they'll tell you that the non-standard classes — better known as *the games* — are where the fun is. Each one has its own unique spin:

- **Jumpers class:** The course in this game is a fast-paced one, consisting of jumps, jumps, and a few more jumps. A tunnel or two may be tossed in for fun, but nothing that slows the pace of the run.

- **Jumpers with weave class:** This course is identical to that of the Jumpers class, with weave poles tossed in to spice things up.

- **Gambler's class:** This game assigns points to each obstacle. Pause or contact obstacles have the highest point value because they take the longest time to complete. In Gambler's class, the handler is allowed to choose the first part of the run, and the goal is to gather as many points as possible. At the end of the first period a buzzer sounds, and the team must finish a set of pre-assigned obstacles known as the *gamble*. This last half of the course must be directed from a distance. Gambler's class is for advanced teams only.

- **Snooker class:** This game is color-coded. A course is set up, and obstacles are tagged with two or more colors. The course may be divided into blue and red obstacles, or the color scheme may be more complicated, with multiple colors used to challenge the participants. Whatever the rules of the day, in a Snooker class, a team must perform a color-sequenced run to play. For example, the rule may be red:color:red:color:red:color, until all the obstacles are complete: Here you would direct your dog over a red-flagged obstacle, then a color, then a red, and then a color until all the obstacles are complete. Sound confusing? It's meant to be. Like the Gambler's class, this one is for teams who have a well-tuned understanding of the sport.

- **Relay class:** In Relay class, multiple teams work together. Teammates may run half the course or each team may run a full course before handing the "baton" off to their teammates. Times are added collectively.

There are two types of team events:

- **Relay pairs:** Two teams work together.

- **Relay teams:** Three or more teams work together.

Signing up

Fun matches rarely have a premium list, and many are okay with drop-ins. These gatherings stress learning, practicing, and troubleshooting.

But when you choose to enter an organized trial event, you first have to write in to get a *premium list,* which includes all the information on the specific event, including

- The entry form
- Where and when the event is
- How many teams can register (Hint: register early)
- Height divisions
- Class specifics
- Awards
- The names of the judges
- Registration fees

Your first registration form may seem like it was written in a different language. Sure, the name and address section is pretty straightforward, but then you get to the class specification section, and that can be utterly confusing!

Each group has its own competition levels and rules for registering for the various classes. If you're new, you'll register for novice or starter divisions. The actual names of the various levels differ depending on the organization: Some simplify the divisions with easily recognizable words, such as beginner, advanced, and masters; others have more obscure definitions. Don't be put off — once you learn the terminology, it will be old hat. Take a few minutes to study the standards for each competitive level.

There will be a registration fee for each trial you enter. The fees run from $12 to $50 per run (this is not set in stone), and generally no discounts are given for multiple classes or more than one dog.

Preparing for a Trial

Once you've signed up for a trial, stay steady in your practice runs. Don't suddenly ramp up the intensity of your workout or increase the duration or frequency of your agility practice. If you change what you're doing, your dog will react either by shutting down (that is, by ignoring you or running off) or worse, injure herself. If you're concerned about a certain obstacle, troubleshoot it far in advance of a trial — not the day before. Nothing temporarily confuses a dog more than a sudden switch in handling, and while it may be necessary to modify your approach, avoid doing it right before a trial. In the following sections I give you some hints on how to get yourself ready for competitions and arrive with a smile on your face and a wagging tail beside you!

Packing for the trip

If you've never been to a trial, prepare yourself. You need to pack for both yourself and your four-legged teammate.

Though the premium list will usually tell you where the event is, consider the location — is it indoors or out? Will the events be run in a large open field, offering little shade or protection from the elements, or in an un-air-conditioned or poorly heated auditorium? Bring along whatever you can to keep yourself and your dog comfortable, such as water, a mist sprayer to cool off your dog's foot pads, and/or a comfortable mat for her to lie on.

If traveling is in the plan, pack an extra set of car keys just in case you need to leave your dog in the car for any reason. That way, you can leave your automobile running with the air conditioning or heat on to ensure your dog's comfort and stability.

If staying overnight is unavoidable, find lodging that welcomes your dog and respect the rules of the establishment. Bring vaccination records, poop bags, bowls, and a crate or familiar bed to ensure your dog is relaxed and in good spirits for your big day.

When packing your overnight bag, remember you're packing for two. Your bag should include comfortable clothing and shoes. Dress for the day: Nothing is worse than being uncomfortable when you're in the spotlight. You'll likely be waiting your turn, so bring a comfortable folding chair, some favorite snacks, plenty of water, and some extra cash. Bring sunblock if it's sunny or rain gear if the weather's iffy. Tuck a copy of the registration form and premium list into a folder for quick reference.

Your dog's bag should include her food, bowls for water, familiar bedding, and a crate (if she's accustomed to one) or a gated pen in case you must leave your dog alone. Bring anything that will help your dog feel at home in this unfamiliar place: favorite toys, a cozy blanket, treats, and so on. Most importantly, keep yourself calm — nothing reassures your dog more than your happy mood.

Before you set out to your first event, check with your veterinarian to ensure your dog's vaccinations (including bordetella or kennel cough) and heartworm testing are up-to-date. Competitions bring together all sorts of dogs: Make sure yours has a clean bill of health coming and going!

Arriving on the scene

The first thing to do when you get to a trial is to take a deep breath. Look around you. Find the registration table, and see where people are setting up their dogs. Be mindful of your four-footed partner — remember, she can't "see" where you are — she needs to sniff about to feel most at ease. Give her a five-minute walk around to sniff her surroundings, and let her relieve herself and settle in before you check in and set up.

Before you unpack, walk to the registration table and check in. Be polite to the stewards, many of whom have volunteered their time — your gratitude will be greatly appreciated. If you didn't receive your confirmation ahead of time, you'll get one at this time. Review it, determine when the judges' briefing and walk-throughs are held (see the upcoming section "Getting to know the course"), and note the running order and locations of the various classes. If you don't get a course diagram, ask where you can view it. Respect the organization's rules and regulations, and arrive on time to allow your dog to get set up before the trials begin.

At the registration table, you'll receive an arm band or sticker that will high-light your dog's class specifics. Wear it on your shirt or shirtsleeve.

Setting up

When you first arrive at an event, you'll need to find an area to arrange your-self and await your run. Find a setup location that's within the allotted "dog" area. Be respectful to those around you; don't crowd others or take up too much space. Here are some other rules:

- Always clean up after your dog.

- Never touch or allow your dog to interrupt another dog without the handler's permission.

- Be mindful of what you say. Stick to the "positive" rule — if you don't have something nice to say, keep quiet.

- When your class is running, watch respectfully. Get to the ring early and check in with the steward. Not only will you be ready for your turn, but your dog will also have a chance to settle into the routine.

- Remove training collars before you get onto the grounds. Many organizations require that dogs run naked (without a collar) or with a flat-buckle collar.

- Speak and act respectfully to the judge. Say hello and follow his or her directions. If your dog acts up or you need to leave the ring early, always ask the judge to be excused.

Helping your dog relax

There are dogs, like people, who are comfortable in any surrounding any time. Mind you, this is the exception, not the rule. Young dogs in particular need more time to relax in new surroundings — older dogs are seasoned by years of experience. Remember, nervousness is contagious! So, breathe deeply. Yes, you. Keep your tone relaxed and comfortable, and stay focused on your surroundings. Act like you've been in this situation before and you know just what will happen and what to do. Your dog will take her first cues from you.

Keep your dog on a leash and limit your commands. Over-commanding your dog pre-trial will put her on edge. The best thing to do is to lead her to a quiet, shady spot if you're outdoors and sit down. Pet your dog calmly when she relaxes next to you.

Give your dog a displacement bone — a favorite chew that she hasn't seen in a while. Like kids, your dog will appreciate having something to do.

Don't stare at or talk to your dog unnaturally. Your focus will trigger her worry. In your dog's mind, your attention communicates that you're unsure of yourself and anxious.

Warming up

Before you perform, give your dog an adequate warm-up. A few laps around the facility or a 5-minute toss will get her muscles moving and ready her for her pending workout. If you're animated on the course, stretch yourself out as well. Gear up for the day by waking both your bodies up gradually. This interaction will also help to offset your jitters and help your dog to relax.

Getting to know the course

Every organization invites you to know the course at some level before you compete. You'll either be invited to walk it solo or with your dog, which is best to do on-leash. One organization, the UKC, allows you to walk your dog through the entire course to familiarize her with their equipment designs and setup. Rules and standards for every organization change, so request and read through the club's rules when you register, and be on time for these pre-performance programs.

Judges' briefing

Before running the course, you and other competitors from your group will have a change to meet with the judge/judges at the *judges' briefing*. How many judges there are is determined by the type of event and the level of competition. You'll hear the rules, course time, and any specific expectations. If you have any questions, this is the time to ask them.

The walk-through

On the day of competition, the judge will arrange the obstacles in a unique pattern. You'll have ten minutes to walk through the course with other competitors to determine your strategy. The course obstacles will be numbered with orange cones to help you organize your footpath more easily.

As you're walking the course, imagine your dog is with you. Try to determine her speed and dependency on your position. Can you send her ahead to jump while you line yourself up at the next obstacle? Where might you need to cross over or cross behind? Have you perfected the *get out* so that you're able to send your dog out to cross the finish line ahead of you?

Agility trials begin when your dog crosses the starting line. If her "Stay" command is rock solid, you can leave her at the start and position yourself near the first set of obstacles; otherwise, you'll need to run with her.

While you can get some clues watching how more experienced handlers orchestrate their performance during the walk-through, their dogs may be capable of different maneuvers than your dog is ready for. Stick to what you know on competition day — don't try anything new!

Familiarization: Bringing your dog in the ring

Some organizations allow you to walk the course with your dog, memorizing the run before the competition begins. You must make careful note of the exact pattern of the obstacles; points are lost if you miss an obstacle or do them out of order. The layout in Figure 16-1 represents a sample novice course with 16 obstacles. A team approaches the starting line. At this point, the handler can stand with his or her dog or leave her in a "Stay" to get a better directing position on the field.

Contact familiarization (AKC)

The AKC allows handlers to take their dogs into the ring ahead of time to familiarize them with the contact obstacles. It's a good idea to do this on-leash because it can be a chaotic mix out there. During this period you're permitted one walk-through per obstacle. If your dog bails or balks, that's it. You had your turn: Don't test the system or you may be disqualified.

This is a good time to work on your dismounts, reminding your dog to hit her contacts no matter when, no matter where.

Course familiarization (UKC)

Here you're able to walk your dog through the course on-leash ahead of time. Determine your footpath and urge her through with the same words you'll use during your trial.

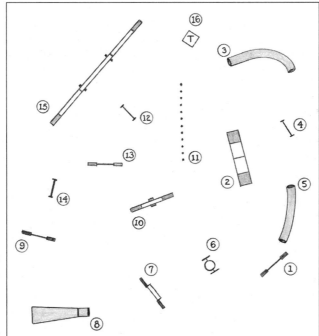

Figure 16-1:
A sample
course
layout.

The UKC organization uses several obstacles that differ slightly from other, more mainstream agility equipment. On UKC courses, you may see a crawl tunnel, a swing plank, and a sway bridge. See the sidebar in Chapter 11 for more information about these obstacles.

Ready, Set, Go! Running the Course

As your running approaches, calm yourself with positive visualization. Remember that dogs can sense your emotions: When you're nervous, you omit a faint but dog-detectable "worry odor." Not only will your dog sense it, it will unnerve her too. (If you find nerves to be a real problem, check out *Conquering Ring Nerves: A Step-by-Step Program for All Dog Sports,* by Diane Peters Mayer [Howell].)

Get to the starting area as the previous dog is midway through her run. When your time is called, remove your dog's leash and/or collar and hand it to the entrance steward.

Give a final good-luck pat to your dog, and get ready to run. Remember, you're not allowed to touch your dog or give her other incentives, such as food or toys, once the clock has started.

On your mark, get set, GO! No matter what happens between the starting and finish lines, you'll both be okay. Life is good. You have each other. Do your best. You'll either have a good run or something will run amuck.

No matter what happens, use every experience as a learning tool. Following are some frequent mishaps. Should they happen to you, you'll be in good company.

- **Course confusion:** Believe it or not, you may get your obstacles mixed up in the middle of a run. When your heart is racing, it happens. Look for the numbered cones, or pause, gather your senses, and reorient yourself.

- **The "oops" touch:** In your head, you know that you can't touch your dog during the run. Those are the rules, no exceptions. But then, oops . . . you can't help yourself. Though you'll likely be disqualified, it happens to the best of teams. Continue your run, politely stopping if the judge signals you. (Politely apologize to the judge — and your dog — before leaving the ring.) It's a truly embarrassing moment — try to avoid it.

  You'll need to handle your dog if she falls off an obstacle and hurts herself. Turn to the judge, acknowledge your decision to leave the ring, and go calmly. Some courses have an onsite veterinarian; in other cases, the workers will direct you to the nearest animal hospital.

- **Failed attempts:** Your dog may refuse an obstacle. Maybe once, maybe twice — maybe until the judge urges you to go on or leave the ring. Perhaps it's the way the sun is shining on the obstacle or the funny smell of coffee that someone dropped while setting up the obstacle earlier in the day. You may never know — you're not a dog. Regardless, repetitive refusal results in a non-qualifying run (also known as an NQ). Let it go, and either go on and finish the course or look to the judge for his or her preference.

- **On-course pottying:** This is a not-too-uncommon faux pas which can often be avoided if you walk your dog five minutes before her turn. Some dogs eliminate in order to release stress. If you're a newbie or you've been traveling or tense yourself, this may be a signal of the novelty. Don't feel too bad — even experienced dogs are known to do this from time to time. You will be excused from the ring immediately, however.

- **Table run-off:** They're the longest five seconds on the agility field — the ones the judge counts out loud while your dog holds still on the pause table. If she jets off, return her quickly and the judge will count again. Remember to wait until the judge says "GO!" to release her.

- **Off-course runs or missed contacts:** While you're running your dog, she may miss a contact, run off-course, or skip an obstacle altogether. Don't stop! While most judges catch every misstep, some don't, and even though your penalties may net you an NQ, give your dog the pseudo-thrill of finishing the course. Your dog won't know the difference. Your positive elation will have a far greater and lasting impression than your getting all bummed out about a few lost points on the score card.

Ask other more-experienced teams how they deal with NQs and how you can help your dog improve. (Also turn to Chapter 15 for some advice on trouble-shooting.)

Relaxing Once Your Run Is Over

Once your run is over, cool down your dog by giving her a few sips of water, spaced a few minutes apart, until she seems content, and then take her on a walk. Like people, dogs' bodies are geared for competition and need a cool-down period to shift back into relaxed mode.

Of course, you're done, so you can pack up your car and go home — especially if you feel you're out of the running — but when possible, stick around. Cheer on other competitors, and learn from their successes or mistakes. Study the judge — you'll likely see him or her again, and it's helpful to learn how each analyzes a run. Most of all, take the time to make some human friends. You'll share a common bond right off the bat! Having friends to offer support, practice with, and learn from makes this sport safer for your dog and a lot more fun!

Judges' signals

During a run, the judge will use raised arm signals to score the performance. Here are a few common signals and what they mean:

✔ **Closed hand:** This signals a refusal.

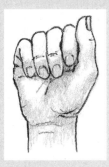

(continued)

(continued)

✔ **Open hand:** In the AKC and UKC, this signals an off-course; in the USDAA, it symbolizes any standard fault.

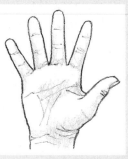

✔ **Two hands raised:** This registers a disqualification in AKC and UKC; for the USDAA, it automatically deducts 20 points from the total score.

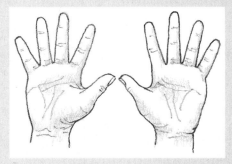

✔ **A "T" symbol (or two fingers raised):** This represents a table fault in the AKC.

If you hear a whistle blow, stop and face the judge. A whistle can mean different things. The judge may disqualify you, he may order a fresh start, or he may have another reason for breaking your run.

Part V
Getting Hip to Hobbies, Events, and Earning Credentials

The 5th Wave   By Rich Tennant

Jerry bought only one type of pet food. NASCAR Kibbles – The High Performance Dog Food.

In this part . . .

Part V covers a host of sporting activities you can engage in with your dog, from ballgames, flying disc fun, and flyball (Chapter 17) to carting, sledding, and joring (Chapter 19). In Chapter 18 I introduce you to obedience, herding, hunting, and tracking trials, plus training your dog to provide protection or to serve as a therapist for people facing challenges. Energizing and fun, these activities involve teamwork and strategy and can be practiced alone or with other enthusiasts. All the activities in this section are for dogs everywhere, purebred or not.

Chapter 17

Sharing Favorite Sports and Backyard Games

Dogs can make the best playmates . . . I remember all the fun I had with my dogs when I was growing up. No matter where we happened to be, you wouldn't have to look hard to find a ball or a flying disc!

If you and your dog love to be active, look around and be creative — there are many ways to experience the rush of activity as you share your mutual enthusiasm. In this chapter, you explore modified versions of games like softball, football, "Hide and Seek," and soccer. You also discover two activities that have evolved into full-fledged dog sports open to pure and mixed-breed dogs. These sports — disc dog and flyball — hold competitive events and invite team sport interaction.

Ball Game, Anyone?

If you're a sports fanatic, why not include your dog in your next practice round? Although your dog may never play soccer, softball, or football in competition, you can invite him to join you in a little backyard play. All he needs are a few retrieval skills (see Chapter 7 for details), a ball, and you — his coach and teammate.

Bear in mind that dogs, like kids, can get injured during play. Rein in your competitive streak, at least when your dog's involved, and remember to have fun!

"Snoopy Soccer"

You need one or more players (plus your dog) and an empty plastic soda bottle or a ball (½ the size of your dog's front leg) to play "Snoopy Soccer." Most dogs love to play with a ball or soda bottle, wrestling and knocking it around with their feet. They also love to use their mouths, which is fine if you just want to mess around. But if you're planning on teaching the next four-legged soccer star, I suggest you go to your local pet store and get an indestructible ball made especially for dogs.

"Snoopy Soccer" is a goal-oriented game. Here's how to play:

1. **Get your dog interested in pawing and nosing at the bottle or ball by knocking it around gently with your feet.**

   Have fun! Kick the toy around with your dog until there's a real challenge to see who can reach the ball first. Interact in random patterns around a field.

2. **After your dog seems focused on this interaction, set up a 6-foot-wide goal.**

   Use trash cans, poles, or anything else you happen to have handy.

3. **Start close to the goal post and stand facing your dog. Run backward or forward toward the goal — whatever encourages your dog to move into the goal zone. Shout "Goal!" as your dog knocks the bottle or ball toward/into the goal.**

4. **Kick the ball or bottle to your dog and say "Goal!"; click (or say "Yes!") and offer a treat for the slightest movement your dog makes toward the goal.**

   In the beginning, click and reward all movements toward the goal. Slowly space out the rewards, encouraging your dog toward the goal before you reinforce him. For details about using a clicker, see Chapter 2.

5. **To get him to go for the goal, kick the bottle or ball toward your dog and 3 feet in front of the goal, and command "Goal!"**

6. **The second your dog crosses the line with the bottle or ball, click and reward him.**

Now try passing the bottle or ball at farther distances from the goal. Pretty soon you can introduce him to the team!

Be careful of your dog's face when kicking things around. If you're just playing soccer to fool around, use two balls and kick the one your dog's not playing with.

Softball

Our dog Whoopsie loves to go to the ball field with our neighbor Ethan, a pitcher-in-training. Ethan's warm-up sessions include three participants: himself, his Dad at bat, and Whoopsie playing outfield.

Though a softball is adequate, you may want to play with a rubber ball, appropriate for your dog's size, so as not to instill an addiction for your game ball. Include your dog at any position, pointing to and leading him to his spot and telling him to "Stay." Each time he chases down a ball, have another player call out "Fetch" to direct his retrieve!

The best position for a dog is the outfield. The risk for injury is much greater when you place your dog in the infield . . . and heaven knows he won't know how to pitch!

Football

Initially use a miniaturized version of a football to get your dog accustomed to the oblong shape. Your first tosses should be short, and you should angle the center of the ball towards your dog's mouth. Gradually angle the ball as you'd normally throw it, then use "Stay" to distance yourself from your dog.

Your next goal is to teach your dog to go out and to run for the goal once he has caught the ball: First use the target flag to teach your dog to "Go long" by placing the flag increasingly farther from you. Next, use the target flag to teach your dog to run through the end post. Place visible poles at the end of the field you're running towards. Command "Target–Touchdown!" as you run with your dog toward the end posts.

Practice this complex sequence inside first (if your mom or spouse will allow it), then alone in the backyard. After your dog has mastered these maneuvers, add more players one at a time until you've united a whole team!

When playing football with a dog, never encourage physical contact. Touch football only!

Inspiring Flying Disc Fun

If you've ever played Frisbee and noticed your dog eyeing the disc eagerly, this could be the game for you! Whether you choose to compete in sponsored disc-dog trials or just play for fun whenever the mood strikes, I promise you one thing: Once you've introduced your dog to the game, you'll never look at your disc, your dog, or your tossing technique the same way again.

The sports version, often called *disc dog,* isn't simply a measure of technical skills. Sure, part of the competition is about pure speed, distance, and accuracy, but points are also earned based on showmanship. A well-choreographed routine set to music, in which you and your dog show off a variety of skills and tricks, not only racks up the points but will also bring the house down. If you want to bond with your dog, this is a great way to practice teamwork — and put all that trick-training to good use!

In this section, I go over basic training as I introduce you and your dog to the joys of the disc. Should the competition bug bite, I explain a little about disc-dog events too.

Spotting a good disc-dog candidate

In Chapter 3, I go into great detail about how certain dog breeds are built for certain activities, and how a dog's personality and passions should weigh into your choice of adventures. Now the time has come to decide if your dog is really a good disc-dog candidate. Some are, some aren't. Here's how you can tell:

- Does your dog love to chase things that move?
- Does your dog have a lot of energy and love to play?
- Is his body well angled and athletic?
- Has he learned a good retrieve? (If not, review Chapter 7 and then read on.)
- Will your dog come reliably off-leash? (If not, review Chapter 4 and then read on.)

This sport is extremely hard on a dog's body! Repetitive jumps and landing really put a strain on a dog's back and joints. Canines with a boxy shape, such as English Labs and Bulldogs, can suffer strain and injury when asked to leap up for a disc in flight. Although these dogs can enjoy the sport, the tosses should not be higher than their heads to avoid the jarring strain of landing. If your dog has dyplasia of any sort (hip or elbow, for example) avoid this activity. This sport is best for well-angled body types who are fit and eager to play.

If you have an older dog at your feet, you're not too late. As long as your dog is stimulated by a flying disc, any age will do. Of course, all dogs must know basic obedience skills to move on to anything more complicated, including flying disc games, but I'll leave that up to you.

You can encourage "disc desire" in puppies when they are 2 or 3 months old by feeding them from the disc and rolling the disc in play, but don't push them to jump and leap. Until puppies are 12 to 18 months, their growth plates are still forming, and injuring them can halt their natural growth. In addition, reliable eye-mouth coordination takes months — sometimes even a year — to set in.

Flying saucers: Choosing your disc

There are many discs on the market: discs with a thumb pad, discs decorated with bone designs, small discs, donut-shaped discs, and fabric discs. The best one for your purposes is a solid disc made of either a fabric or durable plastic. Although solid plastic discs are used in competition, if you're not planning to go for the gold, consider using fabric discs. They're not only softer on your dog's mouth, but they're also safer on a day-to-day basis.

Pups can start with a 3-inch-diameter disc and grow up to a 9.25-inch-diameter disc, the regulation size.

Wash the disc from time to time to keep it clean. Discourage your dog from chewing his disc: Once it becomes punctured or frayed, toss it out.

Training for the catch

In this section, you discover how to teach your dog the basics of catching and retrieving a flying disc. You start with teaching him the grab and then work up to fetching and catching.

The grab and release

According to Peter Bloeme at Skyhoundz (www.skyhoundz.com), follow this basic format when training your dog to catch a disc:

1. **Treat the disc as a dinner plate. It looks like one anyway, right?**

   For a week, feed your dog on the disc, picking it up after each meal to prevent chewing. Wash and hide the disc until the next feeding. When it's time to play, use a new disc that hasn't been used as a dinner plate. Keep the praise high every time he grasps the disc.

2. **Roll the disc on the ground.**

   At first, you want your dog to concentrate on tracking the disc. Doing so is easier if the disc is rolling in front of his nose versus flying by above his head. Once he can snatch it off the ground, you'll be primed for the toss. To do the roll, point your finger along the disc's edge, curl it along your bent arm and then flick it off so that it rolls off your arm and onto the ground. Practice in areas where you won't be distracted, tussling with the disc and praising any interest in it enthusiastically.

3. **Tease your dog playfully with the disc, saying "Get it."**

   When he grabs it, tug _lightly_ to ensure a secure grip before you get him to release it by clicking, offering food, or giving tremendous praise.

4. **Play "Keep Away."**

   Show your dog the disc and run a short distance before allowing him to grasp it. To see whether your dog is sufficiently in love with this new object, turn it upside down and slide it a short distance away from you on the floor. When your dog grasps it, praise him tremendously.

   Initially, your dog probably won't want to give the disc back to you. That's okay; worry about the good retrieving skills after you've nailed the grab.

Don't spin your dog around like an airplane when he has a grip on the disc. Rough tug-of-war matches encourage behavior you don't really want to see in any dog. To teach the fast "Give," use a clicker/treat or second disc. Praise your dog the instant he catches the disc, then produce the reward to entice a quick release. Shout "Give" as he lets it go, then reward him immediately.

Fetching the flying disc

Once you're sure your dog loves the disc, it's time to teach him the return:

1. **While indoors, roll the disc on the ground and encourage your dog to bring it back to your side. Say a release word like "Give" as you click and offer your dog a treat.**

   If your dog isn't food-motivated, you can use another disc to inspire a drop and switch. Practice in a non-distracting room. For more help, review the fetching exercises discussed in Chapter 7.

2. **Practice inside tosses in larger rooms as your dog reliably brings the disc back to you.**

3. **After your dog is cooperating inside, practice outside within an enclosure.**

4. **Practice with five or six discs, encouraging your dog to return each one to you before you toss the next one.**

Tossing tips

This section isn't for your dog; it's for you. If you can't toss the disc predictably, your dog will give up on you. So find yourself a good disc, prop this book open, and dive in!

1. **To grip the disc, place your thumb on the outside edge and curl your fingers under the lip.**

   Don't white-knuckle the thing. A firm grasp will do. Carry it around the house for a couple of days. Now you're talking.

2. **Achieve the proper stance by placing your feet shoulder-width apart. Point the shoulder of your tossing arm at the object you're aiming for.**

Although you'll end up shifting your weight forward as you toss the disc, you should always keep some weight on each foot.

3. **To project the disc forward, firmly grip the disc, thrust, snap the wrist, and release.**

   The toss must be smooth, sharp, and even. Make sure your shoulder stays aligned with your target, your head is up, and your eyes are looking out ahead of you.

   Of course, this isn't the only way to toss a disc, but it's a start. Once you're totally accurate in your toss, go out without your dog and play around with your grip. Practice with a friend who might know some finer points.

If your dog doesn't start bringing the discs back to you, go to a small room or fenced enclosure and roll the disc on the ground. If he looks up and acts confused, encourage him with "Get it" and try one or all of the following:

- ✔ Ignore him; make a call or balance your checkbook. Dogs don't like to be ignored. When your dog picks up the disc, herald the moment!
- ✔ Excitedly grab the disc yourself — you're showing him how to act!
- ✔ Start playing with another disc — in effect, you're saying, "I have a better one anyway."

Wait until your dog starts taking real interest before you progress to more distracting areas. Make or buy a 25–50-foot line and knot the end for easy handling. Progress through your early lessons quickly to remind your dog that he's expected to do the same thing outside that you taught him inside. If he decides to make a break for it, step securely on the end of the line. Don't correct him; he'll do the math when he hits the end. Stop the lesson and ignore him for 10 minutes.

Day-to-day lessons should be short (no more than 10 minutes) and begin with short tosses. Once your dog has figured it out you can progress to the challenging tosses in minutes. Remember, dogs are like people — they need to get warmed up.

Dressing for the part

In his book *Frisbee Dogs,* Peter Bloeme points out from personal experience that appearance, for both you and your dog, really makes a difference for the freestyle round of disc dog competitions. Dress for the weather and coordinate with your dog. For example, red shows off a black dog well: Tie a red bandanna around your black dog's neck, and you'll be the envy of everyone. Just don't get too carried away — a fancy costume for your dog could interfere with his performance! And make sure the rules allow your dog to wear those accessories.

Catching

All this, and the art of catching still hasn't been covered! Up until now, your dog should be fielding grounders and rollers only. To teach the catch, I defer to expert Peter Bloeme again.

Start by bringing your dog to the bursting level with disc excitement. Tease, tug, roll — whatever charges him up. Then do the following:

1. **Kneel down and lightly toss the disc at your dog's nose. If he misses the catch, pick it up.**

   Let him have the disc only if he catches it. His days of grabbing the disc off the ground are over.

2. **Your dog may get frustrated, but continue tossing the disc at his nose until he starts to grab the disc in the air.**

3. **Practice with several discs tossed out 3 feet, and then slowly shorten the time between each toss.**

4. **After he masters the quick toss, slow it down again, tossing the disc to your left. When the left is good, go right.**

To tie in the catching with the running and tossing, begin by holding the disc above your dog's head as you tell him "Get it." Make sure you *always* hold the disc parallel to the ground, the way the dog will see it on the fly. When your dog grabs on tight, let go. Remember, if your dog drops the disc, pick it up silently and start again. No more grounders.

Now make a short toss here and another one over there. Progress slowly, don't be afraid to go back a step or two in the lesson, and remember the two Ws: water and warm-up.

 The most common disc-dog injuries are not sprained limbs or broken legs. They're dehydration and mouth injuries. Many dogs bite their tongue reaching for the disc or cut their mouth on a cracked edge. And I can't stress enough the importance of always offering fresh water.

Introducing disc tricks

Whether or not you and your dog participate in competitions, you can blend your mutual passion for the sport with clever "disc tricks" that are fun to learn and perfect. In competition, disc tricks are showcased in the "Freestyle/ free flight" round. Take a look online, plugging "canine freestyle frisbee competition" into your search engine.

In competitions, points are awarded for many tricky moves, including the following:

- **ZigZag:** In this trick, the dog turns at sharp 90-degree angles to snatch multiple discs being tossed repetitively.
- **Vaults:** The dog vaults off his handler's leg, back, or torso in order to catch a thrown disc.
- **Team Motion:** The handler and the dog must coordinate moves, such as the leg weave and the synchronized spin.

Getting serious with your disc: Disc-dog competitions

Getting good? Want to test your skills in front of a crowd? Go for it! Competitions are usually held at different levels. Community affairs are less serious gatherings, but lots of fun. The home crowd is always the most supportive, too. For true competition, however, you need to travel to events to compete at the Regional and Open levels. Dogs winning at the Open level qualify for World Finals. Too cool!

In competition, there are generally two rounds:

- **Quick Toss:** In this round, each participant is given one disc and 60 seconds, and is scored on the top five best catches. Extra points are given for mid-air catches, and the dogs are further awarded points for three-pawed (in the air) and two-pawed catches.

  In competition, this test is called many things, including "distance," "throw and catch," and "toss and fetch" — no matter the name, the standards are the same.

- **Freestyle:** The freestyle round is a choreographed performance, generally set to music, where each team is given 1 to 2 minutes to strut their stuff. Each team is allowed to carry five discs onto the field for their performance.

  A team of four judges scores each team based on the following criteria:

  - **Overall presentation:** Did it please the crowd? Were the movements synchronized? Was it fun to watch? Was there disc flow? Was there unity between the person and the dog?

- **Athleticism:** Was the dog in shape and up for the challenging moves? Did any of the tosses put the dog's stability at risk? Did the dog fall trying to grasp the disc?

- **Wow factor:** Each performance is judged according to the "Wow" moves — jaw-dropping, radical moves and tricks that are performed amidst long tosses and multiple throws. Expect to see body vaults, trick sequences, repetitive tosses, and full body spins — and if you're watching, let your excitement spill over. Shout "Wow!" when you feel it — your enthusiasm will boost the dog's score!

- **Success:** Success is a relative thing, even in a dog's world. While it does refer to completed tosses, it's not the only guideline. Dogs who are performing difficult maneuvers, and yet occasionally miss a catch, may still score higher than a solid performance with less difficult moves.

Bottom line? Freestyle scores are awarded based on the difficulty and the originality of the material. While you can teach your dog to catch a Frisbee, only a true passion for the sport will shine in the Freestyle competition!

In competition, points are deducted if a movement puts the dog at risk of injury. There are three endangering movements that the judges penalize:

- ✔ **Contortion:** A dog is forced to contort his body to such an extreme as to risk injury.

- ✔ **Slam:** A dog's body slams into the ground at any point during competition.

- ✔ **Buckle:** A dog's legs dramatically buckle upon landing, resulting in a full body collapse.

For more information about training your disc dog for fun or for competition, visit my favorite site for everything flying: www.skyhoundz.com.

Giving Flyball a Whirl: A Retrieval Relay

Flyball is quite unlike anything else you've ever seen. This fast-paced sport combines a relay race, hurdles, and a dog-activated box that launches tennis balls. Seriously. Dogs have to run, jump, hit a trigger to release the ball, retrieve, and race back to the starting line before the next dog can race off.

Of course you don't have to be a competitor to enjoy the sport. Flyball boxes can be purchased or made and are a wonderfully interactive way to play into your dog's passions.

In this section, I explain how flyball works, include a few tips on introducing your dog to the sport, and give you some info on competition.

Flyball history

Flyball was invented in California in the late 1970s. Legend has it that flyball was first introduced to millions of Americans on *The Tonight Show*. Soon afterward, dog trainers and dog clubs were making and using flyball boxes.

In the early 1980s the sport became so popular that the North American Flyball Association (NAFA) was formed. This association is now the worldwide authority on everything flyball. Many other organizations have formed throughout the world. The United Flyball League International (U-FLI) has a large following here in the states. To find other groups devoted to the sport, enter the word "flyball" and the country's name into your search engine. Flyball enthusiasts are everywhere!

Envisioning the course: How flyball works

Here's how flyball is played in competition: Two teams, of four dogs each, race against each other and the clock. Lights, like the ones used in drag racing, flash as a symbol to the teams. Each dog runs one length of the course, which consists of jumping over four hurdles to a ball box (see Figure 17-1). In a dramatic pounce, the dog hits the box with his paw, which releases a ball. A quick catch and the dog races back over the hurdles to the starting point and the next dog in the team is released. Swoosh! The whole jump and catch series happens in seconds. Very exciting!

The team that finishes with the fastest time and the fewest faults wins that series of jumps, known as a *heat*. The winner is the team that wins the best two out of three or three out of five heats.

Before you go to your first gathering, here is some lingo you should know:

- ✔ **Teams:** Each team can include as many as six dogs and as few as four. Although only four dogs are permitted to compete in each heat, they may be interchanged due to strategy or injury, and the jumps adjusted accordingly.

- ✔ **Jumps:** The jumps are set according to the organization officiating the event. Overall the jumps are positioned according to the smallest dog on the team.

- ✔ **Passing:** This is the relay part. Rather than a starter pistol, flyball competitions use lights to indicate the equivalent of "On your mark, get set, go!" The dogs are actually released from a distance behind the starting line, so they're running at full speed when they cross the line. As the first dog returns, the second dog is released from behind the line, so that as the first dog crosses the line coming in, the second dog is crossing the line going out. And so on. The point is that the release must occur at the same time as the return. In a perfect world this would work every time, but it's not a perfect world.

✔ **Faults:** Early passes, missed jumps, and dropped balls receive faults. Depending on the severity or number of faults, dogs must run again. Though it would seem disastrous, often both teams collect enough faults to warrant a second run-through. Funny, but the dogs don't seem to mind!

Deciding whether flyball is right for your dog

Flyball is open to all dogs of pure or mixed heritage that are at least 1 year old and agile and athletic enough to stay the course. To play flyball solo or get in with a group of dogs and form your own four-member team, you need a spirited dog with a slight obsession for tennis balls. Sound like someone in your home? Other advantages are a penchant for running, jumping, and coming when called. Coming when called? Yes! This is one sport that can actually improve your dog's reaction to the "Come" command.

Which breeds do best in flyball? Herding and Retrieving breeds predominate at competitions. Some think small dogs would slow down a team. On the contrary, they're often the heroes. Because the jumps are adjusted to the height of the smallest dog on the team, a small dog's presence improves overall scores.

Getting equipped for the fly

If you'd like to set up a flyball course of your own, the first thing you need to get is a ball box. This contraption, shown in Figure 17-2, releases a ball the instant your dog steps on the lever. The original box had an extending arm that gave a few dogs a black eye. Poor things! Today's boxes are designed to release the ball safely and give your dog the proper footing to turn back toward the finish line.

A flyball box is easy enough to make. How to construct a box is detailed in a great book by Lonnie Olson, *Flyball Racing: The Dog Sport for Everyone* (Howell). Plans for or actual flyball boxes can also be purchased through www.flyballequip.com.

You can buy or make hurdles, too. If you're just playing for fun, try erecting them with a handful of cereal boxes and some brooms from your pantry closet.

For thorough descriptions of the equipment, visit `flyball.org`.

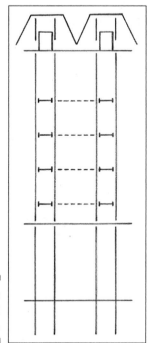

Figure 17-1:
A flyball
course.

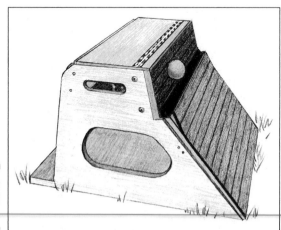

Figure 17-2:
A flyball
box.

Training your dog for flyball

The rest of your dog's flyball career will be affected by his proper introduction to the ball box. Just like any other kind of training, this is a step-by-step process. Your dog should have jumping and retrieval skills — see Chapter 8 for hints on teaching your dog to jump, and Chapter 7 for instructions on a proper retrieve.

Targeting the box

Dogs, like people, develop muscle memory when learning new tasks or games. To teach your dog how to land on the box, review the target training from Chapter 2 until he's reliably touching the disc with his nose or batting it with a paw. Use a bright piece of duct tape for this activity, and have your dog touch it reliably before centering it just over (for nose targeters) or under (for paw targeters) the ball release hole.

Introducing the ball action

Now you're ready to show your dog how the box works with the ball.

1. **Show your dog the box first, with no expectations or training commands. Place a favorite ball on top of the box to be discovered.**

2. **Pop the ball out the hole with your free hand and praise your dog if he grabs it.**

3. **Now hide the ball in your hand, releasing the ball if your dog paws it. Start saying "Hit it" when his response becomes a habit.**

4. **Placing ball after ball in the trigger cup, trigger it again and again, to get your dog used to the action.**

5. **Load the box and let your dog investigate it. Ecstatically encourage any pawing interest.**

   If your dog presses too lightly, trigger the ball for him. If your dog gets hit in the face or gets spooked, adjust the cup hand so that it releases at a different angle, and go back a few steps in the training routine.

Once your dog puts it together, it's time to teach him to make a quick catch.

Making a quick catch

To ensure your dog will be able to catch a ball being hurled toward him at top speed out of a box, make sure he can catch your fastball first.

1. **Start indoors in a quiet room. Take a few balls and toss them at your dog one at a time. Say "Catch" and gradually increase your speed.**

   If your dog needs a food reward to motivate him, give it to him. Most dogs get distracted with food around and are excited enough by the game.

2. **Outside, hold your dog still, command "Stay," and chuck a ball in front of him. Make him wait until it stops moving; then scream "Go!" As your dog gets to the ball, call his name and turn and run away from him at top speed!**

Running the course

Now you're ready to introduce the course. Say "Over" as you start running over low hurdles, placed 10 feet apart, with your dog. Position the hurdles 5 inches below your dog's withers.

The next step involves letting your dog go — gradually! Run over the first three hurdles, saying "Over!", and then let him take the last one on his own. Now let him go after jumping two hurdles, then one. It's easier to master if you've corralled your course or erected it to channel him through the course.

Now ask a volunteer to hold your dog at the starting point, as you stand at the box and call your dog over the hurdles and to the box. Then switch positions and send your dog as your helper eggs him on — and then you call him back!

Repeat the preceding procedure, placing the ball in the box, having the volunteer encourage the dog with the words "Hit it," and calling the dog back over the hurdles. Yes!

To strengthen your dog's focus, work around some distractions. Ask family or friends to mill about and make noise.

Flyball requires so much pumped enthusiasm there's no room for discipline! Redirect your dog's behavior, but don't scold.

Getting your dog used to teammates

If you ever want to make your soiree into flyball a social calling, your dog will need to work around other dogs. Practice with another enthusiast, and hold the dogs side by side as you send them for their balls one at a time. (See Step 2 under the "Making a quick catch" heading.)

Competing in flyball

Are you and your dog quickly becoming addicted to the sport of flyball? It's easy enough to find a local club: Just enter "flyball" into a search engine and brace yourself. Flyball is spreading throughout the nation.

In competition, teams are divided into two classes: regular and non-regular in the NAFA or standard and special classes in the U-FLI:

✔ **Standard/Regular:** In the regular class, the team may consist of four dogs from different backgrounds.

✔ **Special/Nonregular:** Specialty classes include variety, singles, and pairs classes. Non-regular classes include Peewee, Veterans, and Multibreed.

In both organizations winners are awarded honors, but individual dogs can earn points for clean heats (no faults) based on their team's times, whether or not they win. If a team runs the course in 32 seconds, each dog gets one point; under 28 seconds wins 5 points, and under 24 seconds wins 25 points.

If your dog becomes fleet of foot and begins winning titles, you'll have the pleasure of getting to add initials after his name. (How does "Jane Smith, MD, owner of Fido Smith, FD, FDX, FDCh, FM, FMX" look? Pretty impressive, huh?) A dog earns the title Flyball Dog (FD) at 20 points, Flyball Dog Excellent (FDX) at 100 points, Flyball Dog Champion (FDCh) at 500 points, and so on. For a complete list of titles and the points you need to earn them, go to `flyball. org/flyball_titles.html`.

Before you send for your first competition application, send for the official rule book. To obtain a copy of the official rules or to inquire about teams in your area, contact NAFA at: 1400 W. Devon Ave. #512, Chicago, IL 60660. Or find them online at `www.flyball.org`.

Chapter 18

Participating in More Hobbies and Breed-Specific Events

In This Chapter

▶ Putting obedience to the test

▶ Competing in herding, hunting, and tracking events

▶ Doing volunteer work together

Do you have a dog whose instincts won't give her a rest — digging, chasing, herding anything that moves? Whether you have a mixed-breed or purebred dog, there are clubs and hobbyists across the world whose dogs share the same passion and who love to meet, train, and hone their skills — whether competition is the focus or not.

In this chapter, I give you an overview of some of the competitions, certifications, and hobbies you and your dog can check out together. Whether you're looking to earn titles in competition, get a little help on a farm or ranch, or do some volunteer work, you have plenty of options.

Read over the categories in this chapter, see which one fits your dog's drive, and then find a group close by that can mentor and guide you in the learning process. Think of it as another rung on your training ladder: like taking your dog to college. With the basics in place, your dog is ready to learn a profession! And remember: No matter how long it takes for your dog to master a skill, the only things that win brownie points are a good temperament, mindful behavior, and an upbeat attitude, whether you're walking on two legs or four!

Letting other breeds into the mix

It used to be that the American Kennel Club (AKC) only sponsored breed-specific competitive events for purebred dogs. Those days are coming to an end even as I write this. In early 2010 there will be classes for mixed-breed dogs in obedience, agility, and other sporting events. Check out more at www.akc.org.

The United Kennel Club (UKC) also sponsors obedience and agility trials, weight pulls, dock jumping, protection sports (like Schutzhund), hunting programs, and terrier races for dogs of pure or mixed ancestry, provided that they're neutered and have applied for a "limited privilege number."

Visit the UKC at www.ukcdogs.com for more information. The UKC's breed classification for mixed dogs: They lump them all under the heading "AMB" which stands for American mixed-breed dogs.

While both of these clubs (the AKC and UKC) were founded to organize and track the population and certifications of purebred dog registrants, there is an organization that heralds the status of mixed-breed dogs as well. Check it out — visit the Mixed Breed Dog Club of America (MBDCA) at www.mbdca.org.

Showing Off in Obedience

Basic obedience training (see Chapter 4) is something everyone should do — it's a lot like teaching ESL (English as a second language). Teaching your dog the right response to 10–20 words allows you to direct, socialize with, and enjoy your dog throughout her lifetime. Everyone who gets a dog owes his or her pet this much.

But obedience doesn't have to end there. You can enter obedience competitions and show off just how well you and your dog communicate with each other. In this section, I introduce competitive obedience and the more light-hearted sport, Rally-O.

Getting serious with competitive obedience

Competitive obedience takes obedience training to a whole new level. Structured and defined, there are set exercises, a 200-point ideal, and judges who score each performance.

Competition in the obedience ring is divided into three levels, each more difficult than the previous one:

✔ **Novice:** Companion Dog (CD). For this certification, dogs must compete in walking sequences at their handler's side, a long "Sit" and "Down–Stay," "Come" exercises, as well as a few other routines to prove their training and impulse control.

✔ **Open:** Companion Dog Excellent (CDX). Here dogs are expected to work off-leash and retrieve in addition to the skills required for the novice title.

✔ **Utility:** Utility Dog (UD). At this level dogs are to respond to signals only, locate and retrieve articles, and perform jumping skills.

At each level, a competitor is working for an obedience title. To receive an obedience title, a dog must earn three legs in competition. To achieve a *leg,* a dog must score at least 170 points out of a possible 200 and get more than half the points available for each exercise.

Having fun with Rally-O

Like the idea of competing, but a little turned off by the seriousness of it all? Consider rally obedience, or *Rally-O* — a virtual "Simon Says" of obedience. This timed activity consists of doing specific obedience exercises at set stations prearranged by the judges.

Working on a 100-point system, AKC Rally-O awards certification at three levels — Novice, Advanced, and Excellent — with each level graduating to more difficult exercises and off-leash control. Points are deducted if your dog moves outside the assigned area, doesn't complete an exercise, or if you have to touch or correct her. Fast-paced and fun, Rally-O is a whirlwind activity that everyone enjoys. You can find out more about this activity at www. apdt.com/rally and www.canismajor.com/dog/rallyo.htm.

Keeping Livestock in Line: Herding Tests and Trials

Many farmers and ranchers throughout the world still use herding dogs to control their livestock. And many dogs in the Herding group who are living their lives as cherished pets rather than working dogs still take their herding genes very seriously. You can spot them in a minute: They herd their owners from the kitchen, round up the schoolchildren as they get off the bus, and stare transfixed as the Discovery Channel airs a special called *Sheep of the Scottish Highlands.*

Herding dogs come in different types:

✔ **Headers:** These dogs work in front of livestock, usually sheep, and use an intense gaze known as *the eye* to control their herd. The Border Collie and Bearded Collie are two shepherd breeds.

✔ **Drovers/Heelers:** Drovers work behind sheep or cattle herds and drive them forward. They sometimes control the animals by nipping at their heels. Both the Pembroke and Cardigan Welsh Corgi fall into this category, as does the Australian Cattle Dog.

✔ **Livestock guardians:** Livestock guardians do just that: They don't move the flock; they guard it. Bred to work independently, they're raised with the flock and expected to guard it from wolves, bears, and thieves. Livestock guardians are all big dogs, and include the Kuvasz, Komondor, and Great Pyrenees.

✔ **All-around farm dogs:** These dogs are bred to stay around the farm, responding minute-to-minute to any task that comes up including herding and protection. The Collie, Old English Sheepdog, and Australian Shepherd are in this group.

While sponsored herding events do not test differently for each style of herding, titles are earned based on the ability of the dog to work with the handler to move livestock towards a specified goal (into a pen, for example) or around a pre-set course. Competitions aside, many clubs throughout the world gather to simply engage, train, and support their dogs' passions. If you have a dog who clearly has the bug, check it out at www.herdingontheweb. com or www.akc.org/events/herding.

Hunting Dogs: Going after Game

Hunting-dog events are held for dogs who historically have helped man hunt to survive. Though your dog's skills are rarely needed, keep the secret to yourself — your dog takes her passions seriously and, when trained and tested, she will give you her all. Hunting dogs are divided into Hounds, Gun Dogs, and Terriers.

In this section, I discuss hunting-related activities, including digging up burrows, retrieving game, and staying hot on the trail of an animal. You don't have to be a hunter to participate; in many cases, the dogs are simply showcasing their skills by chasing scented lures or finding a critter in a cage.

Earthdog: Digging Terrier trial events

Do you have a Terrier whose digging instincts are driving you crazy? If so, earthdog trials may be the perfect outlet for her. Terriers were originally bred to *go to ground:* to chase vermin all the way into their underground burrows and bring them back, dead or alive.

The breeds allowed to compete include all the small terriers in the Terrier group, as well as Dachshunds and Silky Terriers. Most toy breeds are not allowed to compete in official AKC events, although some, such as the

Yorkshire Terrier, are certainly Terriers and may enjoy themselves at a *fun match* (a non-competitive gathering).

At the test site, a manmade underground tunnel is constructed with wood sides. A caged rodent is secured at the end of the tunnel in an area referred to as the *den.* The dog enters the tunnel at one end (see Figure 18-1), finds the rodent at the other, and barks. (In these tests, the rodent emerges still caged and alive.)

Figure 18-1:
Terriers love
going into
the ground
in an earth-
dog tunnel.

While it might seem as if the dogs get back to nature and let their instincts run wild in earthdog tests, in fact, dogs must be under their handler's control at all times, even when they're underground. Recall and other requirements test the training of even the toughest Terrier.

Tests are run at four different levels. In the first trial, called "Introduction to Quarry," the dog does not receive any qualifications or titles, but simply gets a taste of what it's like to be in a tunnel and scent the prey. After passing this test, dogs advance gradually through the ranks. Titles are awarded for Junior Earthdog (JE), Senior Earthdog (SE), and Master Earthdog (ME).

Each test requires a greater degree of skill in detecting and following a scent, eagerness, and determination than the previous one. The distances from which a dog must locate the den and the complexity of the tunnels she must maneuver in the dark become increasingly more difficult.

For details on these digging events, visit the AKC's Web site at www.akc.org/events/earthdog or the Web site of the American Working Terrier Association (AWTA) at www.dirt-dog.com.

Gun Dogs: Passing field and retrieval tests

Gun Dogs hunt and retrieve small game for their handler, who carries a gun to kill his target. These dogs are further categorized into four classes that specify their genetic predispositions in the field:

- **Pointing Dogs** were originally bred to search fields far ahead of their owners and stop and point if they found a bird. Trials are often run with the hunter on horseback following the hunting dog. A dog on point is a beautiful thing to see.

- **Retrievers** retrieve shot game. In these trials a hunter may shoot one or several birds, and the dog is required to retrieve them from the water or land.

- **Setters** are both excellent pointers, indicating where birds can be found, and flushers, who will rush the bird upon the hunter's command. Ready–set–go!

- **Spaniels** were bred to hunt close to man and flush out birds within gun-shot range. They're also expected to retrieve the game once it is shot.

Each class is trained according to a specific standard, yet trials are run in a variety of ways depending on the kennel club or association holding the events. In each, the dog is judged on its stability during the hunt (barking is an immediate disqualification), its steadiness when *coursing* the field (looking for the game), and its retrieval, including the determination to enter or move through rough terrain/water and tender hold of the game.

In hunt tests, dogs are evaluated against a written standard for following game, alerting the handler, and/or retrieving it. Events are organized by the American Kennel Club (AKC), the North American Hunting Retriever Association (NAHRA), and the United Kennel Club (UKC) under the auspices of the Hunting Retriever Club (HRC).

Each dog that meets this standard earns a pass. This is unlike a field trial in which dog/handler teams compete against one another with only one dog being declared the winner.

For more information, go to www.gamebirdhunts.com or www.akc.org/events/performance.

Hounds: Following prey

If you're a hunting enthusiast and you have a dog who likes to tag along, these events might be for you. There are almost as many kinds of hunting as there are dogs, and the AKC is only one of many organizations that sponsor hunting events. But all have one thing in common: They put hunter and dog back together at a task the dog was originally bred to do. Hounds are divided by the primary sense they use to hunt — vision or smell.

Lure coursing

Sighthounds, who participate in the sport of lure coursing, use their vision to acknowledge and then chase their prey. The goal of this sport is to "preserve and further develop the natural beauty, grace, speed, and coursing skill of the Sighthound."

Lure coursing events don't use live bait anymore. Instead, an artificial lure is pulled along a 1,000- to 1,500-yard course that zigs and zags to test the dog's speed, agility, skill, enthusiasm, and endurance. One of the key players in a lure coursing event is the lure operator. His job is to keep the lure 10 to 30 yards in front of the lead dog, make sure it never gets tangled, and stop it within 20 yards of the lure machine.

All the Sighthounds may take part in lure coursing events, including Afghan Hounds, Basenjis, Borzoi, Greyhounds, Ibizan Hounds, Irish Wolfhounds, Pharaoh Hounds, Rhodesian Ridgebacks, Salukis, Scottish Deerhounds, and Whippets. These dogs have one thing in common: They love to run after game very fast! As anyone who has witnessed a competition can tell you, Sighthounds respond to a lure on pure instinct. They do what they were bred for, which is to chase a moving object.

Sighthounds aren't the only breeds that love to run, of course, and many clubs hold *fun matches* where any breed can enter. If your dog loves to chase, this may be the best way to redirect her energies.

For more information on this sport, visit the American Sighthound Field Association at www.asfa.org or the AKC at www.akc.org/events/lure_coursing.

Scenthounds

Scenthounds use a scented trail to follow their prey and thus don't have to be as fast-moving as sighthounds, who literally hunt to kill. While following a trail is definitely an endurance sport, these dogs are architecturally designed: Their ears are long and flappy to waft scents up to their noses, their lips are soft and subtle to capture and hold scent particles, and their noses are a maze of sensory cells like we could never imagine.

Scenthounds have a signature bay that signals their location to the hunters, who follow either on foot or horseback. Modern suburbanization has urged their silence, but these dogs rarely comply. Happiest following a scent, they like to bellow and share their delight when something smells good.

In trials, gatherings, or competitions, Scenthounds are used to hunt foxes, raccoons, and rabbits either hunting in large groups, smaller packs, or solo. Leggy hounds generally require their hunter to be on horseback to keep up, while some breeds, like American Foxhounds or Coonhounds, have their hunters wait to find them until their baying signals that the game has been run up a tree.

The AKC holds events and judges dogs based on how well they work together and follow a trail. Beagles and Basset Hounds work in packs; Dachshunds work in pairs (called *braces*) and are judged on their ability to run a rabbit into the ground; and Coonhound trials are held to test the hunting skills of several Coonhound breeds, including the Bluetick and Redboned Coonhound.

Similar events are sponsored by other breed groups and clubs as well. If you have a Hound and love the idea of hunting together, research your breed and find out what clubs exist to help you get started.

Tracking: Finding What's Hidden or Lost

Dogs' noses are analogous to our eyes. For dogs, tracking is like what looking around is to us. However, to train your dog to follow a specific trail is no simple feat. *Tracking,* teaching dogs to find missing persons or to detect drugs or bombs, is advanced work and requires a lot of encouragement and patient repetition.

Not only is tracking a great sport, but it can serve other purposes as well: You can train your dog to help with actual search-and-rescue missions. You may even want to teach basic tracking for personal convenience — having a helper to round up the troops for dinner or find a child who's wandered off can be a tremendous asset!

Treating tracking as a sport

You can use tracking as a recreational sport, teaching your dog to find various people or objects in your family, or you can use it as a competitive sport, earning tracking titles.

Training must start with good communication. Positive retrieves, where the leather articles (wallet, glove) are within sight, are the best beginning. As a dog's ability and enthusiasm increase, articles can be hidden from sight in tall grass or around corners.

Exposing a dog to different weather conditions and locations is important in creating a reliable tracking dog. A tracking dog will set to task, and the handler will follow wherever the track leads her.

The AKC offers two kinds of tracking competitions: field and variable surface. *Variable surface* tracking goes across roads, parking lots, and other urban areas, while field tracking is strictly in the wild. Titles for field tracking are Tracking Dog (TD) and Tracking Dog Excellent (TDX), whereas titles for variable surface tracking are Variable Surface Tracker (VST) and Champion Tracker (CT).

To find out more about teaching your dog to track or entering competitive events, check out www.mytrackingdog.com or www.akc.org/events/tracking.

Signing up for search and rescue

Tracking skills also can be used to start dogs with a search-and-rescue group. Search and rescue is not a competition. It's real life — dogs working with their owners to find missing people. These dogs must learn to *air scent,* following a trail created by the natural shedding of microscopic particles from a human's skin.

Search-and-rescue dogs are trained to work in adverse conditions, in inclement weather, day or night, to trail the sometimes tragic repercussions of disasters, both natural (hurricanes, tornados, floods, avalanches, and so on) and man-made, such as bombings or transportation accidents. To find out more about this activity, visit www.nasar.org.

Schutzhund: Offering Protection

Schutzhund is a German word that means *protection.* The training was developed in the early 1900s to determine whether German Shepherds would make adequate police dogs (as well as good breeding stock), though these days the training isn't limited to that breed of dog. Intense training and certification happens at three levels:

- ✔ **Tracking:** Here the dog is set to track a scent, as well as dropped articles, over rough terrain. The trial is run regardless of the weather.

- ✔ **Obedience:** These exercises are similar to those held in competitive obedience; however, rather than involving a gated flooring or yard, they involve football-field-length distances and more elaborate obstacles, such as a wall or high jump.

✔ **Protection:** In this section of the test, the dog is expected to be under the complete control of the handler. Control is tested under stress and the dog must not attack until and unless instructed to or when under a direct attack. While this section of the evaluation has come under a lot of scrutiny (no one should be subjected to an out-of-control attack dog), the trained and padded "criminals" (shown in Figure 18-2) symbolize real-life events. A well-trained Schutzhund dog performs with synchronized precision to the direct commands of her handler.

Figure 18-2: Protection dogs must prove their courage when interrupted by a surprise attack.

Certification for Schutzhund dogs comes at three levels: I, II, and III, with each representing greater challenges to the dog. The finest certification is Schutzhund III: as they say, quite literally: "One in a thousand!"

While I've never trained a dog in the sport, I have worked with trainers and participated as an assistant in classes where such training was done and done well. I've heard, however, that there are some trainers who border on being abusive. Be careful. If the trainer won't let you observe a few classes, go elsewhere. Meet the dogs who are being trained. Are they stable? Are they under control? A good instructor will evaluate every dog and person as well: Be very wary of a trainer who accepts everyone. This is a tough sport suited to a select few.

Earning breed-specific working titles

Believe it or not, there are many other activities you and your dog can do together. Many national breed clubs have designated individual working titles to test for the abilities their breed was first developed to possess.

✔ **The Newfoundland Club of America** sponsors clinics and competitions where dogs can earn Water Dog (WD) and Water Rescue Dog (WRD) titles. They also award the drafting titles Draft Dog (DD) and Team Draft Dog (TDD).

✔ **The Dalmatian Club of America** offers road titles.

✔ **The Alaskan Malamute Club of America** offers titles for weight pulls.

And there are lots more. To discover what your breed club has to offer, write your national club (you can get a list of national breed clubs from the AKC).

Sometimes the best way to deal with your dog's natural instincts is to engage her in healthy competition. Earning a title is only a small piece of the pie. Working with your dog should be your number-one incentive, whether or not you're ever recognized. The best way to get involved in organized activities is to seek out a club of like-minded enthusiasts in your area. Unfortunately, advanced training can't be learned from a book. Although reading helps, it can't replace experience.

Getting Certified for Pet Therapy

No dogs on the couch, please; this section isn't about doggie psychiatrists. *Pet therapy* is the involvement of well-trained dogs who just love to socialize and get attention. Once certified, these dogs play a therapeutic role in such environments as nursing homes, children's centers, prisons, and other long-term care facilities. I've been doing it for years, and I never cease to be amazed by how the unconditional love of a dog can light up a person's life and ease her interactions with the world around her.

Before you call up and offer your services, you need to find out how pet therapy works. I remember my first pet-therapy class, which I took in New York City with my beloved dog Kyia. Together we were exposed to many of the unfamiliar situations that we would eventually encounter on our therapy visits.

I've turned from student into teacher — I now run a class to socialize dogs to the rigors of these environments. The dogs are exposed to wheelchairs, walkers, metal objects, a variety of handling techniques, speech patterns, and people of all ages.

Before therapy dogs are allowed to go visiting, they must be certified by an organization such as the Delta Society or Therapy Dogs International (TDI). These organizations provide ID cards with both the person's and the dog's picture on it and supply each team with insurance should an incident occur.

Is your canine a good citizen?

The Canine Good Citizen test — CGC for short — is a noncompetitive test developed to recognize and certify dogs and their owners as responsible citizens. Although the test was developed and is promoted by the AKC, it's not limited to purebred dogs. Mixed breeds are encouraged to become certified as well.

The CGC measures a dog's social skills and public manners, and is not a competition. The goal of the CGC test is not to eliminate participants, but to encourage pet owners to learn the skills necessary to train their dogs to be safe, well-mannered members of society.

To pass the test, your dog must know the commands "Heel," "Sit," "Down," "Come," and "Stay." The test is composed of ten evaluations. For more information on how to get your CGC certification, visit www.akc.org.

Not everyone is a dog lover. If you're out visiting and someone says they don't want to meet your dog, don't push it. Often, people in care facilities don't get to make many choices. Respect this one.

If you have a dog who is social and loving, yet calm and well-mannered, you may find therapy work very rewarding. Check out the book *Wanted! Animal Volunteers,* by Mary R. Burch, PhD (Howell), or visit www.tdi-dog.org and www.deltasociety.org for more information on how you and your dog can get involved!

Chapter 19

Harness Sports: Bringing Pulling Dogs to the Starting Line

In This Chapter

▶ Carting canines big and small

▶ Sledding in the snow

▶ Joring: Biking, skiing, running with your dog out in front

*T*his chapter is dedicated to the passionate pullers. Those dogs who, when clipped to the end of a leash, become an unstoppable freight train of fur. Harness — literally — this dog's enthusiasm for forward momentum, and you've got the makings of a grand adventure.

While competitive carting, sledding, and joring teams are usually composed of specific breeds — Huskies, Samoyeds, and Alaskan Malamute-types for snow activities and Newfoundlands and Bernese Mountain Dog-types for carting — for the hobbyist, breed doesn't matter a bit. In fact, many of the pulling rigs can be found in miniature, so size and weight don't matter much either. The only prerequisite? That your dog loves to pull!

A Few Caveats

Before rushing into a harness sport, there are a few guidelines that apply to all the sports in this chapter. Following them will ensure your dog's safety.

✔ The harness sports are physically exhausting and thirst-provoking! Keep your dog well hydrated.

✔ Build your dog's endurance slowly. If he's overweight, out of shape, or otherwise compromised due to an injury or accident, get your veterinarian's okay before you begin.

✔ Don't ask your dog to pull anything that weighs more than he does before he's 12 to 18 months old.

> ✔ If you have a young dog between 5 and 8 months, start by teaching him the commands and to harness up. Once he understands the commands, you can have him pull lightweight objects, like a 3-foot-long, 2-x-4-inch wooden plank or an old tire.

Canine Carting

Your dog can pull a cart to take the trash out, clean the yard, bring in firewood, or take the kids for a ride. This activity is not limited to big dogs — one of my editors has friends who've taught their Chihuahua to pull a cart. She has also witnessed a stagecoach drawn by a team of Chinese Crested Dogs, and a Papillon who impressed the judges at a carting competition. Of course, if you have a team of teacup-sized Malteses, you'll have to have them cart table utensils, dirty socks, and other weight-appropriate objects!

I'm a big fan of carting. Though I never carted competitively, all my childhood dogs carted me around. My big red wagon was the vehicle of choice, jury-rigged to a makeshift harness we bought from a dog sledding vendor in the middle of winter. Fortunately, these days you can buy quality products on the Internet, making your ride safer and oh-so-smooth.

As with all other strenuous activities, check things out with your animal doctor before getting your dog involved in carting. Your dog must be conditioned, trim, and skeletally sound.

Getting carting equipment

Before you dive into an overview of the training process, take a look at carting equipment. For more information, do an online search for dog-carting equipment, or check out the top sites I recommend, including `www.black icedogsledding.com` (they sell carts, too) and `k9carting.com`.

Harnesses and lines

You need a harness for your dog. If you thought he was powerful at the end of a leash, just wait until you get him in one of these things! The following list defines the parts of the carting harness:

> ✔ **Front girth:** This piece stabilizes the harness and helps distribute the weight evenly across the chest and shoulders.
>
> ✔ **V1:** This piece must fit snugly on your dog's chest. It distributes the weight over the shoulders. The V should rest at your dog's breastbone.
>
> ✔ **V2:** The second V meets at your dog's withers. It must never fall behind the shoulders, because that would put too much strain on the back.

- ✔ **Shaft loop:** Positioned at the shoulder, this piece balances the cart and prevents it from rolling forward into your dog.

- ✔ **Side straps:** These serve to balance the harness on the dog and help distribute the weight evenly.

- ✔ **Traces:** These connect to the cart.

- ✔ **Rear girth:** This piece centers the harness and falls on your dog's thighs.

Wagon harnesses, which allow your dog to pull more weight (good for the kids!), differ from carting harnesses in that they have a chest strap that distributes the weight forward and a girth strap that positions the harness on your dog. Be sure to look for measurement and fitting instructions, which will ask you for the weight and neck measurements of your dog. Many harnesses have sliders that can be secured for a comfortable (two fingers' room) fit. In place of the rear girth, there's a bar that should be placed under your dog's tail to rest on his thighs. This piece attaches to the *singletree* of the wagon, which is a fancy term for a pivoting bar that gives the dog the flexibility to turn the cart without undue strain.

Carts and wagons

Not only does your dog need the harnesses and lines, but he also needs something to pull. Here's how carts and wagons differ:

- ✔ **Carts:** Carts have two or three wheels and turn nicely. Carts are good for training and competition, coming in lightweight versions or heavier (up to 50-pound) competition styles.

- ✔ **Wagons:** Wagons have four wheels and distribute weight evenly so the dog won't feel off balance, but they're a bit awkward to turn. Wagons are good for county fairs and for heavy yardwork.

Before transforming that dusty old wagon in the garage into a two-wheeled carting machine, turn it around in a circle. Does one wheel stay under the bed while the other projects out? Not good. This forces the weight of the load onto one side, tossing everything (including your dog) off balance. When wagons turn, all four wheels must stay under the flat bed.

If you're planning kid rides or yard help, wagons are a must. A cart can't balance the weight, and if it tips, you might scare your dog off carting for good.

Basic training: Putting the dog before the cart

The first step in training your dog for carting is familiarizing your dog with the harness. Once he accepts having it put on, he should wear it while you review his basic training from Chapter 2 on the following commands:

    ✔ "Wait"

    ✔ "Sit"

    ✔ "Down–Stay"

Your dog will have to learn some new commands too: "Left," "Right," "Fast," "Slow," and "Back." Though it seems like a lot to teach your dog, the commands are just labels for regular actions like moving to the left and right. As you lead your dog during training, label each action with one clearly spoken command. Once you've spoken each command at least a dozen times, ask a helper to guide your dog on-leash as you stand behind him and direct him with these cues. Ask the helper to reward your dog for his recognition. Patient training yields great rewards.

Backing up

Teaching your dog to back up may sound easier than it is. Your dog isn't used to moving backward. To teach him this move, just follow these steps:

1. **Set up a 2-x-4-foot chute in your home.**

   Placing some chairs along a wall will do.

2. **Have your dog stand in the chute, and command "Wait."**

3. **Stand in the opening and face your dog. Hold a favorite treat at the side of his face and move slowly towards him as you say "Back."**

   If he steps back with even one foot, congratulate him. If he sits, no dice. If you're having trouble, check where you're holding his treat: It must be at the side of his face. Above that point, he'll sit. If all else fails, have a training partner *gently* hold his back end up as you encourage him backward. Once he gets the motion ask for more steps backward before offering the reward. After six successful responses, practice this outside the chute, one step back at a time.

Introducing the cart

When your dog has all the basic commands down, you can begin training him to get used to your rig. When first introducing the cart to your dog, you should explore it together. Wait until your dog is comfortable with his new toy before hitching him up.

1. **Place empty traces (harness lines) on your dog and walk along in a straight line.**

2. **Attach a light weight to the traces.**

   Try a large paper bag stuffed with newspaper.

3. **Have a training partner walk by the bag as you steady your dog forward.**

   If your dog is concerned, encourage him along and keep walking.

4. **Attach a heavier item to the traces, such as a wooden plank.**

   To ensure that the weight is distributed evenly, secure two eyebolts and ropes to the wood plank. At this stage, you should be focusing your dog with treats, and your partner should be watching the plank to ensure that it doesn't get caught.

Walking with the cart

A training partner will be an integral part of the process for a while, so don't plan a session without him or her. Here's how you and your training partner can introduce your dog to walking with the cart:

1. **Place your dog in the harness. Have your partner hold the shafts of the cart and walk it into position next to your dog.**

2. **Let your dog sniff the rig and relax with it. At this stage, the cart will not be secured in the harness. Ask your helper to move the cart alongside your dog as you walk forward in a straight line.**

3. **Once your dog is steady, command him "Forward."**

   If the cart disturbs your dog, and you're unable to settle him down, return to attaching a light weight and work at it slowly. During practice, reinforce the steps that your dog is comfortable with before working with heavier weights.

4. **Have your partner occasionally bump into your dog with the shafts while walking next to him.**

   Watch your dog's reaction, keeping him moving along as if it's no big deal. Continue to turn cart and dog separately.

5. **Now you're ready to secure the cart to the harness. Attach the cart to your dog by putting the shafts into the loops only.**

6. **Walk along while your partner steadies the shafts. You can now introduce the words "Pull" and "Halt."**

   Don't turn with the cart yet.

Working on starts, stops, and speed

Now you're ready to connect the traces to the part of the harness called the singletree that secures the harness to the cart, ensuring that the shafts don't slide up as your dog stops. Your helper should continue to hold the shafts to keep them steady until your dog is comfortable with the occasional interference.

1. **Rig your dog and practice your stationary obedience commands: "Stand," "Sit," "Down," and "Stay."**

2. **Continue to work in a straight line as you command "Pull," "Halt," "Wait," "Fast," and "Slow."**

If you have a big dog, you may need a weighted cart to introduce commands such as "Fast," "Slow," and "Halt." Remember, with carts, the weight must be evenly distributed. You can purchase weight bars made especially for this purpose.

Changing direction

To teach your dog turns, you should work in an open parking lot or cul de sac. Start with big left circles, saying "Left" as you herd your dog to the side and lure him with food. Do this until you're sure your dog is having fun with it. Slowly work in smaller circles. Now do the same thing to the right.

The last thing your dog should learn before you take the show on the road is backing up. Of course, he must know what you're talking about before you ask for it in a harness (see the earlier section "Backing up" for details). Calling your partner back to straighten the cart while your dog backs up is useful. It can also help to practice on an uphill slope, where gravity encourages your dog to back up. Soon it will be part of the show.

Once your dog is accustomed to the cart, you can acclimate him more quickly to a wagon, or just have fun with your cart.

Sledding

This section is for snow lovers only! The only thing I loved more than snow as a kid was my Husky dog, Shawbee. One of the greatest gifts I ever received was an official sled dog harness; finally, something we could really get into together!

In this section, I introduce you to a few forms of dog sledding, discuss equipment, and include a few tips on training. If your dog is big enough and strong enough to pull you, he has what it takes to start sledding.

Sledding is a complex activity requiring a fair bit of specialized equipment. Your dog can learn all about it from you, but you need to learn about it from someone else. A basic training course is a must for would-be mushers. To find out about courses in your area — as well as where to buy equipment and other tools of the trade — contact www.sleddogcentral.com, www.isdra.org, or www.blackicedogsledding.com.

Choosing the type of sledding

What's the first thing you think of when someone says "dog sled"? I don't know about you, but I think Iditarod, that grueling 1,150-mile Alaskan race from Anchorage to Nome. The human competitors spend their every waking moment breeding, caring for, and training their dogs, who are arctic athletes extraordinaire.

However, the Iditarod isn't all there is. Here are some of the forms dog sledding can take:

- ✓ **Recreation:** Sledding may be just for fun. Dogs have a natural urge to pull kids around on a leash, so why not redirect this instinct? The sled makes it easier for the dog and more fun for the kid.

- ✓ **Dog sled racing:** Across the United States and in many other northern regions of the world, a huge variety of sledding events are sponsored each year. These competitions may be short or long, regulated for few dogs or many, lightweight or heavy, recreational or for serious contenders only. To get a listing of sledding events, plug "dog sledding events" plus your country's name into your search engine and see where that takes you.

Any large dog can pull a sled, but your dog's build will dictate the kind of pulling he most enjoys. Large-boned, lumbering breeds can pull heavier weights more slowly over longer distances; leggy breeds that are light on their feet can pull less, faster, over shorter distances. When you think of "sled dogs," you may envision a whole team of dogs racing across a field of snow. In truth, though, there are smaller sleds meant for three- or two-dog teams, or even one dog.

Getting the sled and snow gear

First things first. You'll need equipment: Check out www.blackicedog sledding.com or www.alpineoutfitters.net. In this section, I introduce you to harnesses, sleds, lines, and cold-weather clothing for you and your dog.

Harnesses

Harnesses for dog sledding come in several versions: the X-back harness, the lightweight racing harness, and the weight and freight harnesses. The most popular everyday harness is the lightweight racer, made out of nylon and designed to distribute weight evenly across your dog's back. If you're serious about this activity, talk to an expert to determine what's best for you.

Whatever harness you choose, it must fit properly, lying comfortably along your dog's back with the attachment loop falling just above his tail. A poor fitting harness is a pain in your dog's neck, literally — cutting into his fur and causing him to run sideways in an attempt to compensate.

Sleds

There are a few different types of sleds made for the hobbyist and competitors alike. Though you may use your garden-variety sled, these commercial sleds have two runners to stand on, a handlebar that rises from a flat bed where you can put parcels or people, and the all-handy brake to help slow your dog/team down as you bring them to a stop. Following are some choices of dog sleds:

- ✔ **Lightweight sprint or kick sleds:** These sleds are designed for racing short distances and for recreational sledding. Though they have a seat, you generally run or stand at the back of the sled and push the sled to maneuver tough spots. This is the type that my Husky Shawbee and I grew up with.

- ✔ **Toboggan sleds:** Use these versions for sprint sledding and long-distance events.

- ✔ **Freight sleds:** Tow the heavy stuff with these sleds.

Back when I was running my Husky, sleds came in one material — wood. Today's market offers sleds in high-strength aluminum, plastic, and traditional wood. There are pluses and minuses to each material. Cost is a huge factor. The more ergonomically designed, the more expensive they are. The lightness of aluminum and plastic can also work against you if your dog starts to run. Use the Internet to research different types of sleds before you make a purchase. Two of my favorite sites are mushing.com and skidog.ca.

Gangline

What's missing? You have the sled. You've fit a good harness. Now you need something to attach the two. The piece that attaches the dog to the sled is called a *gangline*.

Tugline

In multi-dog rigs, the *tugline* is the piece that connects the harness to the gangline and distributes the sled's weight evenly for maximum comfort

Paw protection

What's hot for the fashionable and safety-conscious sled dog? Booties! Attractive and secure, many mushers use them to protect their dogs' feet. Although the thought of buying booties for your dog may seem silly, professional mushers wouldn't go out without them. Ice and snow wreak havoc on a dog's paws and can cause deep, painful cuts.

If you have a long-coated or wire-coated breed, you need to trim his fur (especially around his feet) so that snow doesn't build up in his coat.

Outfitting yourself

The final thing you need to consider is your clothing. You can sweat profusely after running behind the sled for five minutes, even in subzero temperatures, but you must think smart and dress for all extremes. Here are a few tips:

✔ The fabric of hats and gloves should be lightweight and waterproof.

✔ If it's windy, wear a facemask.

✔ Sunglasses are a must, even on a cloudy day.

Basic training for your sled dog

Start out on a regular leash, and progress to harness training — first just stand behind your dog and direct him, then attach a light weight to get him accustomed to pulling weight. Perfected that? You're ready for the sled!

Teaching sledding commands

Teach your dog/puppy the commands he'll hear out on the trail as soon as possible. "Hike" means hit it: Go forward and lean into it! Say "Gee" for right, "Haw" for left, "Easy" for slow down, and "Whoa" for stop. Say these commands over and over, and your dog will learn them in less than a month. Following are a few teaching tips and a few more commands:

✔ **"Hike":** Take your dog into an open area and, when possible, position someone in front of you to call and bait your dog forward with his favorite toy or treats. This creates a sense of urgency and excitement for this command. Once your dog is catching onto this "Hike" game, shout it whenever you're in the mood for a drag.

✔ **"Gee":** This command tells your dog to turn right. Say it as you turn with him, over and over and over again.

✔ **"Haw":** Same concept as "Gee," but in the opposite direction. Shout "Haw" and hang a left turn.

✔ **"Gee over":** Adding "over" to these directional cues softens the angle. "Gee over" directs your dog to shift to the right or to bear right at a fork. (In competition, you use this command to pass another sled on the right.)

✔ **"Haw over":** This one tells your dog to move to the left, bear left at a fork, or pass another sled on the left.

✔ **"On by":** This oh-so-important command teaches your dog to ignore distractions or to stay straight through a fork. First, review the "Nope" command from Chapter 4. Then set up distractions, such as favorite toys on the floor, and use "On by" as you direct your dog through without even a peek. (Is your dog still distracted? Say "Nope" firmly and correct him with a tug on the leash.)

✔ **"Easy":** This command teaches your dog to slow it down — not stop completely, but shift down a gear or two. Teach it on-leash first, before expecting your dog to understand it once he's rigged.

If your dog has trouble learning this cue, practice on a 6-foot leash initially and/or consider a head collar, which can be controlled by a secondary leash as you're running together. This collar works like a horse halter and will slow your dog with the slightest pressure on it.

✔ **"Whoa":** This one tells your dog to stop: Make sure he has it down pat before you harness him up. Each time you come to a stop on-leash, tell him "Whoa" and then "Sit."

Adding weight

Once your dog has learned the commands, you can attach a tire or a 1- to 2-foot piece of 2-x-4-inch wood to his rig by screwing two eyebolts into the wood and tying the rope to secure it evenly to the harness. The first time you introduce him to pulling weight, you should have a training partner near the wood to make sure it doesn't get stuck. Follow a format similar to that of the preceding section, keeping the lessons short and upbeat: Three to five minutes is a good starting point; then build the lesson time gradually as your dog's focus sharpens.

You may start these lessons with dogs older than 5 months, not before.

Introducing the sled

When you're ready to begin training, head over to a clear field or a golf course so that your dog doesn't get tangled up by all sorts of objects.

During your first outings, you should walk/run in front of your dog and customize him to hearing his new commands. Recruit a helper to stand behind and steady the sled.

1. **Hitch your dog to the sled.**

2. **Leading your dog on a leash, stand at his head and shout "Hike" as you start forward.**

   "Hike" means go, so if he doesn't respond, just keep going. He'll catch on soon! Keep your dog on a long lead and stand at his head.

3. **If your dog wants to run like wild, say "Easy" and keep him at a moderate pace.**

   If he turns to look at the sled, say "Ep, ep" gently as you continue forward.

4. **After a few practice runs, start using "Gee over," to guide the sled to the right. Once your dog starts leading you, practice "Haw over." Then start intermixing the two, but not too often.**

Only "Hike" should be repeated frequently. Telling your dog to turn every five seconds is impractical and annoying.

5. **After a week of beginner practice, you can introduce your dog to pace changes, turns, and pulling in front.**

   For changes of pace, repeat "Hike" to encourage your dog to move faster, say "Easy" for slow down, and say "Whoa" to come to a stop.

   You already know the commands for right and left. Practice turns in just one direction for a few days, then switch to the other.

Giving commands from behind your dog

By now your dog should be pretty psyched to pull his rig. To get him to pull solo, start your usual "Hike" at your dog's side, then drop the lead and drift back, repeating "Hike." If your dog worries, turning to keep sight of you, you may be going too fast. If he's confident but confused, ask a friend to lead him forward until he gets used to hearing your commands from behind.

Practice your control commands by running four feet behind your dog; if he's confused, go on up and help him out. If he makes the transition, praise him wildly, say "Whoa," and give him a hug. Yes!

If your dog is rigged and a distraction causes pause, shout "On by!" and go to his head if you must. If your dog's focus is an issue, review the "Nope" direction from Chapter 4, saying both commands together ten times and then dropping "Nope" for the new terminology "On by."

Progressively drift back until you're able to command from behind the sled. If at any point your dog is confused, either slow up a step or have a friend lead your dog while you command him from behind.

Next, you're ready to begin getting on the sled. When you first step on, it will add a lot of weight to the rig all of a sudden. Work on a downward slope (not a hill) and ask your helper to guide your dog/dogs as you ramp up your enthusiasm and shout familiar directions, like "Hike!" After 5 to 10 seconds of weight-pulling, jump off and push the sled as you continue to direct your dog/dogs.

As your dog/dogs get comfortable with pulling your weight, lengthen the time you remain on the sled as your dog/dogs pull it.

Sledding is a human sport too. Jump off and help push anytime you're moving uphill, or to give your dogs guidance in moving or propelling over difficult terrain!

Joring: Pulling Skiers, Cyclists, Runners, and More

Are you a multi-athletic sort with a dog who hates being left behind? If your dog has any pulling instincts (and what dog doesn't?) you'll have more fun sharing your interests than you ever imagined. Love to cross-country ski? Bike? Run cross-country? Well, hold your huskies — each of these sports has a canine sister sport that you can actually do simultaneously. Let me introduce you to the world of everything *joring*.

No, it's not as crazy as it sounds. In joring, you don't just hold onto your dog's collar and go for a ride. The dog wears a harness, and he pulls you by a line attached to a belt you're wearing, a tow bar (think water-skiing), or even a bike or scooter. In this section, I introduce these pulling activities, discuss some equipment, and help you get started.

Both you and your dog need to train and condition for joring hobbies. And yes, there is some danger involved — if you don't take the training elements seriously, your dog could veer off to chase down a bunny. Ouch! But if you're mindful and you train your dog properly to stay on-course and avoid distractions, what a ride!

Profiling a good joring dog

You don't need a whole team of dogs for these activities — joring is for one to three dogs at a time.

Joring activities are open to any breed or mixed-breed dog over 30 pounds. The only prerequisites are a strong foundation in the basics and an intense passion for pulling. Of course, not every breed of dog is ideal for each activity — you probably wouldn't want to send your unclipped Puli (with his corded coat) out in 6 feet of snow, but you could try out canicross or scootering in the dry seasons!

My favorite quote comes from Kim Tinker of Sandy, Oregon: "There are no bad dogs, just exercise-dependent dogs." And there are few better activities to satisfy your dog than these!

Surveying the types of joring

This whole joring craze began earnestly in Norway as a dog-assisted way to travel on skis. There, severe winters precluded man's finest machinery, and rugged, well-insulated dogs were truly man's best bet as well as his friend.

Like every good idea, joring got more refined and spread like a ripple to all corners of the globe. Other joring activities likely began as a way to condition sledding and skijoring dogs off-season. Regardless of the weather, people everywhere are teaching their dogs the finer art of pulling as a way to both exercise and spend time together.

This section gives you a brief description of joring activities. For more information on each one or for clubs in your area, enter the name of the activity in a search engine or visit dogplay.com or joring.org. And check out some footage on YouTube — it's exhilarating!

Skijoring

Skijoring is where all this joring business began. In *skijoring,* one to three harnessed dogs pull a person on cross-country skis (see Figure 19-1). Imagine dog sledding with the same equipment, a similar training approach, and fewer dogs (no more than three), but instead of pulling a sled, your dog is pulling you — on skis. Call it transportation and hold on tight!

Figure 19-1:
Skijoring.

Skijor in Norwegian means "to plow snow with your face," which is an all-too-common sight when first rigging up with your dog to have him pull you on skis.

You can trail ski with your dog, backcountry it (go where few men tread), or enter competitions — sprint or distance races — comparing your time with others running the same course.

Here are some things to keep in mind as you explore skijoring with your dog:

- Stress your dog's reaction to the "On by" command, especially if you're joring solo. Distractions abound, and skis offer much less control than walking or sledding.

- Dogs need to be conditioned to distance running just as people do. While most dogs can handle running a mile or so, they have to exert much more effort to pull you as they go. When starting out, gradually increase your distance running from a mile to five miles over the course of two weeks. Once you've worked up to that distance, go out with your dog a minimum of once every three days to keep him fit.

- When laying out your clothes, remember that you exercise less when skijoring than when sledding or skiing solo. You also have a tendency to fall more frequently, which means getting wet. Dress warmly, and make sure your outer layers are waterproof. For more information about training your dog for skijoring, check out `skijor.com` and `sleddog central.com`.

Bikejoring

Bikejoring is dog-propelled biking. Envision it: Your dog running at top speed and you sailing along barely pedaling, watching the countryside whiz by. Okay, try not to envision the fall.

This sport is much more serious than dusting off your old bike, holding on, and hoping for the best. In this section, I include a few health and safety tips for this sport, which you can do with one or two dogs. If biking while exercising your dog sounds like a good idea to you, take it seriously. Research the idea extensively, and do what the experts say.

Looking out for your dog's well-being

You need to keep your dog's well-being in mind as you're bikejoring, because dogs can't talk and tell you if they're hurt or thirsty. Here are a few tips on looking out for your dog:

- Dogs must be conditioned to run on pavement. If this is your only option, pay close attention to your dog's pads after each run, speak to your veterinarian about joint care, and begin by slowly introducing the sport 1 to 2 miles at a time. When possible, find a dirt path or trail to ride on.

- Though you may be able to ride 50 miles in a day at 20 miles an hour, your dog cannot. An athletic dog's top speed is about 12 miles per hour.

- Dogs get thirsty! When running your dog, go out at the coolest hours of the day and give him pauses to drink and/or eliminate.

Staying safe

Bikejoring is a serious sport and isn't for the average hobbyist. Though anyone can get caught up in the fantasy of biking with your dog hauling you along, bikejoring requires mindfulness on many fronts: You have to adjust your balance and watch your dogs as you constantly gauge your speed.

Always wear protective gear when bikejoring with your dog. Helmets and gloves are a must. Dogs are not machines. Even a well-trained dog may get distracted, veer off-course, and leave you eating dust. If the prospect sounds too risky, consider scootering with your dog instead, which I explore in the next section.

Watch your speed — especially when you're going downhill! Always play it conservatively and gauge your dog's speed. If your dog loses control, you will too!

One of the most frequent accidents occurs when the towline gets caught in the bike wheel. Just envision this, and then do everything you can to prevent it. Maintain your brakes so they're responsive and quick. Purchase or make a pipe to suspend the towline above the front wheel. Towlines should never be held or tied to the handrails of your bicycle!

Invest in a top-of-the-line mountain bike, and keep it in top condition. The brakes are the most important thing — if you can't stop, well . . . let's just say it won't be a pretty sight for either of you. Bikejoring demands a lot of braking: Is that a squeak you hear? It's likely your brake pads are either wet, mud-coated, or wearing thin. A bike's brakes are a bikejorer's best friend; keep a close eye on yours and replace them when they wear thin. Also keep an eye on your suspension cables and the wheels' alignment. Keep your bike in top working order!

Dog scootering

Bikejoring sound a little too scary? Consider dog-propelled, motorless scootering — the same dynamic with a life-sized scooter and a much easier and quicker dismount.

For dog scootering, think bikejoring with a large, durable scooter. Though it's slightly more cumbersome than a mountain bike, it's a lot safer. Your dog veers off-course? Just step off this one and you're good to go. Though you can use any adult-sized scooter, scooters made especially for this sport are available. Commercial "dogscooters" are made of aluminum with top of the line brakes and shock absorbers, and can tolerate cross-country distance and the wear and tear of being pulled by one or two dogs.

For more information on everything scootering, visit www.dogscooter.com.

Skimjoring

What will those Southern Californians think of next? *Skimjoring* involves dogs pulling a skimmer along the shoreline on a skim board. Dogs love making us happy, so if you can't find the snow, just harness your dog up and head for the beach!

Canicross

"What?" you ask. "There's a sport that actually encourages your dog to pull you, while you're running to keep up? Where can I sign up?"

Canicross is a little more complicated than that — but only a little. It's a one person–one dog sport, likely initiated to keep skijoring dogs in shape during the off season. But like any good idea, it has become a craze. Canicrossers use their dogs for running, speed walking, and even hiking. Some people even use ski poles to keep their arms in shape. Sound fun to you? Read on. . . .

When training with your dog for this activity, remember it's a human speed sport — even if you can cut a five-minute mile, you'll still be on the slow side for your dog.

Here are some general things to keep in mind about canicross:

✔ Your dog must be in complete voice control if you plan to run with him. "Easy" is by far the biggest challenge. A well conditioned runner can run five-minute miles, but this is a trotting pace for a medium- to large-sized dog. The agility required to balance and run leaves little room for explosive tugging.

✔ Many canicrossers use a head collar to slow their dogs, discourage distractibility, and reinforce "Easy" on hills. This is especially recommended when dogs are new to this sport.

✔ If you're a competitive runner, this sport will push your endurance. While you can find canicross competitions in Europe, it might be hard to locate one in the United States. Find races that allow leashed dogs — rig up, get focused, and leave your competitors in the dust!

Don't forget dogs wear fur coats! Your dog will overheat quickly in the heat. To prevent overheating, provide an ample supply of water and a quick swim or spray when possible to keep your dog cool and happy.

Equipment

Special equipment is required for joring sports. First, you must invest in a harness for your dog. For some sports, like skijoring and canicross, you'll need a hands-free rigging for yourself too. Your dog should wear a light-weight pulling harness and comfortable *traces,* which are the ropes you'll hold that attach to your equipment. You can wear a human harness to free your hands once your dog is trustworthy on the trail. (Visit www.blackice dogsledding.com for a great overview of joring equipment.) Following are the basics:

- ✔ **X-back harness:** This harness is fitted to distribute your dog's weight evenly and is designed to allow a fluid freedom of motion when he pulls you along. Different than a store-bought variety, this harness criss-crosses over your dog's back and attaches close to his tail base.

- ✔ **Hip belt:** A hip belt allows hands-free maneuvering and a full range of movement for poling. Be sure you invest in a comfortable model — the best ones are 4 inches wide, adjustable, and come with a quick release mechanism just in case you need to break free from your dog in a hurry!

- ✔ **Towbar:** Holding onto a towbar is an alternative to the hipbelt. It's a handle that fits securely into a nylon cover for comfortable holding and attaches to the towline.

- ✔ **Towline:** This is the line that attaches the dog to a hip belt or tow bar. Most towlines are made of a strong mountaineering rope (polyethylene rope) and range from 7 to 12 feet.

- ✔ **Neckline:** This attaches two dogs side by side.

- ✔ **Line lead:** This lead lines up two dogs front-to-back.

- ✔ **Bridle:** For bikejoring, this is one option for hitching the dog to the bicycle.

When bikejoring, don't tie the dog's towline to the bicycle. The line must be completely centered if you want to remain upright!

Commands

While many of the commands for joring sports are identical to the sledding commands, the most important ones to stress are "Whoa," "Easy," and "On by." Imagine a crisp day with a blue sky and a dog just champing at the bit to run. Everything is fine until — splat — you end up meeting the ground up-close and personal. "Whoa" would definitely be a help here. Or, say you're passing by another joring team or some wildlife appears on the horizon — "On by" is absolutely essential to keep your dog on track. Heading downhill? Feeling like your dog just might propel you airborne? "Easy" reminds him to slow down. Review the training section of the sledding section and search out more detailed training manuals on the Internet.

Teaching a dog to avoid all distractions as he pulls you mercilessly along a snowy or dry dirt trail? "On by!" would be my highest priority! If your dog's predatory impulses are still ripe, review "Nope" from Chapter 4 (saying "Nope" with "On by," until your dog learns the new command), and perfect this lesson before you hit the trail. Get professional help if you need it: Your safety should be your top priority.

Introducing training

The first time you introduce your dog to his rigging or the equipment you're using, let him sniff it. Dogs see with their noses, not their eyes! Let your dog get a full visual before you ask him to pull it. If you're using a bike or scooter, walk him around it, pretending you're seeing this cool thing for the first time too.

Next walk him around as you push it. He may be nervous initially. Keep walking! Act nonchalant, and don't cave to his edginess — if you act like it's no big deal, your dog will mimic your mindset in time.

When initially directing your dog from behind, ask a training partner to lead your dog while you command from the rear. You should be on the equipment; your helper should not.

Part VI
The Part of Tens

The 5th Wave   By Rich Tennant

"He wants the cat for his next trick.
I'd be real careful about this, Eileen."

In this part . . .

Part VI provides three chapters chock-full of helpful "bites" of information! Does your dog like jumping? How about scooting through a tunnel or weaving around poles? Does the invitation to sequence his moves excite your dog or shut him down? And how about you — do you enjoy playing the role of coach? Chapter 20 gives you a sampling of agility moves you and your dog can try together to find out!

Of course, in all your training endeavors, safety should be your number-one priority. Chapter 21 gives you the low-down on sports injuries to beware of. Finally, Chapter 22 tells you what you need to know to keep your dog healthy — from diet and exercise to grooming.

Chapter 20

Nearly Ten Agility Moves Anyone Can Try

· ·

In This Chapter

▶ Getting your dog to jump, tunnel, burrow, and weave

▶ Jumping through hoops and walking the beam

▶ Stopping and holding in key positions

▶ Teaching your dog left from right

· ·

*I*f the sport of agility intrigues you but you're not quite ready to make the leap, look around for some props and try these nine simplified moves at home. If they leave your heart racing with excitement and your dog enjoys them too, consider getting more involved. If nothing else, you'll discover more ways to have fun with your dog — games that you can play wherever your life leads you!

I've listed these moves so that the easiest (and simplest to arrange) come first, but you can try whichever ones you want in whatever order you want.

Jumping Over a Single Barrier

You'll discover lots of jumps when you're out and about: fallen trees, a chain-blocked roadway, and crossing blocks are just a few of the barriers you and your dog can jump over. You can create your own simple single-bar jump, too. All you need are two identical household objects, such as paper towel rolls or cereal boxes, and a broom. Then proceed as follows:

1. **Prop the broom on items of equal height, no higher than your dog's elbow.**

2. **Let your dog sniff the setup, then walk back 10–15 feet.**

3. **Pick a command to say, like "Over," as you point to the jump and trot forward at your dog's natural pace.**

4. **Praise your dog for taking the jump!**

Is your dog reliable off-leash? If not, keep her on a leash unless you're in a safe enclosure! You can gradually diminish the leash escort by using a progressively longer leash and letting your dog run ahead of you to take the jump.

Practicing Spread Jumps

A spread jump consists of two or three horizontal, parallel bars (either of the same height or ascending in height) that the dog must clear in one leap. You can find many opportunities to encourage your dog to leap up and over obstructions during your daily outings. From fallen tree branches or a stream to grates, puddles, or construction zones — each gives you the perfect opportunity to practice this skill.

At home, you can closely arrange three single bars or obstacles, slightly lower than your single-bar jump, and teach your dog to leap across them. Give her plenty of runway: Like an airplane, she needs space to get her momentum going pre-jump and to slow down afterward. For low jumps, pile some books or arrange flat boxes in a heap so that the obstacle is wider than your dog, but no more than 1 to 3 inches off the ground (depending on your dog's size).

Flying through the Hoop

One of the more challenging jumps in agility is known as the *tire,* whereby a dog jumps through a large hoop. While finding a tire may be difficult, a hula hoop or any other large hoop will do. Proceed as follows:

1. **Place your single-bar jump in a door threshold.**

   Position it low — ankle-high for big dogs, on the ground for tiny dogs.

2. **Run your dog over it and back, saying "Over" as you clear the obstacle.**

3. **Now position the hoop behind the jump, placing the low end of the hoop just under the single bar. Let your dog sniff it.**

   Ask a friend to hold the hoop, or hold it yourself if your dog will take the jump on her own.

4. **Say "Hoop–Over" as you encourage your dog to jump through the hoop.**

If she's reluctant, you can toss a toy or some favorite treats through the hoop first.

5. **As your dog gets comfortable with this setup, raise both the bar and the hoop higher.**

6. **Now you're ready to remove the bar!**

   When you do, lower the height of the hoop to increase your dog's success rate.

Running through Tunnels

For many dogs, running through the tunnel is the most exciting obstacle on an agility course. To re-create the feeling, scope out some tag sales or kid shops and purchase a tunnel with an 18- to 24-inch diameter.

1. **Once you've found a tunnel, you'll need to secure both the opening and the exit with two weights to prevent shifting.**

   Gallon jugs filled with sand work great. Collect four and frame both ends one on each side. Tie a tether over the tunnel and secure it to the sand bags.

   Don't skip this step. Your dog may get seriously spooked if the tunnel starts to move while she's in it!

2. **If possible, crawl through the tunnel yourself or hold your dog while a kid demonstrates how it's done.**

3. **To encourage your dog into the tunnel, ask a helper to either stand at the end of the tunnel or hold your dog at the entrance so you can be there to coach her forward.**

4. **Lure your dog through by waving favorite treats and toys.**

5. **Use a command like "Tunnel!" in an enthusiastic voice and praise your dog's every attempt.**

Coming to a Halt

The pause table is a big challenge for many agility dogs. The focus is a full-fledged stop! The dog must leap onto a table, assume a stationary pose, and hold it for five seconds. Once your dog has this move down, you can use it in real life — any time, any place. How handy is that? Just follow these steps:

1. If your dog doesn't know the "Sit" or "Down" commands, flip back to Chapter 4 and brush up.

2. Using treats or toys, practice *quick positioning:* Say "Sit" or "Down" with urgency as you signal with your dog's favorite item by lifting the object above her head or pointing to the ground (see Chapter 4).

3. When your dog pops into position without hesitation, designate a pause place — a low platform with a nonslip surface, a specific mat, or a certain area of the sidewalk or yard.

4. Point to the area, saying "Go," and then say and signal a quick position — either "Sit" or "Down" — once she gets there.

5. Always release with a word like "Okay!"

Navigating the Low Beam

Agility has several raised obstacles that test your dog's balance. Moving across an 8- to 12-foot-long beam, operating a teeter-totter solo, scaling an A-frame: All of these feats await if you choose to get involved.

For now, find an 8- to 12-foot-long, 12-inch-wide board and lay it flat. Let your dog sniff it to "see" it (dogs investigate things by smelling them). When you think your dog is ready, try the following:

1. **Teach your dog to walk across the board by guiding her on-leash.**

   If she's nervous, sprinkle some treats along it.

2. **Once she's comfortable, attach a command to the activity, such as "Cross."**

3. **Reward and praise her after each dismount.**

Always urge her to run off the end. If you let her fudge, she'll become a ditcher — jumping off whenever the impulse strikes. If she does ditch, ignore her and lead her back to the start. Leash her and start over if bad habits start.

Weaving In and Out

The weave poles are the highlight of many agility competitions. A lot hinges on a dog's ability to maneuver the poles properly. To simulate the fun, first teach your dog the leg weave trick found in Chapter 10. Then proceed as follows:

1. **Purchase or gather some poles or sticks.**

   Cut them down to 3 to 4 feet, then prod them into the ground so they're secure. If you have trouble poking them into the ground, whittle one end of each pole down to a point.

2. **Stick four to nine poles in the ground, 22 to 26 inches apart.**

3. **Use a target stick as described in Chapter 2, or guide your dog through the poles by leading her on-leash.**

4. **As your dog begins to get the idea, say "Weave" as you guide her through.**

5. **Pace yourself with your dog — always staying alongside her head, but watching the end pole so as not to distract her to prematurely run out.**

Always run alongside her head — if you hang back or race ahead, your dog may break out of the poles to stay with you!

Mastering "Two On–Two Off"

Like the pause table, this move conditions your dog's mindfulness. You can use it at home to encourage quick responses and increase your dog's self-control.

1. **Lead your dog onto a landing or raised surface, such as a fireplace hearth or low step.**

2. **Lure your dog's front half off the step; then command "Wait."**

3. **As your dog gets familiar with this pose, command "Two On!" as you lure her and praise her cooperation.**

4. **Now test her concentration by tossing toys in front of her as you direct her to "Stay."**

5. **Release her with "Okay!"**

Going Left (or Right)

Agility dogs seem to know their left from their right. When the handler shouts "Left," the dog veers left; when the dog hears "Right," she veers right — as if by wizardry. Miraculous? Well, yes, in a way. But your dog can learn these directional skills too if taught in the right way.

To teach your dog to go left, follow these steps:

1. **Position her at your side on-leash and tell her to "Stay."**

2. **Show your dog a toy or bag of treats, toss it to your left, and pause 2 to 5 seconds to stir her excitement.**

3. **Shout, "Left–Go!" and then signal her with your left arm as you release her collar.**

4. **Praise your dog when she runs to the left.**

5. **Repeat this sequence over and over; then try it during your day-to-day interactions.**

   When you're running to the left, direct your dog with both your voice and arm signal.

6. **Praise her when she gets it right!**

To teach your dog to go right, wait until she understands the left cue. Then, introduce "Right" by repeating the previous steps, reversing them to the right.

Give your dog appropriate directional cues whenever possible: The more you communicate, the more your dog will look to you for direction!

Chapter 21

Top Ten Sports Injuries for Dogs

In This Chapter

▶ Keeping your dog hydrated and rested

▶ Treating bone and soft-tissue injuries

▶ Treating shock

*T*ricks, agility classes, and breed-specific activities are great ways to channel your dog's energy and passions. If you're like most people, you don't think much about injuries when you're starting out on a new adventure. You think about fun and excitement, not ice packs and aspirin. But accidents and injuries can and do happen, especially if your dog is overweight, underconditioned, or not given enough of a warm-up. This chapter describes common sports injuries that can happen to any dog.

If your dog does have an accident during a workout, stay cool. If you lose it, he'll get nervous and go to pieces. Be a rock of confidence. Be mentally tough. Organize. Think. If necessary, get him to the veterinarian as quickly and as carefully as possible.

Dehydration

Dehydration signals more than excessive thirst; it signals an excessive loss of body fluids. If you sense your dog is way off and looking hollow, test for dehydration by pinching the skin on his back. If it remains rigid and does not fall back into place, he's dehydrated. Give him room-temperature water in small half-cup doses to prevent vomiting and go to an animal hospital immediately.

Fever accelerates dehydration; so does vomiting and diarrhea. A dog must drink enough water to offset the fluids lost during activity and prolonged heat exposure. If your dog is panting, give him water — and give it to him often.

Fatigue

Sometimes even dogs get dog-tired. Unable to focus and perform, they need some quick R & R to rebalance. That said, your dog will often let on that he doesn't need a break; he may actually push himself to the point of exhaustion or, worse, injury. Signs of fatigue include the following:

- Stumbling or refusing obstacles
- Gait inconsistency
- Inability to focus
- Distractibility

If your dog seems out of sorts, stop and check him out head to tail. If he appears fine, take a water break, chill out, or go for a quiet walk. Dogs have off days too, and although certain spaciness is understandable, your dog's inconsistencies could signal illness or potential injury. If a short walk doesn't improve your dog's mood, quit for the day and watch your dog's behavior, body cues, and functions. How's his mood? Too much pressure to perform can affect your dog's mental state like a kid who must practice instead of play. Is he eating and drinking normally? Are his stools normal? If not, make an appointment to see his veterinarian.

Fever

Dogs, like people, get fevers. In simple terms, a fever represents that a dog's internal system is in overdrive, like water brought to a boil. When a dog gets hot or is agitated or athletically pumped, the cells inside his body rev up and *voilà* — a fever!

Though dogs' normal temperature is a lot higher than humans' (101 to 102 degrees on average), it fluctuates more rapidly, too. A spike of 1 or 2 degrees in either direction is considered normal. Take your dog's temperature on a good day, noting the healthy readings, so that you can compare.

What brings a fever down? Anything that will cool their insides. A refreshing drink, air conditioning or shade, or a cool shower — or if your dog is seriously overheated, ice packs on his head or thighs.

A prolonged fever or heatstroke signals something more serious and warrants the immediate attention of a veterinarian. If you can't get your dog's temperature to go down or stay down, of if your dog is panting heavily and has a dazed expression, give him a cool shower and call the vet right away.

Back and Neck Injury

Dogs are marvelous animals of movement. Watching an agility dog navigate and twist through and around obstacles is a wonder indeed. Lure coursing, sledding, athletic trials, and other persuasions require that your dog be in top physical condition and that he be warmed up before each event or outing.

The finely tuned musculoskeletal system makes all this motion possible, and when it's working well, your dog's movement looks effortless. A slight injury may only cause a ripple in his motion; however, acute neck or back pain causes the house of cards to fall. Dogs suffering spinal injuries can't move well, if at all.

If you suspect your dog is suffering from back or neck pain, stop everything and see your veterinarian immediately. Best case scenario, a slight bulge in one of your dog's discs is putting pressure on a nerve; time and rest will heal the spasms, though you'll need to be mindful because your dog will be prone to re-injury. Worst case, a disc has slipped or degenerated and is tweaking the surrounding nerves. In this case, your dog's athletic career is over, and he may need surgical intervention.

Symptoms of a back or neck injury include the following:

- Limping, weakness, or paralysis
- Diarrhea or bloody vomiting
- Abdominal pain, often noted in a distended belly
- Loss of bladder control
- Breathing difficulties
- Fever
- Strained neck movement
- Crying when attempting to walk

If you suspect neck or back injury, take every precaution and get your dog to a veterinarian immediately.

Transporting an injured dog

Transporting a dog who has internal injuries is tricky business. He'll be restless and want to move, and your job is to make sure he doesn't. It's best to have someone help you — the other person can drive, and you can comfort and restrain your dog. If transportation help isn't available, however, don't delay in getting your dog to the vet. Try to have someone call ahead so that the hospital is prepared to help upon your arrival.

If you suspect a broken bone, a spinal injury, or internal bleeding, transport your dog on a firm surface such as metal or plywood. Place a blanket over the dog, but don't cover his face because doing so may frighten him. Muzzle your dog for safety either with a professional cover or by using a belt or scarf wrapped over the nose and secured behind his ears.

Broken Bones

A sudden impact, fall, or a twist while a dog is overexerted can result in a fracture. A broken bone is hard to ignore, even for a dog. Serious *compound fractures,* in which the bone is protruding through the skin, are obvious, and without prompt attention, they can cause severe damage and dramatic blood loss.

Although some dogs may attempt to limp through their pain, leash the dog immediately after an accident, fall, or sudden impact. A quick hand examination may reveal the sound or feeling of bone rubbing on bone, or you may need an X-ray to reveal a fracture.

If you suspect a fracture, restrain your dog as listed in the neck and back pain section of this chapter. Apply ice packs to decrease the swelling. If the fracture is in a limb, splint your dog's leg above and below the area. Surround the area using a magazine or piece of cardboard and secure it in place with bandage tape. If you suspect the injury is in the spine, immobilize your dog as much as possible and transport him on a stretcher-like surface.

Foot Injury

I love going barefoot, feeling the dirt in my garden or the sand beneath my feet. That said, it's hard to imagine hot doggin' it 24/7, but that's just what dogs do. Though some hard-core canine athletes wear booties when they run, most dogs arrive at each new adventure with their paws uncovered and at least initially unscathed.

Dogs' paws do have some natural padding. Thickened *keratinous* foot pads (covered with the same substance that makes your fingernails tough) cushion and protect a dog's paws, while intricate nerves act like a computer messaging system, helping the dog recognize and orient to each new terrain.

The more active a dog is, the more susceptible to injury he'll be. Many things can cause injury, including

- ✔ Bee stings
- ✔ Cuts from glass, ice, or rough terrain
- ✔ Cracks from severe weather conditions or dry, rough footing
- ✔ Burns from excessively hot surfaces

In addition, a dog's toenails, if not clipped, can inhibit his gait, leading to injuries such as a toe dislocation or *split nail,* an open wound that's painful and open to infection. Many dogs still have a *dew claw,* a fifth claw located 1 to 3 inches up on their legs, that can get caught unpredictably and lead to painful tissue tearing.

Any one of these conditions can lead to localized swelling, limping, and/or infection if the open wound isn't treated. Be aware of the signs and symptoms of foot injury. A dog suffering paw injury will favor the entire limb, lick the wound, or bite at his pads to remove a foreign body.

A quick look-see often reveals the underlying cause of foot pain, but a veterinarian's attention will confirm the cause. It is important to have a veterinarian wash and disinfect open wounds and stabilize any limb that suffers tissue damage or bone breaks.

To prevent foot injuries, exercise your dog on a variety of surfaces, including grass, pavement (in cool temperatures to prevent pad burns), and sand, pebbles, or rocks to strengthen his pads, and keep your dog's nails clipped monthly.

Strains and Sprains

Strains and sprains result when muscles are overused, pushed past their endurance point, or strained by twitching or wrenching. When working with your dog, set your expectation to what he can tolerate and be mindful that like people, dogs must warm up gradually and have plenty of water to keep fit. To warm up your dog, walk him at a steady pace for ¼ to ½ mile or toss a ball to him in the yard for 5 to 10 minutes. You're giving his muscles a gentle wake-up call!

Table 21-1 names four common soft-tissue injuries that cause limping and subtle changes in your dog's gait.

Table 21-1	Soft-Tissue Injuries	
Injury	*Description/Symptoms*	*Treatment*
Sprains	A *sprain* is a stretching or laceration of the ligaments, which connect bones. Your dog will experience pain over the joint, swelling, lameness, and/or a decreased enthusiasm for activity.	The best cure? Rest and more rest. Ice placed over the area for 20 minutes an hour for the first three hours will help.
Tendonitis	*Tendonitis* is inflammation of the tendon caused by overuse or an accident that involved twisting or wrenching. Movement will be painful and strained.	Rest is the sure cure; a splint may be necessary to stabilize the leg.
Bruises	High-performance dogs can launch into an obstacle at top speed or crash into another dog and suffer a bruise in the same way people do. All a bruise is is a sign of bleeding under the skin.	If the bruising is extreme, place a cold pack over the area to stop the bleeding and swelling. If your dog will allow it, keep the pack on for 10 minutes, wrapping the pack into place.
Muscle strains	A muscle strain comes from an injured or torn muscle and can result from overexertion, a sudden stretch, or an impact to the muscle. Muscles often knot or spasm when injured.	Rest and cold packs will help ease the tenderness. Ice your dog's injury as long as the injury is warm to the touch. Consider wrapping an ice pack over the injury for about 10 minutes.

Your job is to find out what's causing your dog to limp and which body part is in trouble. To figure out just where the pain is centralized, follow these steps:

1. **Observe your dog when he's standing still.**

   He'll lean away from the hurt leg and put pressure on his stronger side. For example, if he hurt his right front leg, he'll lean to the left and put weight onto the two back and the front left legs.

2. **Watch him walk.**

   He'll take a shorter step on his injured leg. His head also may bob up and down to compensate for the pressure he's trying to keep off his injured limb.

3. **To pinpoint the specific injury site, carefully rub your hands along your dog's joints and note any muscle tenderness.**

   If you're still puzzled, gently flex and rotate your dog's joints. If he winces, whimpers, or moves from you, guess what — he's hurting!

4. **Look for discoloration and swelling.**

5. **Take your dog's temperature.**

   Digital thermometers for dogs are now available, and they're safer than traditional mercury ones. They can be inserted in the mouth, ear, or rectally for a most accurate reading (oh joy!). The normal range for a dog's temperature is 101 to 102 degrees. (I know you want to put this book down this very minute and take your dog's temperature!)

Remember that the quicker you or your vet diagnoses an injury, the easier the sprain or strain is to treat and the less likely it is that your dog will need surgery.

Torn Ligaments

Ligaments are swaths of tissue that connect the bones of a joint and give it stability during movement. Ligaments can get partially torn (causing a *sprain*) or completely torn. Tearing is a common injury, especially for athletic or heavily set, large-breed dogs — and it's even more common when dogs are overweight.

The most common injury point for a torn ligament is in a dog's knee: what is in humans called the *anterior cruciate ligament*, or ACL. (***Note:*** It's actually called a *cranial* or *caudal cruciate ligament* in dogs, but to keep it simple, many veterinarians use the human term).

Ligaments generally come in pairs, crisscrossing over a joint to stabilize it and prevent forward-backward mobility. When a ligament tears, the bones are displaced, the knee becomes unstable, and the bones often rub against each other. Ouch!

If a ligament is stretched or torn, you'll need to give your dog a few weeks to months to fully recover. If you push your dog, he'll be likely to suffer a more dramatic injury, as his enthusiasm will far exceed his physical capacities. If a ligament is left untreated, a dog can develop arthritis in the joint and will also place extra weight on the healthy leg, which often puts unbearable strain on those ligaments, resulting in a double whammy.

If your dog is lame and your veterinarian suspects a torn ligament, he'll likely prescribe painkillers and suggest a period for recovery. If your dog is not bearing weight on a leg, a quick manipulating of the area may reveal what's commonly known as the *drawer movement:* the unhinged bones can be easily maneuvered back and forth.

Shock

A dog can go into shock if he experiences a sudden loss of blood, a trauma, or electric shock. Shock is life-threatening if not treated promptly; it causes blood pressure to drop dramatically, which prevents oxygen from circulating in the body. Without oxygen, the body dies.

A dog in shock shows the following symptoms:

- ✔ A fast heart rate, as the heart tries to make up for a drop in blood pressure
- ✔ Rapid breathing, because the body is trying to increase oxygen flow
- ✔ Dilated pupils and a glaring stare
- ✔ Unconscious or semiconscious behavior

Dogs in shock must see a veterinarian. If you suspect your dog has gone into shock, stay calm, keep him still, and get to the nearest veterinarian immediately. Have someone call the animal hospital so that the vet staff will be prepared to help upon your arrival.

Chapter 22

Ten Ways to Ensure Fido's Fit for Tricks and Agility

You've seen dogs bouncing down the street at the end of a leash or streaking across the park after a tennis ball. Nails clipped, coats gleaming, white teeth flashing . . . can dogs actually *sparkle?*

If your dog looks a little unkempt compared to these wondrous creatures, don't despair. This kind of radiant health doesn't require a full-time staff of groomers, nutritionists, and fitness coaches. With a little time, effort, patience, and love, your dog can sparkle with the best of them!

This chapter shows you the top ten things you can do to maintain your dog's health. You discover the healthiest foods, the tastiest snacks, and the best grooming tools to manage the job efficiently and easily. Best of all, you find that canine health and fitness can be fun — you can bond with your dog while you care for your dog. So hang up a wind chime and get started — it's dog spa time!

Give Water, Water, Water

Your dog can live three weeks without food, but she'll die within days without water. Water is necessary for all digestive processes as well as regulating temperature, absorbing nutrients, and shipping things between organs and out of the body.

How much water your dog needs depends on her physical activities and the type of food she eats. Panting is your dog's way of sweating, and if your dog is sweating, she needs a drink.

Dry food also encourages thirst. Because dry food contains only 10 percent moisture, your dog needs about 1 quart of water for every pound of dry food. On the other hand, canned food or home-cooked diets contain more water and require less to rinse and wash down. (This attribute of canned and home-cooked food doesn't necessarily make them a superior food source, however. See the later section "Feed Your Dog Quality Dog Food" for details.)

Water is vital for survival. Make sure clean water is always available for your dog. Provide clean water in a stainless steel dish and change it regularly. Each time you fill your dog's bowl, rinse it to clean off dirt and other nasty particles that don't belong in a fresh bowl.

Encourage Regular Exercise

If your dog hasn't been out for a good run in a long time, you need to ease her in slowly. Conditioning for dogs is like conditioning for people: a necessary evil. To preserve your dog's good health — and before you jump into a new tricks-training regime — you need to make sure she's in top physical shape or has a program to get her there. Just like humans, pushing your dog too far too fast can lead to trouble.

Start with conditioning for tricks and obedience. Most of the stunts I outline in this book don't require tremendous amounts of physical exertion. However, if your dog has been off the training wagon for some time, do the following:

- ✔ **Keep the lessons short and upbeat to start, no more than 3 to 10 minutes.** She doesn't have to master a trick a day. You can have practice sessions three times a day if your schedule allows, but short lessons are best.

- ✔ **Start with tricks that are easy for her to master and that make you laugh.** Laughter is great encouragement.

Conditioning for athletic activities is another issue. Are you pumped up to start racing that dog of yours over every tree and up ladders? Whoa, Nellie! Your dog will want to try everything you introduce her to, but is she ready? If your dog can't tell a tree stump from an ottoman, start small. There's no need to conquer the world in a day. First, take a couple of weeks to make sure your dog can handle the excitement. Go for half-mile hikes, building the distance over time.

Growing pups are in the majority where sports injuries are concerned (see Chapter 21 for info on sports injuries). A 4-month-old pup will run until her legs can't carry her, but all that exercise can permanently alter her growing body and cause problems later in life. A young dog's energy and enthusiasm can be quite misleading: She'll want to try everything and give no thought to the consequences. Overly strenuous activity, slippery footing, or excessive jumping causes trauma to bones and joints. During your puppy's growth phase — 4½ to 9 months — keep her activity level regulated and don't encourage jumping. I know — teaching your dog new stuff is a lot of fun, but you need to be the parent here and do what's best for your dog.

Feed Your Dog Quality Dog Food

Aren't all dog foods basically the same? No, Virginia, they're not. The only true similarity is in the percentage of components required to meet a dog's daily allowance, which is governed by the AAFCO (Association of American Feed Control Officials). To pick the right food, you need to know how to read ingredient labels. You may discover that the most costly, aggressively marketed, or cleverly labeled food isn't necessarily the best.

To pass regulatory standards, dog foods must contain six essential elements: protein, fat, carbohydrates, vitamins, minerals, and water. But that's where the similarities usually end. The makers of dog foods diverge on which ingredients they use to reach the minimum daily requirement (MDR). For example, some use soy (a vegetable protein) to meet the daily protein requirement, whereas others use animal protein. This section looks at the essentials one at a time.

Protein

Protein is the most expensive ingredient in dog foods, and its source often determines the quality of the food. Animal sources are superior. Unfortunately, there's not enough meat around to satisfy all the pet dogs in the world, so the producers often substitute vegetable protein.

Rationing treats

During trick training, you often hand out treats in great abundance (to say the least). Pick a sugar-free breakfast cereal or morsel of a light dog snack to keep calories down, and reduce your dog's regular meals slightly to compensate. Whatever you choose, remember it's not the amount that counts, but the act of giving — you don't need to give a lot to show reward.

The difference between vegetable and animal protein? Vegetable protein is often harder to digest, and the dog has to consume more of it to meet her needs. More food equals more stool. My advice is to find a food that uses more animal protein than vegetable protein and requires smaller rations to meet the MDR.

Next, consider your lifestyle. Do you have a lot of free time to train your dog and engage in high-energy activities? Performance foods with high levels of crude protein provide lots of energy to burn. Puppies also need higher amounts of protein for their growing bodies.

Carbohydrates

Some dog-food manufacturers meet the MDR for protein by using primarily vegetable matter. Vegetable sources of protein also contain high levels of carbohydrates — not a bad diet for humans, but what's good for a human isn't always good for a dog. The reason humans digest carbohydrates well is that they start digestion in their mouths, chewing and breaking down the food. Dogs don't chew, they gulp, and their digestion doesn't begin until the food gets into their stomach.

Fats

Please don't ever buy fat-free dog food. I know it sounds tempting, but your dog needs plenty of fat to keep her skin and coat healthy and for overall body functions.

Fat gives your dog energy and keeps her cool when it's warm and warm when it's cool. How does it do this? Fat is an insulator, protecting the body from extremes in temperature. Neat, huh?

The recommended amount of fat is 15 to 19 percent, and many nutritionists will say for dogs, more fat is better! Why? Because carbohydrates are what add bulk for dogs, whereas fat gets utilized for body functions in dogs.

Vitamins and minerals

Have you ever wondered what vitamins do and why they're necessary for good health? Vitamins do two things: unlock nutrients from food and make energy. Fascinating, huh? Minerals are a lot like vitamins: They help the body maintain its normal daily activities, such as circulation, energy production, and cell regeneration.

Do not supplement your dog's diet with vitamins and minerals unless directed by your veterinarian. Too many vitamins or minerals can cause health problems.

Brush Up on Grooming: The Peanut Butter Connection

Grooming can be your worst nightmare or your best friend. If the thought of brushing your dog troubles you, try this approach:

1. **Start with a soft-bristled brush.**

   You may use a firmer brush when your dog is more accepting, but soft is better when starting out.

2. **Call your dog aside happily and give her a treat when she comes.**

3. **Take some peanut butter and rub it on the refrigerator at your dog's nose level.**

4. **While she licks it off, say "Stand" and brush gently.**

   Praise, too!

Begin with short grooming sessions, quitting once your dog is through licking off the spread. Gradually extend from 30 seconds to several minutes, giving your dog treats or a bone to occupy her while you gussy her up.

The peanut butter trick also works wonders when you have to towel-dry or wipe a dog's paws. If early association with the activity is positive, your dog will be much easier to handle down the road. If your dog's not a big peanut butter fan, try some soft cheese, yogurt, or meat broth.

Give a Bath

Every dog has to take a bath sometime. Short-coated breeds need a bath less often than long-coats — unless, of course, they're avid excrement rollers.

To make the bath a positive experience, lay a towel on the bottom of the sink or tub for your dog to stand on comfortably without slipping, and spread peanut butter around the edge to occupy your dog while you scrub. You can bathe small dogs in the sink; large breeds fit best in a tub or can be hosed outside on a warm day.

Shampooing a malodorous mutt makes her socially acceptable, but it also strips away natural oils in a dog's coat. Shampooed too often, the coat will dry out and become brittle, so bathe your dog only about once a month.

Cut out mats or ask a professional groomer to do this for you. Mats are extremely annoying and painful — like having a knotted tangle that pulls on your skin all day. Distracting and irritating, a mat won't bring out the best in any dog!

Keep Your Dog's Nails Clipped

If nails grow too long, they can crack, break, or become ingrown. Ouch! Unfortunately, dogs don't relate to the whole manicure thing the way some people do. Using treats or peanut butter can calm the most savage beast.

Nail clippers for dogs look like a downsized guillotine — sharp and defining. The hand-clasp action provides the power needed to cut through a dog's nail. Don't try human clippers — they're not strong enough.

When clipping, make sure you clip the very tip of the nail, just as it starts to curl. If your dog has light-colored nails, you can see the delicate blood vessel inside; that's the part you want to avoid!

Don't overlook dew claws or hind nails. Though they grow more slowly, they still need your attention.

If your dog isn't comfortable having her feet handled, make it a part of your everyday interactions. Handle the feet when giving a treat, petting, or feeding. Tell your dog how wonderful her feet are. Kiss them when she's sleeping. (Okay, you don't have to kiss your dog's feet, but you can.)

Be very careful to avoid cutting into your dog's tissue! Aside from being excruciatingly painful, the wound can bleed for hours. To prevent excess bleeding, get a clotting solution, such as styptic powder, from your veterinarian. It works like magic. In a pinch, you can use a little bit of cornstarch, but the clotting solution is better.

Be Easy on the Eyes

Dogs don't spend as much time on their looks as you do, but that doesn't mean their facial features should go unnoticed. Eye irritations can blur their vision and cause disorientation. Soulful, sweet, comic — your dog's eyes tell it all. It's up to you to keep the eyes healthy, bright, and clear.

If you have a longhaired breed, carefully clip the hair surrounding the eyes — the better to see you with!

If your veterinarian prescribes eye medication, administer it carefully. Use peanut butter on the fridge or a bowl of broth in a friend's lap to occupy your dog while you medicate her. Place your hand carefully under your dog's chin and pull the lower eyelid down until you see the white part. Squeeze the drops in there.

Keep the Ears Clean

Ears mesmerize me. I can lull myself into a trance petting a dog's ears, and it doesn't seem to matter what shape — uprights, floppy, short, or cropped. Dogs seem to love the ear massage, too.

Different dogs require different cleaning schedules, from every couple of weeks to daily. Your dog's activity, diet, and the weather also influence the frequency of cleaning. If your dog is an Olympic swimmer, I suggest daily cleaning before bed. In most cases, twice a month is sufficient.

To clean the visible surface area of your dog's ear, ask your veterinarian to recommend a commercial ear solution that will prevent infection. Soak a cotton swab with the solution and wipe the visible surface area of your dog's ear.

Never, never, never use a Q-tip or poke your finger into your dog's ear. You can do irreparable damage to your dog's inner ear.

Protect the Nose

When I was growing up, people used to say you could tell a dog's mood by touching her nose. If it was hot, the dog was sick; too dry, the dog was depressed. The truth is there's no truth to that old wives' tale. A dog's nose can heat up in a warm environment and can dry out when the air is dry. If you want to know if your dog's running a fever, take her temperature — rectal style!

A dog's nose can become discolored from the sun, from an allergic reaction to a food dish, from hypothyroidism, or from household detergent. In such cases, use a stainless steel feeding bowl and clean house with environmentally safe products. And when your dog goes out into the sun, protect that nose with SPF 45 sunblock!

Avoid a Foul Mouth

I have one obsession: It's my teeth. I love brushing, flossing, and going to the dentist. Odd, I know. Based on this, you probably know what I'm going to suggest before I even write it: You must take care of your dog's teeth. Though dogs are less prone to tartar buildup than you are, they're not immune. Sure, they have more concentrated saliva and they chew bones and things, but this doesn't take the place of dental care. Without a little help from their friends (that's you), they'll suffer from tooth decay, abscesses, periodontal disease, and tooth loss.

To keep your dog's teeth healthy, do the following:

- ✔ Provide chew toys.

- ✔ Brush your dog's teeth once a week, using special canine peanut butter-flavored toothpaste. If your dog won't settle for the brush, use your finger.

- ✔ Avoid human toothpaste; fluoride and dogs don't mix. Many human formulas also contain Xylitol, which is toxic to dogs if swallowed.

Index

Business/Accounting & Bookkeeping

Bookkeeping For Dummies
978-0-7645-9848-7

eBay Business
All-in-One For Dummies,
2nd Edition
978-0-470-38536-4

Job Interviews
For Dummies,
3rd Edition
978-0-470-17748-8

Resumes For Dummies,
5th Edition
978-0-470-08037-5

Stock Investing
For Dummies,
3rd Edition
978-0-470-40114-9

Successful Time
Management
For Dummies
978-0-470-29034-7

Computer Hardware

BlackBerry For Dummies,
3rd Edition
978-0-470-45762-7

Computers For Seniors
For Dummies
978-0-470-24055-7

iPhone For Dummies,
2nd Edition
978-0-470-42342-4

Laptops For Dummies,
3rd Edition
978-0-470-27759-1

Macs For Dummies,
10th Edition
978-0-470-27817-8

Cooking & Entertaining

Cooking Basics
For Dummies,
3rd Edition
978-0-7645-7206-7

Wine For Dummies,
4th Edition
978-0-470-04579-4

Diet & Nutrition

Dieting For Dummies,
2nd Edition
978-0-7645-4149-0

Nutrition For Dummies,
4th Edition
978-0-471-79868-2

Weight Training
For Dummies,
3rd Edition
978-0-471-76845-6

Digital Photography

Digital Photography
For Dummies,
6th Edition
978-0-470-25074-7

Photoshop Elements 7
For Dummies
978-0-470-39700-8

Gardening

Gardening Basics
For Dummies
978-0-470-03749-2

Organic Gardening
For Dummies,
2nd Edition
978-0-470-43067-5

Green/Sustainable

Green Building
& Remodeling
For Dummies
978-0-470-17559-0

Green Cleaning
For Dummies
978-0-470-39106-8

Green IT For Dummies
978-0-470-38688-0

Health

Diabetes For Dummies,
3rd Edition
978-0-470-27086-8

Food Allergies
For Dummies
978-0-470-09584-3

Living Gluten-Free
For Dummies
978-0-471-77383-2

Hobbies/General

Chess For Dummies,
2nd Edition
978-0-7645-8404-6

Drawing For Dummies
978-0-7645-5476-6

Knitting For Dummies,
2nd Edition
978-0-470-28747-7

Organizing For Dummies
978-0-7645-5300-4

SuDoku For Dummies
978-0-470-01892-7

Home Improvement

Energy Efficient Homes
For Dummies
978-0-470-37602-7

Home Theater
For Dummies,
3rd Edition
978-0-470-41189-6

Living the Country Lifestyle
All-in-One For Dummies
978-0-470-43061-3

Solar Power Your Home
For Dummies
978-0-470-17569-9